D1163464

EWAN BUTLER

AMATEUR AGENT

In war, moral considerations make up three-quarters of the game: the relative balance of manpower accounts only for the remaining quarter.

NAPOLEON BONAPARTE

NEW YORK
W · W · NORTON & COMPANY · INC ·

COPYRIGHT © 1963 BY EWAN BUTLER
First American edition 1964

Library of Congress Catalog Card No. 62-10095

PRINTED IN THE UNITED STATES OF AMERICA

PROPERTY OF
BASE LIBRARY AFL 2057
UNITED STATES AIR FORCE
BROOKS AIR FORCE BASE, TEXAS

For
PHYLLIS NAYLOR
in gratitude

CONTENTS

Note

All of the leaflets are from the collection of Mr R. G. Auckland, of Sandridge, Hertfordshire, and photographs of them are published with his kind permission.

I. THE LAST, LOST YEARS

Most men carry a key-ring in their pocket, and the manufacturers of key-rings have seen to it that every possible taste and hobby, superstition and sentiment, is reflected in the very personal little trinkets which they offer for sale. Some rings have a tag which bears the sign of the zodiac under which its owner was born, others sport regimental emblems, the burgees of sailing-clubs, miniature champagne bottles, or the coats of arms of the cities in which they were bought. My own key-ring is weighted down by a German 5-mark piece, minted in 1930. The obverse side of this handsome coin, which is as large as one of our 5-shilling pieces, shows the Eagle of Germany perched defiantly on a bridge. Round the rim of the disc this motto appears, in strongly raised relief: *The Rhine, Germany's River, not Germany's Frontier.*

This old coin, with its menacing message, rests in my pocket, day after day, because it has been my destiny to be haunted by Germany for the greater part of my life, and I am still haunted. My father, himself a former student of the University of Heidelberg, first sent me there to learn the language in 1927, when I was sixteen years of age, and since that time the course of events in the world has seen to it that I should never get Germany out of my system. I became a journalist in later years, and in 1935 *The Times* sent me to New York as their assistant correspondent in the United States.

There were, goodness knows, plenty of things to think about in the America of 1935–37, but to me none of them seemed vital. The " Depression " had ended, and the Roosevelt Administration was wrangling with the Supreme Court over the means by which this had been achieved. But in Germany, too, unemployment had been overcome, and there was no wrangling. In September 1935 the Nuremberg Racial Laws were promulgated, and, in comparison with that sinister piece of legislation, what was happening in the United States seemed insignificant. Six months later Hitler's Wehrmacht reoccupied the Rhineland, and I had a long conversation, over several schooners of beer, with the man who tended the boilers of the apartment house in which I lived.

" I had four years of it last time," my friend said, in a cockney accent which years of residence in New York had in no way modified. " Sixtieth Rifles. Think we'll be called up again ? I'm still a British subject."

" I'm afraid we shan't be called up now," I replied. " I wish I could think that we should. I hold a commission in the Reserve. But it won't be long before we shall be forced to fight, and every year that passes will make the going tougher."

" We ought to stop that bastard Hitler *now*," the stoker asserted, and I agreed with him.

Although I was fascinated by life in America, the grim march of events in Europe lent, as far as I was concerned, an air of unreality to the life of which I was, for a time, a part. The letter from London which posted me to Berlin as assistant to James Holburn, newly promoted chief correspondent after the expulsion from Germany of Norman Ebbutt, seemed to be no more than another inevitable link in the chain which bound me to the Reich. My anxious thoughts had been in that doomed country for years past, and now my body was to follow them.

The British journalists who served in Berlin in the years which preceded the outbreak of the last war, and who still survive, feel, and feel with justice, that for them the fight against Hitler began some time before their fellow-countrymen became involved in the conflict. Certainly we were unpopular with the Germans, since most of us took few pains to conceal our aversion to the National Socialist philosophy. When Holburn was transferred to Moscow, early in 1939, I took over from him as acting chief correspondent, but in the meantime I had become involved in a piece of work which was to have an important effect upon my future.

In June 1938, as the Czech crisis moved towards the sorrowful anticlimax of Munich, I was on leave from Berlin. I found, to my dismay, that most of the people whom I met in England cared very little about what was happening in Germany, and thought that war against her was out of the question. A few of my acquaintances, notably Lord Vansittart and Sir Stephen Tallents, did not share this facile optimism, nor did Robert Byron, whose death in the war of which he so clearly foresaw the advent was an incalculable loss to British life and to British letters.

As a labour of love, Byron, Tallents, and I sat down, during my leave, and wrote a long memorandum on propaganda to Germany in the event of war. Tallents, who knew about most things that happened in Whitehall, told us that no serious thought had been given to this vital matter, and undertook to ensure that what we wrote would at least be read by a few people whose opinions carried weight with the Government.

Our document fell into three parts. As a civil servant of great experience, Tallents wrote a section which suggested the practical steps which must be taken to establish a Government department which would be responsible for propaganda to the enemy. Byron contributed a section on the general theory of propaganda, about which he knew a great deal ; and I was responsible for one which dealt specifically with the problem of how we should set about the job of hammering home-truths into the heads of the infatuated German people.

Sir Stephen bore our memorandum away, I returned to Berlin. The Munich crisis drove all thoughts of my holiday

task from my mind. I marched, sick at heart, into the Sudetenland, with the triumphant German Forces, and slunk, dis-
gusted, back to Hitler's capital. Only when Robert Byron
joined me there at Christmas was I reminded of our memorandum.

When the Munich crisis finally burst upon an unprepared
and resentful Great Britain our document, Robert told me,
was the only thing of its kind in existence. For a few days it
became a State Paper, portentously secret, and was eagerly
studied in high places. Then Mr Neville Chamberlain
brought back " peace in our time " from Germany, and our
memorandum was filed away in some undiscovered drawer
from whose bourn no document returns.

Yet I suspect that two years later, when the Germans, whose
peaceful intentions in 1938 had been so evident to all save
warmongers like myself, were preparing to invade the United
Kingdom, somebody remembered that memorandum and
that I was one of those who had signed it. In remembering, if
my suspicion is correct, this unknown civil servant charted for
me the course which my service was to follow for the rest of
the war.

The year 1939 was a sickening one for us in Berlin. In
March I stood with Edward Beattie, of the United Press of
America, on a balcony of the Hotel Ambassador in Prague,
and watched German armoured cars roll down the street
below us. We both wept, unashamed, and in this we were in
good company, for most of the people in the crowd which
stood huddled beneath us in the cold light of early morning
were weeping also. A few men threw snowballs at the Nazi
juggernauts.

After that shame came the British guarantee to Poland, and
I enlisted in the Polish Army as a private soldier. This was
the result of a bet with the Polish Military attaché in Berlin,
who had remarked, bitterly, that our guarantee was worthless,
since we had no intention of fulfilling it. We would not fight
for Poland, he said, as we had not fought for Czechoslovakia.
I assured my friend that he was wrong, and to back up my

assurance I said that although I held a commission in the British Army Reserve I was prepared to volunteer for service in the Polish Forces in any capacity in which I might be thought useful. I stipulated, though, that I should be released from my obligations to Poland as soon as my own country declared war on Germany, as I was confident that she would. The Military attaché rang a bell, a clerk brought in some incomprehensible papers, I signed them, and we drank a glass of vodka.

In Berlin one could almost feel the ground growing hot beneath one's feet as Hitler stoked the fires of war, yet some things I remember from that time with pleasure. I recall for instance a party at the Kasinogesellschaft, Germany's most exclusive military club. It was a Jungherrenabend, or Young Gentlemen's Evening. By long-established custom the older members left the club immediately after dinner, leaving the field clear for the young officers to enjoy themselves. On this occasion they acted a charade in which one youngster, his glossy black riding-boots looking singularly out of place beneath an ancient mackintosh, disguised himself as a travesty of Hitler, delivered a ludicrous mock oration in the Führer's best style, and danced a singularly inelegant minuet with another officer, who, draped in a tablecloth and with tulips in his hair, was supposed to represent Madame Horthy, the consort of the Regent of Hungary. There were only two foreigners present, of whom I was one, and I asked one of the young aristocrats how he and his friends dared to commit this gross act of *lèse-majesté* in the very heart of Berlin. " Oh, don't worry," the boy replied. " All the club servants are old servants of one or other of our families. They won't split to the bloody Nazis."

I remembered that party five years later, on July 20, 1944, when many of the men with whom I had drunk and laughed that night were involved in the plot against Hitler's life. The British prejudice against " Prussianism " is one which cost us dear in the last war.

At last even my masters in Printing House Square, who had

steadily refused to believe that war was inevitable, realized that it takes two to make peace, and that Hitler was determined to destroy Poland. A discreet man called at my office and handed me my calling-up papers for the Polish Army. I told him that I hoped to reach Copenhagen and was instructed to report to the Polish Military attaché there on arrival.

Five British journalists remained in Berlin on August 30. The British Embassy could not, or would not, offer us any protection, and so, since the frontier was already closed for normal traffic, we negotiated a *laissez-passer* with Reinhard Heydrich, of infamous memory, who was the head of the Gestapo.

I had met Heydrich on several occasions, and had indeed, on his insistence, once drunk Bruderschaft, or Brotherhood, with him at a dinner-party at which he was my guest. I could therefore address him by his Christian name, and could, in speaking to him, use the familiar *thou* instead of the more formal *you*. This distinction is very important to every German.

In negotiating the *laissez-passer* we pointed out to Heydrich that whereas there were only five of us British journalists in Berlin nearly a hundred of our German opposite numbers remained in London. If we were interned all our German colleagues would suffer the same fate, and this would be a poor exchange from the German point of view. Heydrich agreed, and gave us an impressively stamped document which not only enabled us to leave Germany but allowed us to smuggle out two Polish colleagues who would otherwise have certainly been arrested, and probably murdered.

We left Berlin in a body, and set foot, with feelings of unspeakable relief, on Danish soil one day before the German Army and Air Force were unleashed against Poland.

I reported to the Polish Legation, and to my embarrassment found that I was looked upon as something of a hero. I reported to the British Legation, and found, as I had expected, that I was looked upon as more than something of a bore. I was assured that there would be no war, and they were indignant when I expressed disbelief.

The days which intervened between the German assault on Poland and the Franco-British declaration of war were agonizing. One afternoon Ralph Izzard, my colleague of the *Daily Mail*, and I sought to kill time by going to the Tivoli Gardens, and there we carried out what was, I suppose, the first propaganda raid on Germany. We bought several dozen balloons, and spent a happy hour in composing offensive messages to the Führer, and attaching them to the balloons. A brisk breeze was blowing towards Germany, and our missives were soon bowling southward before it. Ralph spent the next six years in the Navy, and I in the Army, but this was our first act of war, and it filled us with childish satisfaction.

At 11.15 A.M. on September 3, 1939, we heard, clustered round a radio in Ronald Selkirk Panton's room at the Angleterre, the tired, sad voice of Neville Chamberlain. We were at war, and we drank to victory in champagne. Then I went downstairs to the bar, and there ran into two stout, prosperous Danish businessmen whom I had met there on the previous evening. " Ah ! " they cried cheerfully. " So you are at war ! Come and have a drink ! " I joined them. We were to meet again six years later in very different circumstances.

Nothing remained but to buy a ticket to Bergen, in Norway, where it might be possible to find a ship which would take me home, and to take my leave of the Polish Legation. I had won my bet, and the Polish colony in Copenhagen paid up handsomely. They insisted on coming with me in force to the station that evening, bearing an embarrassing assortment of food and drink to fortify me on my journey. I said good-bye to them with real regret and pity, but also with relief. I was glad to be going home to my own army. A week later I was in uniform, and a month after that I had joined the British Expeditionary Force in France as an intelligence officer.

My own job in France was, inevitably, one of intelligence ; first in the section which dealt with the German order of battle, and later in charge of a subsection which, commanded by Lieutenant-Colonel Gerald Templer, was responsible for security, morale, and liaison with our French Allies.

The months spent in watching the formidable build-up of enemy forces were extremely depressing. The British Expeditionary Force had no tanks, few anti-tank guns. We were required to hold an open stretch of the Franco-Belgian frontier which was almost entirely without natural obstacles to an advancing enemy, and equally devoid of man-made defences. These, throughout a long winter of bitter cold, the B.E.F. set itself to build, as best it might, while beyond the Rhine the German divisions, armoured, motorized, infantry, each a clump of sinister black pins on the great map in our Order of Battle Room, seemed to multiply like rabbits. A silly song, *Run, Rabbit, Run,* was very popular with our troops at that time. At General Headquarters we were well aware that our chances of making these particular rabbits run in the direction of Berlin were, for the present at any rate, not at all promising.

Nor did things look any brighter when I came to deal with our relations with our French Allies, which was the job of my little section.

We were, in some ways, rather a distinguished subsection. One of my intelligence officers was the present Duke of Wellington, then Lord Gerald Wellesley. He had been a diplomat throughout the Kaiser's war, but he was now determined to uphold as best he might in middle age the great military traditions of his family. As a somewhat elderly ensign of the Grenadier Guards, the breast of his tunic bright with distinguished, if unmilitary, decorations, Gerry Wellesley's diplomatic skill was invaluable in dealing with our Allies on every level. The mayor of an Artois village in which British troops had misconducted themselves was as impressed by " Milor " Wellesley's charm and tact as was the local archbishop or a French Army commander.

Alec Waugh, a veteran of the First World War and as determined as was Gerry Wellesley not to miss the second round, was another of my officers. In tiny, meticulous handwriting, always in green ink, in which had been set down so many novels and short stories, he now drafted reports on the wide range of subjects which our duties covered, and many of them made glum reading.

It was impossible, in the face of the evidence which came pouring into our little office, to accept uncritically the confidence in the French Army and Government which our politicians continued to profess, as indeed they were bound to do officially. But, as later events were to show, this confidence was not confined to public utterances. The warnings which the Duke of Windsor frequently sent back from the French Grand Quartier Général were blandly ignored, as were our own humbler reports, and it was not long before we were all required to pay the penalty for wishful thinking.

One of my pleasanter duties at this time was to accompany my general to Paris, once a fortnight, for a series of conferences with our French opposite numbers. These visits were often frustrating, since French G.Q.G., the Government officials whom we met, and the members of our own embassy, seemed to live in a fog of unreality which we were powerless to dispel, doggedly though we tried to do so.

General Noel Mason-Macfarlane, the Director of Military Intelligence of the B.E.F., had been our Military attaché in Berlin until shortly before the outbreak of war, a fact which explains my presence at G.H.Q. As correspondent of *The Times*, I had made a regular practice of visiting " Mason-Mac " at least once a week, and we became very friendly. Sometimes I was able to give him information which was of some value—I once succeeded in identifying a German division which nobody had known to exist—and the colonel, as he then was, could always be relied upon to give me something useful.

Now I was one of Mason-Mac's junior officers. With him and Lieutenant-Colonel Gerald Templer, who was in charge of security, I travelled to Paris twice a month for a series of conferences, most of which we found, as I have indicated, extremely frustrating. My brief was a somewhat varied one. At one moment I might find myself, as I did, explaining to the wives and *chères amies* of most of the French Cabinet Ministers that we could not allow them to establish Anglo-French canteens behind the lines, in which the troops of both nations could mingle, waited upon occasionally by these important ladies, rigged out in charming uniforms designed by Lanvin or Paquin.

This was not a pleasant gathering, and I do not blame even such intrepid officers as Mason-Mac and Gerald Templer for shirking it. I was obliged to explain to this group of authoritarian ladies, who, in one way or another, had a large say in the policy of the French Government, that the gross discrepancy in pay between the British and French armies made establishments of the kind which they planned most undesirable.

The British soldier was, Heaven knows, not any too well paid, but he was rich compared to his French ally. If the canteens which the Comité de Solidarité Franco-Britannique proposed to set up had been actually established they would have done far more harm than good. French soldiers would have seen British troops regaling themselves on beer and eggs-and-chips while they themselves could afford, at best, a cup of coffee. This, I advised my superiors, was hardly calculated to make for Franco-British solidarity. "All right," they said brutally, "you go and tell the bloody women so !" I did, and it was an experience which I shall not forget.

On the other hand, I was called upon, also in the interests of Franco-British solidarity, to play a part in setting up an establishment of a very different kind. One of my duties as General Staff Officer (Third Grade) was to attend a weekly conference. My rôle was to advise, when called upon to do so, on our relations with our French Allies.

At the end of one conference I was told to wait behind after my brother officers had left. Two letters were then produced, one from General Voruz, who commanded the French Liaison Mission at our G.H.Q., and a copy of our reply. The French general had inquired about a dive in Lille, the only large town in the B.E.F. area, and as such the Mecca of our troops when they got a leave pass. This was known as the Officers' Club, and was, notoriously, a brothel. The French Mission inquired whether this haunt was under the official control of the British Army.

I was told to go to the French and rub in what was said in our letter. Of course we had nothing whatever to do with the place. The Archbishop of Canterbury wrote about three times a week about the morals of the troops. It would be pretty crazy if we took any official notice of a—a whore-house.

I saluted smartly, and, on my return to Arras, visited Colonel de Vogüé, head of the great champagne firm of Moët & Chandon, who was General Voruz's chief of staff.

The colonel had received our letter, and was not at all pleased about it.

" Look here," he said, " we wish that your Army *would* take some interest in brothels ' pour la protection de la population feminine du région.' At the moment there are dreary, sleazy brothels in every town in this area—Lens, Douai, here in Arras, and, of course, in Lille. The other ranks are swept out at 9 P.M., and by that time the officers are pretty well queuing up outside. This is bad for discipline and bad for the respectable girls of the area, because the troops, without enough—ah—outlet, are inclined to seek satisfaction elsewhere."

I replied that we were well aware of this, and that I had indeed made several reports on the subject.

" Very well then," said Colonel de Vogüé, " you go back and say that the French Mission would very much welcome the opening of one or two establishments under full military auspices. I should suggest one ' maison close ' for officers only, as a start."

" I'll see what I can do, mon colonel," I said, and went to consult with my G.I.

The outcome was that we would give no formal recognition, but we would clap the telescope to the blind eye. The existing system was not only bad for discipline, it was dangerous to health.

I returned to the French Mission in triumph. They were delighted.

" We'll send for Monsieur Valentin," they said, " and hold a little conference."

A week later I was summoned to the conference. Monsieur Valentin was a dapper little man, very suave, very well dressed. He owned the celebrated Sphinx, in Paris, and a chain of high-class ' establishments ' all over France. He grasped our problem immediately.

" What you need, messieurs, for a start," said M. Valentin, " is a large house of the second class. Oh, I assure you that it will be very comfortable and well run—but not de luxe, you understand. Officers cannot afford de luxe prices, but at the same time the rates will exclude the other ranks. I shall set about renting premises at once. Of course," M. Valentin added thoughtfully, " it will require a certain transfer of personnel."

M. Valentin lost no time. In a matter of days he had taken a lease on a country house, not far from Arras, known as La Maison Blanche. The personnel was transferred a few days later. I was walking down the main street of Arras one afternoon when several small cars, each crammed with beaming young women, drove past. The girls were waving gaily at every British soldier in sight. " Bonjour, chéri ! " " Bonjour, chéri ! " Most of those to whom these greetings were addressed were baffled by them. I was not. I knew that M. Valentin had been as good as his word.

A week or so later a grand party was held at the Maison Blanche, to which I was invited. The place was not open for business. That would be for the morrow. This was a purely social occasion, with Madame very grand in spangles and black lace, and the girls all wearing discreet evening gowns. A good deal of sweet champagne was drunk, and the conversation could not possibly have been more refined.

" Will you allow me to offer you another glass of wine, mademoiselle."

" You are too kind, mon capitaine ! "

A few weeks later, when the Germans attacked us, the Maison Blanche justified its existence, if it never had before. The Madame and her girls behaved like heroines. Fiercely patriotic, like most French prostitutes, *boules de suif* to a girl, they defied the German invaders, hid British soldiers from them, helped them to escape, and, one way and another, made themselves quite a sizeable thorn in the side of the Wehrmacht. It is only fair that this should be said now.

One Englishman whom we always saw on our visits to Paris was refreshingly free from illusions. A section of the British Press took a perverse delight, throughout the so-called " phoney war," in publishing from time to time malicious stories about the life of fashionable ease which, it was alleged, Noël Coward led in Paris. It was reported that Mr Coward, disguised as a lieutenant-commander R.N.V.R., was contributing to the war effort by flitting from cocktail-party to cocktail-party, and that he had found a comfortable sinecure through influential friends.

Nothing could have been further from the truth. Mr Coward was engaged, and successfully engaged, in an exacting job of liaison. The highlight of our visits to Paris was a regular meeting of senior French and British officers and functionaries over which Mr Coward presided with the suave aplomb which millions have admired on the stage and screen, and which he was able, without apparent difficulty, to transfer to real life.

After these meetings, the emissaries from British General Headquarters were often entertained by Mr Coward in his flat. To hear our host sing, to his own accompaniment, some of his own compositions which, for reasons which were as clear to us as they would have been to the Lord Chamberlain, could never be performed on the British stage, was a rare delight and privilege.

It was not, however, a privilege confined to generals and staff officers. Whenever he had a free evening (doubtless from all those cocktail- and dinner-parties) Noël Coward would drive northward from Paris. We had furnished him with a list of the most isolated units of the B.E.F.—a detached company of infantry here, a battery of gunners there, a Field Company of Royal Engineers, a " mobile bath unit." The qualification for Noël Coward's list was that the troops concerned should be far from any centre of population, with little hope of ever seeing a visiting concert-party or even of going to a cinema.

To these seemingly forgotten men, isolated on the dismal border which separates France from Belgium, Noël Coward would suddenly appear, having driven perhaps two hundred miles to find them.

" My name's Coward," he would say to the commanding officer. " I gather your chaps don't get much fun up here. If you've a piano anywhere I wonder if they'd like me to put on a little show for them."

Night after night, in the grim winter which preceded the real war, Noël Coward gave our troops a cabaret show for which people in London and New York would have paid almost any money. Then he drove back through the dawn to his real job in Paris. It is only right that, after many years, this should be recorded.

In the first hours of the morning of May 10, 1940, Guardsman Yule, my soldier-servant, roused me from sleep with a piece of news which we had been expecting for weeks past.

" They're in, sir ! "

Expectation notwithstanding, it took me a moment to grasp his meaning.

" Who are in, Yule ? "

" The Boche, sir. They're into Belgium."

The three weeks which followed were a confusion of fighting and boredom, of an early advance into Belgium, followed by a sickening retreat. The last days of May 1940 saw me back in England. The ' miracle ' of Dunkirk was not ended when I landed at Dover, and my general, who had also been ordered to England, was asked to deliver a postscript to the nine o'clock news on the night of his return. General Mason-Macfarlane was a man who did not mince words. Together we sat in his club and composed a grim factual script in which the general warned his hearers that the greater part of the B.E.F. might still be lost. It was useless to lay all the blame for this on the Army, which had been systematically starved for years, by successive Governments, of the weapons and equipment which it needed. If disaster overtook the men who still remained in France, then new and greater armies must be raised to avenge them, and this could be done only if the British people trusted its military leaders.

I dined that night with Lieutenant-Colonel Gerald Templer, my immediate superior in France, who, had we known it at the time, carried a field-marshal's baton in his knapsack, and together we listened to the general's broadcast.

" By God," said the colonel, " the ' top-hats ' aren't going to like this."

They did not like it. This was the first, but by no means the last, war-time broadcast in which I had a hand which earned official disapproval.

On the morning after the broadcast General Mason-Macfarlane telephoned to me.

" I've been sent for by the Minister of Information," he said. " You'd better come along too. Come and have breakfast first."

We ate a large breakfast—rationing was still no more than a cloud on the horizon in June 1940—and drove to keep our appointment with Mr Duff Cooper. The Minister was angry. How dare General Mason-Macfarlane criticize the Government for deficiencies in arms and equipment ? Did the general not realize that the present Lord President of the Council (Mr Neville Chamberlain) was Prime Minister during much of the critical period when, as the general had asserted, the British Government was starving its Armed Forces ?

Mason-Mac's large square jaw seemed to shoot forward a couple of inches. I knew the storm signals, and the storm came.

" I'm afraid I can't help that, sir," he said. " You're speaking as a politician. I spoke as a soldier. And what's more I spoke the truth."

He swung round on me.

" Didn't I, Ewan ? "

" You did, sir," I replied.

" We've just come from France," Mason-Mac added.

" Yes, I know, General," the Minister said, " but we can't afford broadcasts which damage civilian morale."

" Damage civilian morale, my foot," the general retorted. " If you tell people the truth they'll do what's required of them—and what is required is the hell of a lot of work."

The interview petered out. Neither side would yield, and at last the general rose to his feet.

" Come along, Ewan," he said, " there's nothing more we can do here."

We bade Mr Duff Cooper a formal farewell, and walked out. Before closing the door Mason-Mac said to me in a loud voice, which was certainly heard, as he intended that it should be, in the Ministerial office, " Well, I know what *I* think of our bloody Minister of Information ! "

And the general stumped off down the corridor.

For a few days I waited at my parents' home near Reading, expecting to be sent back to France, south of the Loire. I was " on two hours recall " to Aldershot, but the summons never came.

My father was at this time regional commissioner for the Southern Region of England. Had invasion come—and it was more likely to come in his territory than in any other—he would have had all the powers of the King, and could have carried on the Government in the name of His Majesty if the Southern Region had been cut off from the rest of the country. Until we were invaded the regional commissioners (there were eight of them in all for the whole country) were in supreme command of the police and civil defence forces and, of course, in close liaison with the Armed Forces.

My father's headquarters were at Reading, in the gaol which Oscar Wilde made immortal, and which is now a super-Borstal for particularly tough young prisoners. In 1939, when crime was much less prevalent than it now is, the gaol was closed down, but it reopened to house the regional commissioner and his staff. My parents had bought a house in the pleasant Thames-side village of Sonning, four miles from Reading, a little time before the war, knowing well that war was coming and what my father would be called upon to do when it did.

I did not feel like lurking about in uniformed idleness while the Battle of France was being fought out to its tragic conclusion, and I asked my father whether he could not find me some useful job. He replied that the police were raiding the homes of suspected fifth-columnists every night, and that the chief constable of Berkshire was short of staff who could read and evaluate the documents seized, particularly those written in German, as many of them were. If I would care to help in this work I should be very welcome to do so.

And so for a week I sat and ploughed through masses of paper, and very queer stuff a lot of it was. The police brought in a tin uniform case of highly incriminating evidence, which they had dug up in the garden of an Oxford don. A bank clerk in Surrey was found to possess two sets of S.S. uniform, an extensive file of correspondence with the German Embassy in London, and a very tidy little armoury of pistols, whips, and ammunition, not to mention a library of books on torture.

We devised a system of classifying this evidence so that it could be easily seen, at a rough glance, whether the suspect was really dangerous or not. But no arrests took place. At last I tackled my father about this.

" The Home Office have been sticky," he said, " but one of my colleagues in the other regions ordered a lot of arrests on his own authority last night, and if he can do it so can I. We're going into action to-night."

I suppose they did so, but, of course, I never heard what happened, and rightly so.

When the news of France's capitulation came over the radio my parents and I were in the drawing-room of their house in Sonning. " This calls for champagne, to cheer us up," my father said, and went to the cellar to fetch a bottle. We drank to the greatness and deliverance of France and to our own deliverance, and then I decided to go down to The Bull, the most homely of Sonning's three inns, to see how the news had affected the local population.

The bar was in an uproar. Everybody was buying drinks for everybody else and everybody was in the best of good spirits. " Now we know where we stand ! " people said. " No more bloody foreigners ! " Earnest souls were explaining to eager listeners that if one poured candle-grease into a 12-bore cartridge it would blow the stomach out of a German paratrooper at 300 yards. Other strategists were devising booby-traps of lethal intent and, probably, doubtful efficacy. Everybody was having a lot of fun.

I blessed this heavenly stupidity. We should not fail while we had such people in Britain.

Soon afterwards I became a schoolmaster, my job being to instruct officers in the interrogation of German prisoners of war, first at Swanage and later in the overpowering atmosphere of Smedley's Hydro, at Matlock. In September I was ordered to London.

My job in France had been officially classified as " Military Intelligence," but that term covers a multitude of duties, not all of which are particularly secret. Now, in the autumn of 1940, I began to be drawn into " Intelligence " in the sense in which the public understands the term.

The essence of intelligence work is that the fewest possible people should have an overall picture of it. In some ways it may be compared to the production line in a modern factory. Thousands of workers are employed, each one of them tightening a particular nut again and again, soldering a piece of wire to a strip of metal, punching a rivet into one particular hole. The individual worker may have no idea of how his tiny job fits into the total pattern, but at least he can see the finished product, the car or the television-set which he has helped to make.

Those who work in intelligence can never do this, for there is never a finished product, and if there were, great care would be taken to ensure that those who made it did not see it, or recognize it if they did see it. Each man does his own job, and leaves it to others to fit the pieces together.

That is why no book about any branch of intelligence can hope to give more than a very incomplete and inevitably distorted picture of even one small aspect of the whole design—if a design can be said to exist in something which, by its very nature, is bound to be fluid.

In 1940 our intelligence system, permanent, hardly less active in peace than in war, found, to its dismay, that another prop had been added to the edifice. The organization which has become celebrated under the name Special Operations Executive, or S.O.E., was, as they say in the Navy, strictly " hostilities only." When the war ended it was disbanded, to the undisguised relief of its ' professional ' counterparts, although to-day even a visit to the handsome club-house of the Special Forces Club in London might suggest that S.O.E., while sleeping, is by no means dead.

The Office of Strategic Services, or O.S.S., S.O.E.'s American counterpart, hastily created, with our co-operation, after Pearl Harbour, has not been disbanded, and now forms part of the Central Intelligence Agency in which are combined all the functions of intelligence. This is contrary to British practice, since we maintain that the gathering of information and counter-espionage should be completely divorced from sabotage and subversive operations. We were therefore obliged to improvise S.O.E. at short notice, and to dismantle it at the end of the war was the logical outcome of this doctrine, since we assumed, wrongly, that the end of the war implied the beginning of the peace.

Much has been written about S.O.E. and O.S.S., whereas very little has been written about the British intelligence organizations. The reason for this is plain enough. The latter were, and are, staffed by ' regulars. ' S.O.E. was manned almost entirely by people who, in the First World War, when snobbery was even more rife in the British Services than it was in the last conflict, would have been termed " temporary gentlemen." And a very queer collection we were.

Among the colleagues in S.O.E. whom I knew personally were, for instance, an eminent young actor, a professional burglar, a man who sold rubber goods in Bucharest, two Peers of the Realm and a sprinkling of baronets, a pimp, two or three prostitutes, a jockey, an art expert, a publisher, and several journalists. This is a list assembled at random from personal contacts. We had some much queerer fish than these in S.O.E., and the organization was, as might have been expected, regarded with deep suspicion by the more orthodox organizations beside which we presumed to range ourselves. But S.O.E., like Combined Operations, another irregular body which was no less disliked in some quarters than were we, confounded its critics by actually doing the job which it was designed to do.

Notwithstanding the spate of books which have been written during the past fifteen years by brave men and women who served S.O.E. " in the field," the reason for the existence of S.O.E. is not generally understood. It was summed up by the Emperor Napoleon in a passage from a letter which he wrote in 1808, and which is quoted on the title-page of this book. " In war," Napoleon said, " moral considerations make up three-quarters of the game : the relative balance of manpower accounts only for the remaining quarter."

Somebody, it is not unreasonable to suppose, remembered those words in the weeks which followed the providential escape of the bulk of the British Expeditionary Force from the beaches of northern France. The " balance of manpower " could scarcely have been less favourable to us than it was then. We had managed to retrieve most of our trained soldiers, but they were totally unequipped. In any case, with France out of the war and with no immediate prospect of recruiting any allies, apart from the governments-in-exile, which were trying to settle down in London, we could never hope to match, man for man, the armies of the Third Reich. One answer to the problem was to attack the morale of the enemy.

The men who, from a small office in Fitzmaurice Place, a

few yards from Berkeley Square, in London, set themselves to grapple with this daunting task in the autumn of 1940, had no illusions, which was more than could be said for those who manned some other 'secret' establishments. One of these, comfortably snugged down at Woburn Abbey, the country seat of the Dukes of Bedford, employed a large staff of propagandists whose mission in life it was to undermine the morale of the German people. During the long, cold winter of the phoney war British aircraft had been risked on missions whose sole purpose was to drop copies of Mr Neville Chamberlain's speeches on the German people. If the object of these costly sorties was to add to the sufferings which, according to the 'experts' in London, were being inflicted by the Nazis upon their fellow-countrymen, these "leaflet raids" may, in some small degree, have served their purpose. The leaflets were little models of ineptitude, and they must have bored to extinction any German who bothered to read them.

Even after the fall of France, when Europe lay prostrate at the feet of a victorious Germany, the psychologists in " the Country," as Woburn was generally called, insisted that Great Britain had " 60,000,000 allies " in Germany. These were the " German workers," who were, it seemed, heartily sick of Hitler and all his works, and awaited only the necessary stimulus from Bedfordshire to overthrow their master.

To Colonel (now General Sir) Dallas Brooks and the small band of officers who had joined him at Fitzmaurice Place, this reading of the situation seemed not only false but dangerous, since it appeared to be founded on wishful thinking. The plain, if unpalatable, fact of the matter was that in the eight years which had elapsed since Hitler's seizure of power most Germans, to borrow a phrase which Mr Macmillan was later to make famous, had " never had it so good," or at least never since the defeat of 1918. Germans might grumble mildly, in 1939, about shortages of butter or of this or that commodity, but they did not grumble about shortage of work, as they had, and with good reason, before Hitler's advent to power.

Whatever the methods may have been by which Hitler

lifted Germany from despair to a new and overweening national pride, the Führer had kept his promise to give Germans bread and work. If Great Britain and France had stood firm when Czechoslovakia was threatened in 1938, or had they, better still, opposed the German march into the Rhineland in 1936, Hitler might indeed have been overthrown. Then there were men in Germany who would almost certainly have opposed him, and who had the means of doing so effectively. To suppose that the " German workers " would be either able or willing to topple the Führer from his throne was to misread German history. " I'm all right, Jack ! " is an expression which is easily translated into German.

And now, Colonel Brooks and his staff maintained, it would take more than a shower of leaflets to shake the allegiance of a people which was still rubbing its eyes at the glittering victories which Hitler had laid at its feet. It was futile to talk, as many of our broadcasts did at that time, of the wickedness of the Gestapo to an audience whose only actual contact with the Gestapo would be likely to take place if they were found listening to enemy broadcasts. To most Germans the Geheime Staatspolizei was no more than a name. Such dealings as they had with the police were with the " Green Police," the ordinary uniformed " Schupos."

Hugh Dalton, the Minister of Economic Warfare, had been told by Winston Churchill that it was the duty of S.O.E., for which he bore Ministerial responsibility, to " set Europe ablaze." Presumably Germany was still a part of Europe, even though a hostile part, and every effort must therefore be made to obey the Prime Minister by kindling such sparse brushwood as might be found there. It did not look as though the spark for this conflagration was likely to come from Woburn.

Propaganda more telling and biting than that purveyed by " the Country " was needed, and propaganda must be accompanied by action, on however small a scale. " The Country " would continue its courtship of the German people. In Fitzmaurice Place an embryonic organization was planned whose purpose would be to attack the morale of the German

Armed Forces by sabotage in occupied territories and by special propaganda and, conversely, to raise and maintain the spirits of those living under German occupation by the same means. Finally, and most important of all, the new organization would actively recruit and help resistance movements in all occupied territories, and would organize sabotage.

This was the genesis of S.O.E., and it was to this organization that I was called in the autumn of 1940.

2. "DON'T LET'S BE BEASTLY TO THE GERMANS"

WHEN I REPORTED for duty in London I was told that the War Office was dissatisfied with the German broadcasts of the B.B.C. They might be good enough for civilians, about whom the War Office did not profess to have much knowledge, although even this was doubtful. They were certainly not the stuff to give to the million-odd German troops who stood poised along the northern coast of France, awaiting the order to invade the British Isles. Something a good deal more positive was needed, the War Office felt, and I was ordered to collaborate with Major John Baker-White, later Member of Parliament for Canterbury, in devising a programme which would have some appeal to the German Army of Invasion. The B.B.C. would give us fifteen minutes each night, and we should be our own masters.

John Baker-White was an excellent propagandist although he did not claim to any special expertise where the Germans were concerned. This I was supposed to supply. Between us we worked out a formula for our programme which is only worth mentioning here because I am still vain enough to believe that it was a good formula in the circumstances.

The B.B.C. German services at that time were largely, and quite understandably, manned by refugees, mostly Jewish, from Germany. We decided to have nothing to do with any of them—with one exception. It could be taken for granted, we argued, that a German soldier would resent hearing a German voice speaking into an enemy microphone. He would, moreover, believe, however wrongly, that the speaker was a Jew. Monstrous though the anti-Semitic teachings of the Nazis were, they had penetrated a great deal more deeply into the minds of Germans than the experts at Woburn were prepared to admit. It was agreed that three German-speaking British officers would put the programme on to the air. If our accents were not perfect so much the better. At least that proved to our German audience that we were not traitors. We introduced the programme jauntily, and on a note of deliberate defiance, to *The British Grenadiers*, played with all the *brio* which the band of the Grenadier Guards can bring to their own Regimental March. Then, as Goering's bombers droned sullenly over the derelict roller-skating-rink in North London which sheltered our studio, somewhat dubiously, beneath a glass roof, we announced ourselves : " Hier ist England ! Hier ist England ! ! Hier ist England ! ! ! Es sprechen englische Offiziere an die deutsche Wehrmacht ! "—" Here is England ! British Officers speak to the German Army ! "

And speak to them we did. Our news-reader, contrary to our general rule, was a German and a Jew. But Mr Behrmann had, in the First World War, achieved the fabulous rank (for one of his race) of regimental sergeant-major in the Prussian Guard. He was, moreover, a skilled broadcaster, and news-reading is not a job for amateurs. Mr Behrmann's voice had the authentic rasp of the Prussian warrant-officer, which automatically brings a German soldier to attention, and evidence which we later collected showed that it did just that. Stephen Haggard, one of the best young actors in London, then a lance-corporal awaiting a commission, and a wonderful speaker of German, went to work with me.

We had access to intelligence sources, and could therefore chat to our listeners with some confidence. Why, we might inquire, in a nightly gossip column called " Things we should like to know," had the 2nd Battalion of Infantry Regiment 76, stationed at Wimereux, had no leave for a month ? Could it be that their commanding officer, Major Schmidt, was so obsessed by the charms of Mlle Odette Dupont, who lived at such-and-such an address, that he had no time to attend to leave-rosters ? We gave our listeners a recorded serial which recounted the unhappy life of Gefreiter Hirnschal, or Corporal Numbskull, a keen but somewhat addle-pated Nazi, who somehow always managed to make unintentionally outrageous remarks about the Party in his letters home, which, in consequence, never got past the censors. The programme played out to a splendid pastiche of a German marching-song, composed and recorded for us by Geraldo and his celebrated orchestra. The tune opened with all the pomp of a hearty military march, blaring brass accompanying cheerful, confident voices, and died away at last in the plaintive whine of a mouth organ receding into the distance, as the German armies marched farther and farther from home.

We learned later that *Wir wollen Heim ins Reich* (*We want to come home to the Reich*), a slogan of Hitler's which we turned against him, had caused a lot of Germans to feel pangs of homesickness, which was just what the song was intended to do.

We also introduced guest speakers to our audience. Captain Thomas Troubridge, R.N., later to become Admiral Sir Thomas and Fifth Sea Lord, who had been British Naval attaché in Berlin until the summer of 1939, sometimes had a few words to say to the German Navy. Many German naval officers knew Troubridge, who indeed had occasionally written, unofficially, Fleet Orders for Hitler's Kriegsmarine, and they recognized his booming voice. His German accent was atrocious, but the meaning of what he said was painfully clear.

The general burden of these talks was that it would be a pleasure for the Royal Navy to blow the Germans out of the water, and that it was really rather unkind of Admiral Raeder to deny that " band of brothers " this simple satisfaction. The same theme ran through all our broadcasts. " All right," we said, " just try to invade us and see what happens to you ! "

Towards the end of the war we captured an order, dated December 1940 and issued by the German commander-in-chief in France. It pointed out that a programme " skilfully designed to appeal to the weakest side of the German soldier's nature " was broadcast from London every evening at a certain time, and all officers were enjoined to ensure that the troops under their command did not listen to this dangerous transmission.

But we soon discovered there were people at home no less eager to see the end of the " Programme for the German Forces " than were Hitler's generals. The supporters of the " 60,000,000 allies " school of thought felt, or professed to feel, that the often rather brutal tone of our programme, its defiant attitude, might alienate the affections of the Germans from Great Britain ; a curious point of view when it is considered that at that moment the German Army, with the ardent support of the whole German nation, was preparing to invade and to enslave us.

A statement, which I broadcast myself one evening (and which was perfectly true), to the effect that Reich Marshal Goering had secured for himself the virtual monopoly of the manufacture of contraceptives in Germany for a payment to the Jewish owner of the firm, who had fled abroad, of £10,000 in sterling, gave the opposition a chance of denting our rather thin armour. Was vulgarity of this kind to be allowed to sully the pure ether of the B.B.C. ? they asked the Minister of Information. The Minister, briefed by us, replied that the broadcast had been phrased in such a way that nobody who was not familiar with the goods in question, as all German soldiers were, would have known what we were talking about. Baffled but undaunted, the opposition withdrew to await another *casus belli*.

They did not have long to wait. One November night, as the bombs thudded around Maida Vale, causing the glass roof of our studio to shiver, and shaking the microphones, we introduced to our listeners a colonel in the Polish Army. This officer came from Poznan, which at the time of his birth had been Posen, and a Prussian city. He had served as an artillery officer in the German Army in the Kaiser's war, and had joined the Polish Army after the liberation of his country. I wrote the script which the colonel delivered.

" I was proud to be a German soldier then," the colonel said. " When one of our men was killed it was my duty, as battery-commander, to write to his wife or to his parents and to express my sorrow, which was perfectly genuine. But I cannot help wondering whether the men with whom I fought more than twenty years ago were the same kind of men as you, who are listening to me now. I believe that they were, and that the ordinary German soldier is still the decent chap that he used to be. But, in that case, how can you stand shoulder to shoulder with the brutal S.S., who have made martyrs of the Polish people, and who are now bringing their rule of torture and oppression to every European nation which you—and not the S.S.—have conquered? We are going to win this war, however long and bitter the struggle may be, and I warn you all that, unless you now make it clear that you will have nothing to do with the atrocities of the S.S. henceforward, we shall, when we have beaten you at last, make no distinction between you and the S.S. All will carry the same load of shame, and all will suffer the same punishment."

The menacing tone of this address was too much for those who believed, flying in the face of all the evidence, that the Germans, with the exception of Hitler and a few misguided followers, were really rather fond of the British. A Member of Parliament asked a question in the House of Commons. Did the Minister of Information not realize, he demanded, that the threatening tone of this broadcast was likely to give offence to many Germans? Apparently the Minister did realize this, and it seems that his heart bled for the wounded feelings of our enemies. At all events, we were forced to surrender control of the programme no more than six weeks after its inception, to the indignation of the War Office.

I was told one day, a week or two after we had left the skating-rink in Maida Vale, that the chief feature of the " Programme for the German Forces " had been, on the previous evening, a talk in which the speaker drew a telling comparison between the kindness with which the British authorities treated conscientious objectors and the cruelties to which their German counterparts were subjected by the Nazis. Broadcasts of this kind could, of course, be warranted to cause no offence whatever to any German, soldier or civilian. In fact, they may have given those who cared to risk their life and liberty by listening to them a hearty laugh. By that time I had been formally drafted to Fitzmaurice Place, and was a full member of S.O.E.

If I have told the story of the " Programme for the German Forces " at what may seem to be exaggerated length it must be said, in extenuation, that the virtual suppression of this programme had several important consequences. It convinced the War Office that it was almost hopeless to aspire to hit at the morale of the German Armed Forces if the channels of communication with them were subject to close political control. The policy of the B.B.C., which was to establish a reputation for absolute truth both with our friends in Europe and with our enemies, was a perfectly correct one, as was proved in the latter years of the war. But soldiers, whatever their nationality, speak a language of their own, and that language was not understood either in Senate House, the immense white stone headquarters of London University, from which the Ministry of Information now operated, or by those who toiled among the Duke of Bedford's Old Masters and herds of rare animals at Woburn.

Moreover, the purposes which the military authorities sought to achieve by propaganda were often incompatible with the kind of long-term directive under which, quite properly, our official information services were required to work. It was sometimes necessary for the services to seek a quick tactical advantage by the use of propaganda of one kind or another, and to do so, the military authorities felt, they must possess some organization, however modest, which was under their own hand. This applied particularly to propaganda directed against the German Army and Air Force.

At Fitzmaurice Place, as might have been expected, very little attention was paid to work against the Germans, military or civilian. Both categories of the Master Race, as far as could be judged, were in a highly inflated frame of mind, thanks to a series of sweeping and quite unexpected victories. Furthermore, there was no sign of any real resistance to the Nazis in Germany. It was known, of course, that diplomats such as Ulrich von Hassell and Albrecht Bernsdorff, saints like Dietrich Bonhöffer, and certain regular Army officers of very senior rank were opposed to Hitler. But it was evident that there was no cohesion between Hitler's enemies at home.

In any case, it was quite unrealistic to suppose that any force except the Army could overthrow the Nazi dictator, and it was hardly likely that the Army would take any steps in that direction for some time to come. They had, in little more than a year, conquered Poland, Norway, Denmark, Holland, and France, and were now eagerly awaiting the order to spring at the throats of their last enemies, the British. They were drunk with victory, and they expected that Hitler would give them further doses of that heady brew. The German people expected this also.

There were, of course, many refugees from Germany who went about London claiming to anybody who would listen that a German Resistance Movement existed, that they were in touch with it, and that it was liable to depose Hitler at any moment. These optimists, whose motives for inventing such fairy-tales ranged from pure self-interest to equally pure wishful thinking, were welcome allies to those Britons who placed their faith in the " German worker." It was largely thanks to their intervention that the "Programme for the German Forces" had been driven off the air in its original form, and it was a relief to find that at Fitzmaurice Place they could be ignored, or virtually ignored.

Not that we did not maintain a formal, if not a cordial, relationship with "the Country." Once a week a splendid Daimler saloon purred up to the unobtrusive entrance to our offices. It collected me and, sometimes, the late F. A. Voigt, who knew more about Germany than almost any Englishman, and who got little enough credit for his expertise either during the war or after it. Colonel Brooks regarded these duty visits as a waste of time.

"Tell 'em to stop lurking about forty miles outside London and to come in and get bombed every night like the rest of us," he would say. "It might fill them with righteous anger if they saw what the Germans are doing here, and a bit of anger is what we need in our propaganda."

We never passed this message on. The limousine drove up to the abbey, sending the deer scampering across their paddocks and announcing its arrival with a melodious blast of the horn. We dined in a large canteen, watched by noble portraits whose originals would certainly have regarded us as a very odd lot indeed. I generally used to sleep in a small room which contained, as far as I can recall, two Dürer drawings and a lovely little Murillo. When the light was switched off, and the blackout curtains drawn back, the night sky to the southward, lit by the twinkle of anti-aircraft shells, glowed as Hitler lit his funeral pyres in London, and searchlights stabbed the distant darkness. A night away from the London Blitz was certainly a relief, but Brooks was right in believing that this immunity from the realities of war added to the air of unreality which our propagandists breathed in those days. Some of them continued to breathe it until 1945.

In the meantime General Wavell had, by the middle of December 1940, driven the Italian armies from Egypt, and Hitler decided with some reluctance that he must help Mussolini to retrieve his losses. Germans, the advance

guard of the Afrika Korps, began to appear in Libya, much
to the astonishment of some people at G.H.Q. Middle East,
in Cairo, whose thinking had become so conditioned to dealing
with Italians that they were almost incapable of imagining
any other enemy.   In any case, there was hardly anybody in
the Middle East who knew much about Germans, though
Italian experts grew on date-palms.

As spring approached, it seemed to those who were in
charge of my fortunes at Fitzmaurice Place that I might make
myself useful in Cairo.   There was little scope at home, and
my efforts to join the French section, which was already
sending agents into France, were politely rebuffed.   There
were, it seemed, plenty of better volunteers than I for that
dangerous work, but comparatively few people who knew
much about Nazi Germany and its inhabitants.   I was therefore ordered to Cairo by the quickest available route.   My
brief was a very vague one.   Cairo needed people who knew
something about Germany.   I knew something about Germany.
Therefore Cairo needed me.   This simple reasoning proved
itself to be correct only in a very limited degree, as it turned
out.

The " quickest available route " turned out to be a passage
to Freetown, Sierra Leone, in a light cruiser.   Thence, in
theory, I should be flown across Africa in less than no time,
and arrive in Cairo within a month of leaving London.
Delighted to be going abroad, I took a train to Plymouth in
high spirits.

I have sometimes felt that I was a Jonah for Plymouth.
On the very night of my arrival there the Luftwaffe switched
its attack from London to the Devon seaport, and for three
nights Plymouth was subjected to bombing very much more
concentrated than anything which I had known in London.
It was a great relief when H.M.S. *Dunedin* sailed.   The
Scharnhorst was at sea at this moment, and the pessimists in
the wardroom thought it highly probable that we should
encounter her.

" That'd keep you busy, Pongo," they said.   (All soldiers

are " Pongo " to the Royal Navy.) " You'd have to do a bit of stretcher-bearing then. She'd sink us without our being able to get within range, even."

That might well be, but at least there was a prospect of being able to sleep until we were sunk, which was more than there had been ashore in recent nights. Although my bunk was immediately above the starboard propeller shaft, I found the vibration very soothing indeed.

3. WAR OF WORDS

THE JOURNEY TO Cairo lasted longer than anyone had expected. *Dunedin*'s course carried her almost to the coast of Brazil before at last we headed eastward for Sierra Leone. The wardroom pessimists were quite disappointed to find that we had, in spite of their forebodings, escaped destruction from the 15-inch guns of the *Scharnhorst*. For two rather anxious days, though, it seemed that these Jeremiahs might be justified, since we received a signal from the Admiralty announcing that the Germans had reported our position to *Scharnhorst*. *Dunedin* was an old ship, a 6-inch light cruiser completed just after the First World War, with a top speed of about 22 knots. For two days her engineers drove her at a knot or two above this maximum through a fierce storm in the Bay of Biscay, which caused the wardroom furniture to perform a devil's dance, and once brought a sofa and the three officers who were sitting on it down upon my head, a mishap which amused everybody, including " Pongo the Passenger," very much indeed.

But of the *Scharnhorst* there was happily no sign, and three weeks after sailing from Plymouth *Dunedin* dropped anchor in the fine harbour of Freetown. I said good-bye to my ship-mates with great regret. If I had known that, within six months, *Dunedin* was destined to be torpedoed in the mouth of the river Plate, and that there would be virtually no survivors from her splendid ship's company, there would have been a poignancy in my leave-taking which, since the future was mercifully hidden from us, was actually rather a gay affair. After a special dinner we played rugger up and down the wardroom and parted at last vowing that we would meet again in London.

Freetown gave me my first sight of a British colonial possession, and I was not impressed. The transit camp at Wilberforce, high above the town, was a pleasant place enough, but Freetown had little to show for some 150 years of British rule.

A transit camp in war-time is, one imagines, a very plausible imitation of purgatory, an abode of lost souls condemned to wait hopefully for release and in the meantime exposed to excruciating boredom. Once a week some of us drove cheerfully out to a rough landing-strip which had been hacked from the bush, and watched for the aircraft which was to carry me across Africa. It always arrived more or less on time, but it was never able to continue its flight. Once the undercarriage crumpled and collapsed before our disappointed eyes, on another occasion a cylinder head blew off, and a third attempt to leave Freetown was frustrated by a buckled propeller.

Each mishap meant a further sentence of at least a week in purgatory. There was nothing for it but to sip tepid beer on the balcony of the Grand Hotel, which was a good deal less grand than its name implied, and to lay wagers on whether the colony's anti-aircraft guns would manage to hit the Vichy French reconnaissance aircraft which flew up from Dakar dead on schedule every morning, circled the harbour defiantly while the guns put up an ineffective barrage, and made off again. By the time we had watched this performance on several successive mornings nobody was prepared to bet on the skill of the gunners, and the spectacle lost whatever element of suspense it may once have held for us. Some weeks later a Spitfire arrived in Sierra Leone and shot the Frenchmen into the sea. We missed this climax, but when I was told of it I remember feeling that it was rather unsporting.

The British authorities themselves were quite aware of the colony's deficiencies. After I had been marooned in Freetown for about three weeks, thereby qualifying as the oldest resident of the transit camp, the governor very kindly asked me to lunch. He explained that the colony was by no means as he would like to see it. The shanty-town of shacks built of petrol-tins which disfigures Freetown was, the governor admitted, a disgrace. But what could one do with a revenue of only £1 million or so a year?

One could not, I suppose, do much. But I could not help feeling that we might ourselves have developed the iron-ore field which was being worked by an American company, and that we might have shown more imagination about the possibilities of Sierra Leone's diamond industry, as we have done since the war.

I spent a fascinating week-end at Port Loko, the head-quarters of the Sierra Leone Regiment, Royal West African Frontier Force, where I saw a witch-doctor—he was a lance-corporal—in action. His job was to detect a thief in one of the platoons. The culprit was already under suspicion. The lance-corporal laid five long feathers, each tipped with a small ball of clay, starwise on the baked earth of the parade-ground. He then covered the feathers with a half-gourd and ordered the suspect to take two paces forward.

"Now," said the witch-doctor. "You tell truth. If you not tell truth one these feathers he stand up!"

The man gave a long account of his innocence, and the gourd was removed. One feather rose and stood rigid on its clay tip. The man was ordered to give a better explanation, and was warned that if he did not do so two feathers would stand up. They did. Finally, after four feathers had risen from the ground, the man confessed and produced the stolen property. I have never ceased to wonder how this was done.

At last, despairing of ever leaving Sierra Leone by air, I managed to get passage in a small ship, the *New Northland*, which would creep down the coast to Takoradi, the port of Accra, where one might hope for better luck. The *New*

Northland was a Canadian vessel, built for service in Arctic waters. This did not make her the ideal ship for cruising up and down the coast of West Africa in a temperature of more than 100 degrees in the shade, which was matched by high humidity. She was without fans, and her cabins, which must have been delightfully snug in an Arctic winter, were hellish in an African summer. The presence aboard of a large contingent of doubtfully " Free " French Senegalese troops, who had deserted from Dakar and who claimed to be filled with enthusiasm for the cause of General de Gaulle, did little to make life in the *New Northland* any pleasanter, and there were no regrets when we finally went ashore at Takoradi, in the Gold Coast.

A Hudson aircraft took me on to Lagos, the capital of Nigeria, and thence, at long last, across Africa to Khartoum. Here a Sunderland flying-boat awaited us on May 11 for the last leg of the journey, which followed the course of the Nile. I spent some of the time during this long flight in the cockpit, in desultory conversation with the captain and first officer of the aircraft. Our talk was suddenly interrupted by the wireless operator.

" We've got Hess, sir ! " he called to the captain.

" What do you mean—' We've got Hess ' ? " the captain demanded.

" Rudolf Hess, sir. Hitler's Number Two. He's landed in Scotland, and we've arrested him."

The captain expressed incredulity by uttering a single word of five letters.

" It's quite true, sir," the wireless operator insisted. " I've just heard it from the B.B.C."

I hurried back to the main cabin, where General de Larminat, one of the most gallant and successful of de Gaulle's commanders, was sitting.

" Mon général, it seems that Rudolf Hess has landed in Scotland and been arrested there."

" You mean Hitler's deputy ? " the general asked.

" Yes, sir. The W/T operator has just picked the news up."

"Ah, ça non, mon garçon. Ce n'est pas raisonnable, voyons."

"Apparently the B.B.C. have broadcast the news. It seems to be true."

De Larminat shook an admonitory finger at me.

"I do not believe it. You must be careful of spreading rumours. But if the news is confirmed when we reach Cairo I will buy you a bottle of champagne."

A few hours later we killed a bottle of Heidsieck on the terrace of Shepheard's Hotel. It tasted wonderful.

The authorities in London, who had supposed, in their innocence, that because I had some knowledge of Germany and the Germans I should be welcome in Cairo, proved to have been much mistaken. Nobody was in the least interested in my arrival, nor had the officers of the small branch of G.H.Q. to which I had been ordered to report the smallest notion of how I should employ my time. They had taken over a small block of modern flats in Sharia el Hadiqua, a couple of hundred yards from the massive building known as Grey Pillars, which housed most of General Wavell's staff.

When I arrived in Cairo we had been repulsed in the desert and the battle for Crete was about to begin. A certain General Erwin Rommel had made his appearance in Libya, and had told the Italian commander-in-chief there that the Afrika Korps, an army of seasoned German troops which was rapidly assembling under his command, would advance whenever he, as a German general, saw fit and not on any orders from the Italians.

But while all these grave matters were exercising the minds of the officers at Grey Pillars an atmosphere of happy unreality prevailed at Sharia el Hadiqua. The offices in that little block of flats were magnificently equipped. Refrigerators and fine new electric fans ensured cool drinks and cool air, handsome American limousines stood parked outside the building. Behind the block was a garden, bright with flowers.

The whole tempo of the office was conditioned to dealing with the Italians (who had, in fact, already been effectively dealt with by General Wavell). If the atmosphere was not precisely one of *dolce far niente* there was certainly an air of lassitude about the conduct of affairs. Not that I ever really knew what was going on. My knowledge of Italians and of things Italian was elementary, and nobody in Sharia el Hadiqua was interested in the Germans.

Nevertheless, any effort must be made to reach the minds of the Germans who were pouring into Libya in menacing strength. The first step was to recruit an assistant. London had blandly assured me that I should have no difficulty in finding in Cairo a paragon who combined an excellent knowledge of German with unshakeable loyalty to the British cause. In fact, it proved quite impossible to discover anybody of this kind. There were plenty of Levantines who spoke and wrote German well enough, and who claimed to be able to type and take short-hand, but it was painfully evident both to me and to our security authorities that if the formidable General Rommel ever did fulfil his promise of entering Cairo in triumph most of these people would be the first to rally to his banner, taking with them all the secrets which they had learned from us.

Then, one morning, Major Guy Tamplin, one of the few officers in that strange little department who was working really hard and who seemed to know what he was doing, mentioned that his wife had just arrived in Cairo.

" That's a stroke of luck for you," I said. " Where did she come from, for heaven's sake ? "

" From Riga," Guy announced calmly. " I was manager of the British Overseas Bank there. Luckily for me, I was in London on business when the Russians came into Riga in 1940. I've got a Bolshevik death-sentence hanging over my head, as a matter of fact, because I served with Denikin's Whites against the Reds in 1919. I was born in Russia, you know."

" But how on earth did your wife get from Latvia to Cairo ? " I asked.

" Oh, Nina's a very determined person," Guy replied. " She simply bullied and nagged the Russians until they gave

her a passport. She came out through Turkey. But the thing
is that she must get a job in Cairo. Otherwise she'll be
deported to Kenya with the other non-productive females. I
gathered that you were looking for some one to help you."

" I am indeed," I said. " Does your wife speak German ? "

" Like a German—and she does German shorthand. She
also speaks Russian, Polish, French, and, of course, Lettish."

" And she's a British subject and the wife of a British officer.
When can I meet her ? "

" I'll send her along to you to-morrow," Guy promised.

On the following morning a vision of beauty entered my
office. Nina Tamplin wore an elegant chiffon dress and an
immense picture hat. She looked as though she was about to
keep an appointment at the Ritz Bar in Paris—in fact, she
looked far too *mondaine* to be true. My heart sank. This
was not at all what I wanted. A girl with those good looks
and those very un-G.H.Q. clothes just could not be efficient.

I sat Mrs Tamplin down at a typewriter and dictated two
or three paragraphs of German at high speed. Nina rattled
them off with contemptuous ease. She then took a couple
of pages of shorthand and transcribed them. My fears were
allayed. Nina was just what I wanted.

As we got to know one another, I discovered that Mrs
Tamplin had a subtle and ingenious brain. It was not in the
least surprising that she had managed to outwit and bluff
the Soviet officials in Riga, and to make her way alone across
Russia, which was then still allied to Germany. It would
have taken a very tough commissar indeed to get the better of
Nina Tamplin.

Now, at least, there were two of us in the German section,
and it remained for us to make a job for ourselves, since
nobody else was interested in putting us to work. One day
Nina had an idea.

On her way to Cairo from Turkey Nina had spent a little
time in Jerusalem. There she had met three Polish officers
who had, before the war, been employed by the Polish national
airline LOT. In escaping from Poland, these men had taken

with them a small wireless transmitter. It was a feeble affair with an output of only half a kilowatt, but surely, Nina suggested, we might use it to broadcast to the Germans on frequencies which the enemy employed for his normal signals traffic. Nina was sure that the Poles would be willing to let us use their transmitter, and one of them was a radio engineer who would be able to service and maintain the set. We set off together for Jerusalem to investigate this possibility.

The Poles were more than anxious to help. They had installed their transmitter in a small suburban house. If the British authorities would pay the rent of this place, and cover the cost of maintaining and operating the set, they themselves were entirely at our disposal and so was their equipment. The Polish Army confirmed that they would not object to three of their officers being employed in this way. Sharia el Hadiqua, only too glad to get me and my boring obsession with Germans out of the way, agreed to foot the very modest bill for our tiny broadcasting-station, and arranged for my posting to Jerusalem with unfeigned relief. Then they more or less washed their hands of us.

In order to broadcast two programmes of fifteen minutes each day we should, even though Nina and I worked like slaves, need one more helper. This time we found him without difficulty. Lieutenant Kurt Gottlieb, Nottinghamshire Yeomanry (The Sherwood Rangers), was stationed in Palestine with his regiment. A Viennese, Kurt had, in the years before Hitler's ' liberation ' of Austria, represented his country in most of the great show-jumping championships, including the Royal Horse Show at Olympia, in London. When the Nazis came to Vienna Kurt had escaped to England, and, more fortunate than many Jewish refugees, had been warmly welcomed by the British friends whom he had made through his prowess as a horseman.

A few months before the outbreak of war Kurt had joined the Sherwood Rangers, then still a horsed yeomanry regiment, as a trooper. He had called himself Trooper Godfrey, and none of his comrades in the ranks of the regiment seem to have

realized that he was a foreigner. They simply assumed that he
came from some remote part of England, which would account
for his slightly unusual accent. After the war was some months
old, Kurt, who had a strong personality and a capacity for
leading men, was sent to an officers' training-unit. After he
had passed out, his regiment paid him the compliment, rather
unusual where a foreigner and, technically, an enemy alien was
concerned, of insisting that he be commissioned into their
ranks. " Trooper Godfrey " became Second Lieutenant
Gottlieb.

Kurt, who had a mordant wit which was as biting in
English as it was in German, was just the man we needed, and
the Sherwood Rangers agreed, with some reluctance, to second
him to me for a limited time. The Poles had, in the meanwhile,
been doing mysterious but, apparently, successful things to the
transmitter, and, on an evening in August 1941, we went on
the air for the first time, addressing ourselves to the Afrika
Korps.

It would be presumptuous to claim that our broadcasts did
much to shake the morale of the German Forces in Libya, and
we ourselves were keenly conscious of our inadequacy. Yet
within two weeks of the first broadcast we discovered, to our
delight, that our transmissions were being jammed by the
enemy, which seemed to indicate that somebody, at least, was
listening to us on the other side, and disapproved of what we
were saying sufficiently to try to prevent it being heard. Still,
this was only negative comfort, though comfort it was, of a
kind.

While we were launching our little station Kurt and I shared
a tiny house in the German Colony, one of the pleasantest parts
of Jerusalem as it then was, with Major the Prince Aly Khan.
Aly was a gay and charming companion, completely unaffected
and without any trace of ' side.' It would have been impossible
to guess from his manner or from the way he lived that this
was one of the richest young men in the world. He paid his
share of the household expenses, ate our simple food with
apparent relish, and worked hard.

One evening I was drinking the first gin of the day, and Aly was having a shower, when I saw a party of Indians coming timidly up the little concrete path which led to our front door. The leader of the party carried what seemed to be a box, wrapped in a silk scarf.

I called out to Aly in the bathroom, " Aly, I think some of your constituents have come to look you up."

Without even bothering to wrap a towel about himself, Aly strode to the front door, flung it open, and stood stark naked before his co-religionists. They, quite overwhelmed, prostrated themselves, and Aly said what were evidently the right things and accepted the gift which they offered. Then, with a few more kind words, he sent his visitors on their way. He then returned to the bathroom, put on a robe, and poured himself a pink gin.

" You might have put a towel round your middle," I said reproachfully.

" Don't worry," Aly replied. " They loved it that way. They'll talk about it to their dying day."

And I expect that they did.

The Palestine Broadcasting Service, which owned a relatively powerful medium-wave transmitter, and whose chiefs had, naturally, been informed of our activities, took advantage of the presence of Kurt and myself in Jerusalem to enlist us to broadcast a weekly programme in German from their studios. These broadcasts were not aimed at the enemy (although Kurt and I hoped that some German soldiers received them), but at the German-speaking Jewish residents of Palestine.

In June General Wavell's assault on the Italo-German Forces had failed. Rommel had advanced, Tobruk was invested, and the 15th Panzer Division had become something of a bogey, not to the soldiers only, but to many civilians in the Middle East and, most of all, to the German Jews who had found refuge in Palestine. They knew very well what their fate would be if the German Forces broke through to Cairo, and if they did not know the enemy radio stations lost no opportunity of reminding them. Kurt Gottlieb and I, speaking as British officers, tried, in a small way, to counteract these very understandable fears. We were told that we were not entirely unsuccessful in doing this.

It is typical of the muddle which dominated many of our military and para-military activities in the Middle East at this time that while we were broadcasting hopefully over our little transmitter on the outskirts of Jerusalem another tiny radio station, of whose existence we had no knowledge whatever, was piping away from Jenin, a few miles to the north. But whereas we broadcast in German, the Jenin station spoke Arabic. It was operated by Captain John Connell Robertson, who is better known to a large public to-day as John Connell, author, critic, broadcaster, and television personality. His resources were, if anything, even more meagre than our own, which was strange, for the purpose which his station was intended to serve was very much more ambitious than anything to which we aspired.

Some farsighted planner had realized that if the enemy should carry out his avowed intention of driving us out of the Levant it might be an advantage for us to control a radio station which already enjoyed the confidence and even, perhaps, in some degree, the affection of the Arabs. Such a station could be operated, if the worst came to the worst, from the Sudan or even from Kenya, and would help to stimulate Arab resistance to the invader and to pave the way for our return to the Arab lands.

Jack Robertson, in Jenin, was as little satisfied with the results which he seemed likely to achieve with his laughably inadequate equipment as were we in Jerusalem, but neither side was aware that it was not alone in its frustration. The frustration, however, was not to last very much longer.

One morning I found a signal awaiting me in the little room which served us as an office. I was to report to Cairo immediately. This was surprising, since for weeks past my own particular masters in Cairo had shown no interest in our existence, but for good or ill I decided that I must be in Cairo

that evening. Thanks to the helpfulness of the Royal Air
Force, I reached Sharia el Hadiqua just as the short-lived
Egyptian twilight was falling. I sensed an atmosphere of
uneasiness about the place.

"Ah, yes," said an urbane major. "Butler, eh? And how
have you been getting on? Everything all right in Jerusalem?
Now, you're to report to Mena House at nine this evening.
A fellow's just arrived from London. I won't give you his
name. Just tell the reception clerk who you are and you'll
be shown up."

Mena House is a very fine hotel indeed. It lies in the
shadow of the Pyramids, and is, in peace-time, much favoured
by the wealthier class of tourist. Now the great white building
was almost empty. Coal-black Sudanese servants stood about
in a deserted lobby, while in the garden the palm-trees stirred
in a sharp desert breeze. I gave my name at the reception
desk and was at once taken to Mr Terence Maxwell.

It took about ten seconds to decide that this tall, strikingly
handsome civilian was a man who knew what he wanted and
intended to see that he got it. His first question was brief and
to the point.

" Well, Butler, do you think you're doing a good job? "

To this there was only one possible reply.

" No, sir," I replied.

" Why is that? " Maxwell asked.

Under his questioning the story of our impotence came out.
I was not proud of the story. Probably we should have
asserted ourselves more, have insisted on being allowed to do
the job which needed to be done. Maxwell listened quite
impassively. At last he said, " Well, I've been sent here to
reorganize things completely. You'll take over command of
all our ' black ' propaganda, not only to the Germans, but to
Greece, Turkey, Yugoslavia, Rumania, Bulgaria, and Albania
and to the Arab world as from to-morrow morning. Put up
the badges of rank of a lieutenant-colonel before you come to
the office. Good night."

I entered Sharia el Hadiqua next morning with much the

same feelings, I dare say, as those which might be experienced by the boss of a local Soviet, in the remote fastnesses of, say, Georgia, who has suddenly been told by Mr Khrushchev that he is to become Foreign Minister of the Soviet Union. The extra ' pips ' which I had just added to the twin crowns on the shoulder-straps of my tunic seemed to weigh me down, and I felt extremely selfconscious. This feeling was not dispelled by the consternation which prevailed in what had been, so recently, a very snug little offshoot of the General Staff. Several officers were being sent home to the United Kingdom immediately, others had been warned that they would be posted far from the delights of Cairo. It was a relief to find that a small, hard core remained, and that this would include my old friend Christopher Sykes, who would work with me, and Guy Tamplin, now also a lieutenant-colonel, who would henceforward be in charge of operations, as I should be of propaganda.

As to how far we succeeded, it is perhaps enough to say that between that day, in the late autumn of 1941, and April 1943, we had erected and operated two powerful broadcasting transmitters.

Our first transmitter was, I am afraid, stolen, although we paid cash for it later. We learned that a new 10-kilowatt American transmitter was lying crated on a sun-bleached jetty at Bandar Shahpur, in Persia. It had been ordered by Reza Shah, whom we and the Russians had just deposed, and, knowing something of Persian efficiency, we were pretty certain that it would be left to rot on the dock at Bandar Shahpur until it withered away. It seemed better to kidnap the whole outfit.

Accordingly my signals officer, Major Jerry Parker, set out by road for Persia with a small body of troops in six half-ton lorries. Via Baghdad and Kermanshah, across mountains and deserts, Jerry led his little convoy safely to the Persian Gulf, and, by the mercy of Allah, the transmitter was there.

Kurt and I awaited it in the mess of his regiment in Jerusalem. The officers of the Sherwood Rangers must have noticed that

we were both on edge. Jerry had made a signal that he might
be expected in Jerusalem about 10 P.M. He arrived almost
dead on time, and with him the transmitter which, when
assembled, was about as large as a small bungalow.

Jerry assembled it, but he did better than that. Having
studied the booty (for which we paid the Persian Government
with handsome apologies), Jerry built us a duplicate. How
he did so must be one of his mysteries. He scrounged components from equivocal Arab merchants in Damascus, from
Jewish technicians in Tel Aviv, from Army stores. He made
many of the more intricate parts himself. But in an astonish-
ingly short time a new transmitter was ready to go on the air.
The original booty was earmarked for broadcasts to Europe.
The duplicate would transmit to the Arab world.

From our studios in Jerusalem teams of men and women
from Germany, Austria, Italy, and every German-occupied
country in Eastern Europe were on the air for a total of about
sixteen hours a day. Generally speaking, each country which
we addressed boasted two teams—a right-wing (sometimes
monarchist) group and an extreme left-wing group. The
members of these groups hated the sight of one another, and
Major Anthony Kendall, and his excellent staff of British
officers, each an expert in the language and politics of a particular country—did their best to ensure that the rival teams
met as little as possible. But since each team broadcast on a
different frequency and purported to be transmitting from
within the country which they were addressing, few restrictions
were placed on any attacks which they might make on each
other. We only insisted that all our broadcasts should assail
the common enemy, albeit from different standpoints. This
allowed everybody to let off some steam.

Thus it often came about, for instance, that " The Free
Voice of Greece," as our left-wing Greek station was called,
would urge its listeners to ignore the scoundrelly outpourings
of " For King and Country," a station which favoured the
exiled Government of King George of the Hellenes. This
station, the " Free Voice " would say, did admittedly oppose

the German and Italian invaders, and to that extent deserved
support, but its politics were beneath contempt. In the
meanwhile, in a studio only a few steps away from the room
in which this broadcast was being made, the " For King and
Country " team might be putting the finishing touches to a
broadcast with which they would go on the air in a few minutes,
and which would flay " The Free Voice of Greece " scarcely
less severely than the Germans and Italians.

This system worked well for a surprisingly long time. The
Greek colonies in Palestine and Egypt, who listened religiously
to our broadcasts, firmly believed that they actually were made
from Greek soil, and this applied to the people of other East
European countries also. Every now and then we arranged a
dramatic ' raid ' by the Gestapo on our studios. The announcer, his voice shrill with apprehension, would declare
that the enemy were at the door and that the station would
be forced to go off the air.

" Watch for us, watch for us ! " the announcer would cry.
" We shall be back on the air. We shall not desert you."
Then there might be a couple of pistol shots, the crash of
an overturned microphone, and silence, which would last for
a day or two until the station went triumphantly into action
again.

I had just left the studio after one of these little comedies had
been played when I fell in with a Greek acquaintance. He
had heard our programme and was horribly concerned about
the fate of the broadcasters.

" I happen to know the very address in Athens from which
they broadcast," he assured me earnestly. " The Gestapo
will do terrible things to them."

I expressed my anxiety for these heroes, and almost wished
that I could have told my friend that at that moment the
broadcasters were finishing a bottle of Cyprus brandy which
I had brought to the studio to revive them after their amateur
dramatics.

In the meantime the Arabic station which Captain Robertson
had founded in Jenin was in process of becoming a monu-

mental affair. The transmitters both of our European and Arabic stations were at Beit Jala, near Bethlehem, connected by land-line with studios in Jerusalem for the Europeans and in Jaffa for the Arabs.

Our policy with " Mahattat el Sharq el Adna el Arabiya," or " The Near East Arabic Broadcasting Station," was a simple one. This was no clandestine operation. On the contrary, we wished as many Arabs as possible to know that in this station the Arab world had a transmitter of its very own, staffed and operated by Arabs. The only Europeans in the handsome old house which contained the station's studios and offices were its first director, Wing-Commander Alfred Marsack, R.A.F., an officer who had devoted the greater part of his life to Arab affairs, and who was a devout Moslem, and the general manager, a British chartered accountant. The rest of the crew—programme staff, engineers, and artists— were Arabs. Some of them came from as far afield as Kuwait and Saudi Arabia.

Since Arabs love a display of comfort and opulence, we furnished the studios with good carpets and handsome furniture, and our servants and drivers were equipped with a smart and distinctive uniform. In the lobby which led to the studios hung an almost priceless illuminated page from the Koran, which we managed to borrow. The Koran reader who opened our programmes each day with a recital from the Holy Book was well worth the £120 a month which he received, for there is no greater attraction to Arab listeners than the Koran, beautifully intoned. Our " reader "—although this is not quite the right term, since the man was blind and knew the Koran by heart—already had a reputation which extended far beyond Palestine. Now we brought his beautiful voice every morning to tens of thousands of homes and coffee-shops, in Palestine, in Egypt, and even in the Sudan and the Persian Gulf. Men began to know and trust " Sharq el Adna," and, if the Germans ever broke through, they would continue to listen to us, wherever our transmitter might be.

It was our policy to offer our microphones to any prominent

Arab who would like to use them, and scripts were very little censored. We did not object to criticism of the British—was this not, after all, an Arab station—but we did draw the line at praise of the Germans. Subject to that proviso, our speakers were free to say what they chose, within very broad limits.

The station's dance band and classical orchestra became quite celebrated, and when they gave concerts in aid of comforts funds for Arab soldiers the largest cinema in neighbouring Tel Aviv was not large enough to hold the audience. We booked locally celebrated artistes on contract, and Vera Lynn's popularity as a singer with British troops and civilians was at least equalled, as far as the Arab world was concerned, by that of our Mary Jubran, " the Nightingale of the Lebanon."

On the political side we were lucky in being able to engage a notorious (and quite charming) rabble rouser, who had an extensive and well merited reputation as an anti-British agitator. He was also a holy man, which added greatly to his prestige in the Arab world, but this had not prevented the British authorities in Palestine from imprisoning Sheikh Muzaffar half a dozen times in the years before the war. His spells of imprisonment did not seem to have done the Sheikh much harm—indeed, they had given him a chance of learning English of a sort ; but they had greatly enhanced his reputation with those who, like himself, were bitterly opposed to all Jewish immigration to Palestine—that is to say, all Arabs.

If Sheikh Muzaffar did not particularly care for the British he cared for the Germans even less, and, unlike most Arabs, he had, in his youth, had quite a lot to do with Germans. He had been a mufti—that is to say, a chaplain—with the Turkish Army which opposed us in Palestine and Mesopotamia in the First World War, and in the course of his duties he had met many Germans and had hated them.

When, therefore, Great Britain declared war on Germany in 1939, Sheikh Muzaffar immediately presented himself to the High Commissioner in Palestine, Sir Harold MacMichael, and offered his services to the Allied cause. This he did on the clear understanding that as soon as the Germans were soundly beaten he would resume his activities against the British. For Sheikh Muzaffar, the matter was simply a choice of evils, and the British were the lesser of the evils.

Hearing that an Arab broadcasting-station was about to go on the air, the Sheikh hastened to offer his services, and I accepted them eagerly. The old man, with his fine features and noble white beard, would have been a great figure on television, but even on sound radio his whole personality came across the ether. He was quite tireless, and almost every day he delivered a commentary on current affairs as they concerned the Arabs, in which the Germans and Italians were scarified with sarcasm, humour, and straight invective. The fact that the Sheikh was broadcasting from " Sharq el Adna " was, to many thousands of Arabs, a guarantee of the authentically Arab character of the station. It was surely inconceivable that the British would have ever allowed him on the air.

Apart from our broadcasting, we controlled two presses in Cairo, and we built up throughout the area in Syria and the Lebanon, Iraq, Persia, and Turkey, a little network of propagandists, managed in each country by a British officer. We felt that we were beginning to earn our keep.

Life in those days consisted of three weeks a month in Cairo and a week in Jerusalem. But sometimes I was called farther afield.

Soon after we and the Russians had occupied Persia and deposed Reza Shah, in 1942, it was necessary for me to visit " Our Man in Teheran." I was fascinated by the Persian capital, which I have since come to know much better, and by the British Embassy, where I spent most of my time—the Hotel Ferdowsi did not tempt its guests to linger about its dingy premises.

The embassy, built in the heyday of Victorian complacency, resembles a minor British public school—a compound, surrounded by a high wall of yellowish brick, and containing a number of buildings made of the same materials, a swimming-pool, tennis courts. The atmosphere, too, under Sir Reader Bullard, our extremely able Minister, was astringent.

One day I was sitting in the lobby of the embassy waiting to lunch with the Minister. I had a couple of days to waste, since I was waiting for a signal from Cairo in order to complete my mission. I was told that His Excellency was in conference with the Soviet Ambassador—the Russians rated an Ambassador in Persia even then—and that I must wait.

Presently the Russian Ambassador emerged, accompanied by our Minister. I saw to my astonishment—why had I not checked on this ?—that the Russian Ambassador was none other than Grigori Smirnov, who had been Soviet Press attaché when I was in Berlin, and also correspondent of Tass, the Russian official news agency. We had been good friends and, until the German-Soviet Pact, had made rather a point of teasing the Nazis together.

Disguised as I was in long military greatcoat, Scottish bonnet, and the rest, I decided to give my friend a shock. I rose to my feet.

" Du, Grigori ! " I said, in our only common language.

The Ambassador swung round. His face broke into a broad grin. He strode across to me and flung both his arms around my neck.

" Ach, Du, Ewan. Was machst Du denn da ? "

I explained in a few words. Smirnov insisted that I come to the Soviet Embassy next day, and said that we would have a private party, all on our own.

When the Soviet Ambassador had left Sir Reader Bullard led the way into lunch.

" I gather that you had met the Soviet Ambassador before," he said, dryly.

On the next morning I reported to the Soviet Embassy. It was formidably guarded and more than a little forbidding. But the warmth of Smirnov's welcome, notwithstanding a concrete bust of Stalin which glared down at us, was enough to dispel the gloom. We drank a great deal of vodka and ate a lot of caviar. At last, after much gossip about old days in Berlin, I put to the Ambassador the question which I had wanted to put.

" Look, Grigori," I said, " I've got a couple of days to waste here. I shouldn't be wasting one of them if I might go up and see some of your troops."

Smirnov threw up his hands in horror.

" Don't expect me to give you a letter of introduction," he said. " As far as I'm concerned, the Army is a nuisance. They create incidents which I have to sort out. But if you put a Union Jack on your car and drive sixty miles north to Kasvin, which is our headquarters, I don't think anybody would shoot you."

" Right," I replied, " I'll do just that."

" Our Man in Teheran " telephoned to Kasvin that afternoon and arranged that an interpreter should meet us at the local *chaikhani*, or inn, at 10.30 A.M. on the following morning. Along roads slushy with melting snow, with unmelted snow on either side, we jolted over appalling potholes to Kasvin. At the tea-house the interpreter, who bore the improbable name of Hannibal, awaited us. He was a direct descendant of Peter the Great's celebrated Negro slave, a relative of Pushkin. His father had been an admiral of the Russian Imperial Navy. He was now a Persian subject.

We explained that we wished to present our compliments to the commander of the Soviet garrison.

" Nothing easier," said Hannibal, who spoke English as he spoke Russian, perfectly. " I will telephone and arrange it."

Hannibal returned five minutes later.

" At eleven-thirty," he said. " They expect you."

We drove, our Union Jack whipping in a chill wind, to the entrance of a series of barbed-wire perimeters. A little Mongol sentry, shabbily but warmly dressed in a padded cotton tunic, presented arms smartly and let us through. We drove through three more circles of barbed-wire and at last came to a tiny bungalow. The door opened without our having to knock, and we were shown into a room about the size of an English suburban ' lounge.' Eight officers confronted us, dominated, I was alarmed to see, by a lieutenant-general. I was glad that we had all taken the trouble, in Cairo, to learn Soviet badges of rank.

Since " Our Man in Teheran " was in plain clothes, it was for me to do the honours. I gave them the smartest salute I could manage, and said to Hannibal, impassive at my elbow, " Will you please tell these officers that I come, quite unofficially, from the Army of the Nile. I am sure that my commander-in-chief would be most displeased with any of his officers who happened to be close to our Allies and who failed to extend, from us all, congratulations and good wishes."

Hannibal ripped this off in a flurry of Russian, and I was disconcerted to see that my little speech seemed to have had entirely the wrong effect upon our hosts. Already glum, they now looked even glummer. At last the general spoke.

" Any questions you have to ask," he said, " we shall be happy to answer."

Apart from the fact that this was an obvious untruth, since nothing could have exceeded the sense of suspicious security which brooded over that little room, it was a relief to be able to answer this crack with a good conscience.

" I have no questions to ask," I replied, through Hannibal, who interpreted so swiftly that one was scarcely conscious of not talking Russian. " I come only to convey our good wishes for a common victory."

The whole atmosphere of the room was transformed by those words. A bell was rung, and mess waiters in smart white linen jackets wheeled in trolleys of vodka and zakouska—the delicious hors d'œuvres with which Russians accompany their drinking.

Away we went—toast after toast—King George VI, President Roosevelt, Marshal Stalin, " Death to Hitler," " On to Berlin," and so on. After about eight toasts and a good deal of chatter I decided that it was time to leave, and I asked Hannibal to convey this to our hosts.

He did so and was shouted down by the general.

" Certainly you may leave now," he said, " but we shall repay this visit. Where can we find you an hour hence ? "

I looked desperately at Hannibal. After all, he knew the local scene.

Hannibal replied in rippling Russian. I saluted smartly, the Russians bowed and we departed.

As we entered the car Hannibal said, " I told them that they would find us at the *chaikhani*. We must order lunch and plenty of vodka."

We drove back to the *chaikhani*. Although Kasvin is an important town by Persian standards, the inn was a poor, broken-down place, like most Persian hostelries, yet charming, in its dirty, tumbledown way. Hannibal summoned the inn-keeper and ordered chello-kebab—a delectable dish of rice and meat, when properly cooked—vodka and, boldly, some bottles of the wine of Shiraz, of which our host said that he had a stock at the very peak of perfection.

Persian wine at its best is excellent, and one assumes that that old toper Omar Khayyám enjoyed nothing but the best. But nowadays one bottle may taste like nectar and the next, from the same bin, like the worst kind of vinegar. Consistency is not a Persian virtue. Nevertheless, Hannibal ordered the wine.

Presently we heard the tramp of heavy boots on the bare wooden stairs, and up came our guests, led by the general. Off we went again. King George VI, Marshal Stalin, President Roosevelt, " Death to Hitler " . . . the toasts continued. At last the general, having drunk a good deal—as had we—and eaten a certain amount of a very good kebab—as had we, mercifully, also—drew me aside into a corner. Hannibal, as always, stood at my elbow.

" Tell me, Colonel," the general said, " why does your King send traitors to represent him in Moscow ? "

To say that I was taken aback would be an understatement.

" Traitors, sir ? What can you mean ? " I said.

" Your Ambassador in Moscow, Sir Stafford Cripps. He's a Red, isn't he ? "

I bridled.

" The Ambassador is a Socialist, sir. But he is a member

of the King's Privy Council, and a most trusted servant of His Majesty."

" Oh, I dare say. All the same he isn't typical of Britain."

" Well, sir," I retorted, " who would you like as Ambassador ? The Duke of Gloucester, perhaps—the brother of our Tsar ? "

The general beamed and turned towards his junior officers, who were eating and drinking on the far side of the large, shabby room. Hannibal hissed a translation into my ear as the general spoke.

" This chap says," the general boomed, " that we might get the brother of their Tsar as Ambassador in Moscow."

A little hum of excitement went up from the other side of the room.

" I didn't say that, sir," I hastened to interpose. " I asked whether you would *like* him as Ambassador."

The general snatched another glass of the Shiraz—thank God it was not corked !

" Of *course* we should welcome the brother of your Tsar. We are tired of Red intellectuals in sandals."

I recalled Sir Stafford, an impeccably dressed barrister, if ever there was one, and smiled inwardly.

" But you're a Red, aren't you, sir ? " I inquired, guilelessly.

" Of course *I'm* a Red," the general retorted. " But we wouldn't send a White to represent us in London."

I saw the point, and the general rubbed it in.

" Frankly," he said, " we're getting a little tired of being treated like people who don't know how to use the right knife and fork at meals. Now that we're allies we'd like to see something really typical of your country in Moscow—and the more aristocratic the better. Because that's the sort of people you British are."

I did not wish to shatter the general's illusions, and so I agreed with him. Presently he said, " Now you're coming down with me to make a speech to the garrison. They've never seen a British officer any more than I have. It'll do them good."

By that time vodka, Shiraz, and chello-kebab were forming a not yet unpleasant mixture within me. I did not feel ill. I just felt that I did not care any more.

" Of course, sir," I said, through Hannibal's obedient lips.

The troops were drawn up—a couple of thousand of them, I judged, before a little platform, which stood at the head of a barrack square. The general mounted the platform with me, and I found that I was facing a microphone.

The general said a few felicitous words . . . " Allies " . . . " common enemy " . . . " Army of the Nile " . . . and left the microphone to me.

In desperation I turned to Hannibal.

" What's the Russian for ' Death to Hitler ' ? " I asked.

He told me, and I bawled it into the microphone in the best imitation of his pronunciation that I could manage.

" What's the Russian for ' Long live the Anglo-Soviet Alliance ' ? "

He told me, and I parroted it.

" I want to say that we shall soon meet in Berlin."

Hannibal told me what to say, and I did my best to say it. After that I felt that I had done my duty. The troops cheered like mad. They must have understood.

Then everybody, starting with the general, began to kiss me. After that I had to shake hands, solemnly, with a lot of very junior officers who had not come to our party. At last we were allowed to enter our car and to drive back to Teheran.

I was soon overcome with an acute attack of what is sometimes called " boozer's gloom." The liquors and the food which I had taken in were by now reacting powerfully. Before the yellow-brick walls of the British Legation loomed out of the night I had managed to convince myself, notwithstanding the assurances of " Our Man in Teheran," that I had wrecked Anglo-Soviet relations for good and all.

As things turned out, I had not.

I skulked miserably in Teheran for another day, expecting at every moment a summons from the Minister in order that I might explain my behaviour in Kasvin. None came.

I returned to Cairo, and lived there in an atmosphere of steadily diminishing dread. Nothing was said. I was not called to account.

The only sequel occurred two years later. My old general, now Sir Noel Mason-Macfarlane, had been hustled away from England at the earliest possible moment. Perhaps the interview with Mr Duff Cooper still rankled in high places or, more probably, a whole series of similar interviews with other Ministers, of which I knew nothing.

At all events, Mason-Mac had been Governor of Gibraltar for some time when the entry of Russia into the war on our side gave Whitehall an ideal chance of sending this stormy officer even farther afield. He was ordered to head the British Military Mission to the Soviet Union—a complete sinecure, since Mason-Mac was allowed to see nothing.

However, I met the general in 1943. He grinned and crushed my hand. Then the big jaw shot out.

" You're the —— who harangued a lot of Russian troops in Kasvin a couple of years ago, aren't you ? I might have known it ! "

Here it came ! Nemesis.

" Yes, sir, I'm afraid I am. Did I make a fool of myself ? "

" On the contrary. We got a glowing report about the whole thing."

" Have a drink, sir," I said.

Trouble blew up in the summer of 1942, and it was caused by our Greek left-wingers. Taking advantage of the fact that the British censor officer, who vetted their scripts, had suddenly fallen sick, " The Free Voice of Greece " delivered an unrestrained attack on the Greek Government in Exile, in London. Its members, the station announced, were all criminals who deserved to go to prison. There was a celebrated prison called Dartmoor in England, the broadcaster added, and this would be a very suitable residence for the Greek Ministers during the rest of the war.

I, in Cairo, did not hear this broadcast, but unhappily the Greek Government in London did. King George II of the

Hellenes personally asked King George VI whether the station from which this scandalous transmission was made was under British control, and the authorities finally admitted, mistakenly, I think, that it was. This confession led to a trip back to England for me. When I returned to the Middle East after some weeks of rather inconclusive discussion in London the stations survived, but it was clear that they would not remain under our control indefinitely. In any case, the whole pattern of the war was changing. The victory of El Alamein was followed by the Allied landings in North Africa, and it was certain that the enemy would soon be driven from the African continent. When, in the early days of 1943, we surrendered control of our network we hoped that it would remain a going concern.

In fact, much of it did. " Sharq el Adna " lived on, first in Palestine and later in Cyprus, until the Suez crisis of 1956, as one of the most powerful broadcasting stations in the Eastern Mediterranean area.

With the German threat banished once and for all by General Montgomery's Eighth Army, Cairo sank back into lethargy. It was time to move on. I was surprised and pleased to find that I had been given a priority air passage to London. It was April 1943.

4. AN ILLIBERAL EDUCATION

THE FLIGHT HOME was a delight. When the last Sunderland flying-boat went out of service in 1961 I was one of the many to whom the disappearance of these splendid aircraft brought a pang of sorrow. Steady, spacious, reliable, our Sunderland bore us from Cairo to Khartoum and thence to Stanleyville, on the Congo River, and to Leopoldville.

Since we were faced with a delay of two days in the capital of the then Belgian Congo, I deserted the ferro-concrete and chromium plate of Leopoldville, which seemed uneasily out of place there, even then, and crossed the river to the relative simplicity of Brazzaville, the capital of French Equatorial Africa. There an old colleague from my days in Berlin, Géraud Jouve, was in charge of the radio station, one of the most powerful instruments of propaganda in General de Gaulle's hands, since its short-wave transmissions were easily received in Europe. I told Géraud something, though not by any means all, about my own activities.

When he had shown me over the station, of which he was justifiably proud, Géraud glanced at his watch.

" It's time to introduce you to another propagandist," he said, and we set off in his battered car.

A youngish officer in British uniform welcomed us at the door of a pleasant bungalow and led us into the garden. Here, shackled to his perch, was a fine African grey parrot. The major, who was British liaison officer with the Free French Forces in the colony, gave us drinks and the bird a slice of banana, and presently the parrot burst into speech.

" —— General X ! " the parrot cried, vehemently, naming a British officer, who was at that time rather less than popular with the Free French Forces. " —— General X ! —— General X ! ! "

" Where did he pick up that horrible word ? " I asked the bird's master. The young major almost blushed.

" Well," he said, " as a matter of fact, I'm afraid I taught it him. Just as a joke, you know. The trouble is that the joke's a bit too widely known now."

" How's that ? "

" You see, every evening, at exactly the same time, the wild parrots fly across the garden from the jungle—swarms of them. Coco here gets very excited, and he shouts his slogan at them at the top of his voice. One or two French officers enjoyed the performance, and told their friends, and pretty soon Coco was putting on a nightly cabaret turn. It would have been all right," said the major, " if we could have kept it at a more or less junior level."

" —— General X ! " the parrot screamed.

" The trouble was," the major continued, " that the G.O.C., General de Larminat, heard about Coco and insisted on listening to a performance. Still, he seemed to enjoy it. . . ."

The major took a pull at his drink.

" After Coco had done his stuff," he went on, " the General said, ' You must release that bird at once, mon Commandant ! ' I was a bit shaken. ' Why, sir ? ' I asked. ' Because,' de Larminat said, ' if he is free he will go back to the jungle and teach *all* the parrots to —— General X. And that, my boy, would be splendid propaganda ! '

" I only hope to God old X never hears about it, that's all," the major added fervently. I have often wondered whether he ever did.

From Leopoldville we flew to the Ivory Coast and on to Accra. Here I was arrested as a German spy. The local transit camp, a pleasant enough place, housed its guests in large shimbeks, huts of bamboo and palm leaves, which were cool and comfortable, at least by the standards of 1943, when air-conditioning was hardly known in Africa. These huts were each shared by several officers, and, since every sound was audible through the woven partitions, the fact that I delivered a long harangue in German in my sleep was noted with interest by my fellow-guests. In the morning I was hauled before the commandant to explain myself, on suspicion of being a German agent. It took ten minutes to establish my innocence and the better part of a crate of beer to persuade those who had denounced me, and who were now filled with remorse, that they had acted very sensibly indeed, and that they should not hesitate to do the same thing again in similar circumstances. The incident also served to rub in the elementary lesson that people engaged on intelligence duties should sleep alone, if possible, or at any rate that they should be very careful indeed with whom they do sleep.

At Freetown, whose transit camp was much inferior to that at Accra, one of our party broke a leg by falling into a pothole, ten feet deep, in the dark, and three of us spent a wakeful and frustrating night before we arranged for his admission to hospital. It was a relief when the Sunderland swept down on the Tagus and we saw the lights of Lisbon through the scuttles.

As a lieutenant-colonel, I was almost the junior of our party. Only a submarine commander, returning from the Mediterranean after sinking a vast quantity of enemy shipping, was of lower rank than I, technically, and in fact a lieutenant-commander R.N. was far senior to a strictly temporary half-colonel. This officer was extremely proud of his luxuriant red beard, so proud, in fact, that his suspiciously new passport, issued to carry him through neutral Portugal and Eire, described him as an " artist," a flight of imagination which he was soon to regret. The rest of us were ostensibly " Government officials," belonging to unspecified departments.

We were a pretty shabby lot, too. Even the admirals and generals among us—and there were several of them—could, for the most part, muster no more than a pair of flannel trousers and a tweed jacket in which to land in Lisbon. The Portuguese Policia Internacional did not bat an eyelid, however, nor did the conductor of the electric train which bore us from Lisbon to Estoril within a few minutes of our landing.

" British officers, eh ? " he said, waving aside our proffered escudos. " No pay, no pay ! "

I had one saddening encounter in Lisbon. Leslie Howard, a fine actor and a delightful man, whom I had got to know in France during the phoney war, and who had later asked me to act as technical adviser in his film *Pimpernel Smith*, which I was unable to do, was, like us, passing through Lisbon on his way home. I looked him up at the Hotel Aviz, to my mind the best hotel in Europe, and now, alas, closed. We drank to a further meeting in London. Leslie was to fly on that same night, we on the following evening. We said au revoir, confident that we should meet in the Savoy Bar three days hence, and having made arrangements to do so. A few hours later Howard's aircraft had been shot down into the sea, and there were no survivors.

It has been suggested that the Germans believed Mr Churchill would be a passenger in that aircraft, and that they singled it out for destruction for that reason. Mr Churchill, in his Memoirs, has subscribed to this belief. Another theory is that the enemy felt that the propaganda campaign which Howard was waging against them with his films was too effective to be comfortable, and that it would be as well to put him out of the way. This is also a plausible explanation, but perhaps poor Leslie Howard was just unlucky. Another victim of this disaster was the wife of Raymond Burr, " Perry Mason " of television.

We were more fortunate. The Sunderland droned on un-opposed towards Ireland, and, as we neared Foynes, the submarine commander began to have misgivings about his

passport. The Portuguese had accepted the fact that he was
an artist without question, but would the Irish be as gullible?
The officer, who, as his record proved, must have been quite
imperturbable in a submarine, became almost panic-stricken
at the idea of a brush with officialdom. He hurried round the
flying-boat seeking advice and consolation.

"Yes, but look here, supposing they ask me what *kind* of
artist I am? What do I say?"

"Tell them you're a Dadaist, old boy."

"What the hell's that?"

"Well, I *think* it means that you don't have to know how to
draw. You just scribble a few lines on a bit of paper, if they
ask you to, and say that it's *The Soul's Awakening*. They can't
contradict you."

Only very slightly consoled, the sailor went in search of
further comfort.

At Foynes we were interrogated, in the most casual possible
fashion, by a middle-aged captain of the Irish Army. We had
all agreed, before the Sunderland touched down in the
Shannon, that when asked, in the usual way, to which Government department we belonged we would, to a man, claim
to be in the service of the Forestry Commission. The captain
made no comment whatever on this appalling series of lies,
contenting himself with entering our ostensible occupations
on a list. The submarine commander had modestly placed
himself at the end of the queue, but when the captain's eye
scanned his passport it must have brightened. By the time
this interrogation took place we, released from bondage, were
having a drink in the pub which faced the customs shed. The
commander finally joined us in a state of pitiable agitation.

"By God, I've given the whole show away!" he said,
before he had even raised his pint of Guinness to his lips. He
drank deeply and continued. "Well, that chap in there
asked what sort of an artist I was, and I said an impressionist,
and he said, damn him, 'Well I'm an impressionist too, and
my impression is that Admiralty would be nearer the mark
than Artist.' And, like a fool, I said 'Yes,' without thinking,

and the chap grinned. They'll be livid about this at the Admiralty."

At that moment the Irish captain entered the bar, and the commander rounded upon him.

" That was a damned dirty trick you played on me ! " he protested. " You . . . you trapped me."

The captain was quite unperturbed.

" Look," he said, " I got an M.C. in the last war, only I'm not allowed to wear the ribbon now. Go in and beat the bejesus out of the Germans, and see if I care ! "

After that the commander bought his tormentor a drink.

To our disappointment we were held at Foynes for the night by weather, and a bus took us to a comfortable hotel in Limerick. When I had written my name in the register the girl at the reception desk glanced at it and then at me.

" You're proper Irish, aren't you ? " she said.

I admitted that, by blood, I was.

" Well," said the girl, " you won't have to pay for a drink as long as you're in this hotel."

When I finally went to the bar I found that orders to this effect had indeed been given. Feeling rather guilty, and supposing, rightly enough, that this generosity would apply only to my own personal drinks, I asked two Irish officers, a major and a captain, both in uniform, to join me. At least I could pay for their drinks, and I did.

" Where," the major asked, after we had bought a round apiece, " are the old regiments ? Where are the Connaught Rangers, where are the Dublin Fusiliers, where are the Irish Rifles ? "

" You know perfectly well where they are," I replied. " They were disbanded in 1921, and their colours hang, I believe, in Canterbury Cathedral."

" Yes," said the major, " but shouldn't they be in there fighting now ? Isn't it a shame that they have no part in this war ? "

" *I* think so, of course, but surely you don't."

" But we do," said the captain.

"Why," the major inquired, in tones of the utmost reasonableness, "don't you raise those old regiments again North of the Border?"

"But good heavens!" I cried, "you're supposed to be neutral! What on earth would de Valera say if we did that?"

"Ah, to hell with Dev!" the major said, testily. "If you'd only raise those old regiments we'd run excursion trains of recruits to join them. I'd desert myself, come to that."

As I lay in bed that night I reflected that there were some lessons to be learned from the events of the day which had just ended. Would it have been conceivable that twenty senior German officers, arriving in plain clothes in a neutral country, even in a neutral country with which they had the rather special relationship which we have with Ireland, would behave as had we servants of the "Forestry Commission"? The idea was quite inconceivable, partly because senior German officers would regard such a childish joke as beneath their dignity and an offence against discipline and good order, and partly because they would see no fun in it.

And then I remembered that party, in 1938, which now seemed so long ago, at the Kasinogesellschaft, in Berlin, of which mention has already been made, and I was willing to admit that some German officers have a sense of humour.

But then, again, what German would ever believe in the possibility of my conversation with the two Irish officers in the hotel bar? While the Germans made every effort to exploit the sorrows of Ireland, which, goodness knows, the Irish had proclaimed loudly enough, here were Irish officers actually insisting that the regiments which had been disbanded when British rule ended in their country should be raised again by their oppressors. It occurred to me that even had Poland not been involved in the war it was hardly likely that Polish officers would have suggested to a German visitor the re-establishment of the West Prussian regiments which vanished when Pilsudski freed his country.

On the next day we flew on to Poole in brilliant sunshine.

To our amazement a special train, which consisted simply of two Pullman cars, was waiting to take us to London. For the first, and probably the last, time in my life, I felt myself to be a Very Important Person.

My orders were that I should proceed at once on ten days' leave, and I wasted no time in London. In Hertfordshire, where I had a tiny cottage, I lounged in the peace of an English spring. Every one, I found, was far more cheerful than they had been during my last brief visit, a year before. Nobody then had doubted that we should win the war, but, equally, nobody quite knew how we should do it. Now, the Battle of the Atlantic was nearing its end, Africa was cleared of the enemy, and people speculated where and when we should strike at Hitler's Europe. But preparations for the Village Fête and Flower Show were already afoot, and the dramatic society had just presented *Outward Bound*. The proceeds had gone towards Mrs Churchill's Fund for Russia, instead of the Organ Fund, otherwise life seemed to go on much as usual, except that there were no young men left in the village, and the beer at the Red Lion was poor stuff.

When I reported for duty it was not to Fitzmaurice Place. During the past two years S.O.E. had expanded enormously. Its agents were in the field in every country occupied by the enemy, from Norway to Burma. The organization had its own training establishments and laboratories, its wireless network, its flights of aircraft, and an intricate system of liaison with our Allies. Headquarters were now in Baker Street, housed in a modern red-brick office-block which professed to shelter the " Inter-Services Liaison Department." But we spilled out into many of the rather glum warrens of Edwardian flats which cluster round the northern end of Baker Street.

The men and women who worked for S.O.E. in London have been given little recognition, official or otherwise. Most of the books which have been written about the organization are the work, naturally enough, of people who were actively engaged in operations abroad, and many of them are inclined to take a critical view of " Baker Street." This is perfectly understandable. Few regimental officers have a good word to say for the General Staff, a fact which the War Office took into account at the outset of the last war, when it sought to protect staff officers from the contempt of their comrades by equipping them with detachable brassards in place of the gorget-patches which had singled them out indelibly during the Kaiser's war.

Perhaps one day an official history of S.O.E. will be written, which will, at long last, give those who worked in the obscurity of Baker Street the credit to which they are certainly entitled, for without them there would have been no operations in the " Field," and no exciting books to be written about them. In 1944, thanks to S.O.E. and their American colleagues of O.S.S., Europe was indeed set ablaze, as Mr Churchill had ordered in 1940, and it was in Baker Street that the staff work which made this possible was done.

It would not be easy for a historian to write such a work, for S.O.E., like any other organization of its kind, was divided into watertight compartments, which worked independently of one another, and were co-ordinated only at a high level. It was a breach of etiquette, as well as of security, for the French Section to inquire in any detail about the activities of, say, the Norwegian Section. Even within the " Country Sections " themselves curiosity was actively discouraged. It is a safe rule of intelligence work that nobody should know more than his immediate duties demand.

I reported to Baker Street hoping that I might now be transferred from the German to the French Section, which was extremely active, and which had recently suffered some heavy losses. The hope was stillborn.

" You're going to Stockholm," said the major behind the bare trestle table.

" To *where* ? "

" Stockholm—capital of Sweden. Don't say you've never heard of it."

" Well, of course, but why Stockholm, for God's sake ? "

" To take over the German Section there," the major explained. " Let's have some lunch."

If the Gestapo had at that time placed a powerful charge of explosive beneath the Wallace Head public-house, which stands in Blandford Street, W.1, and had timed its explosion for about 1.15 P.M. on any day except Sunday, they would have saved themselves a great deal of trouble during the last two years of the war. In the bar, munching Spam sandwiches and washing them down with watery war-time bitter, half the headquarters staff of S.O.E. could be found at any lunch-time. Conversation was about anything except the subject which obsessed them all to the exclusion of everything else.

A newcomer in uniform was introduced to captains, majors, and colonels, some of whom indicated that they had already heard of him, while to others he was, at least ostensibly, unknown. The newcomer, if he had any sense, forebore to make inquiries about these new acquaintances. Mr Asquith's much abused motto " Wait and See " might also have been the motto of the Wallace Head.

After lunch the major described, in the very minimum of detail, the job which lay ahead. Owing to a misfortune which he did not at that time specify, the German Section in Stockholm had been dormant for nearly two years. One able young woman had remained in the British Legation as a care-and-maintenance party, but the section had undertaken no operations or propaganda for many months. It was felt that the time had now come when greater activity might be shown. The Russians had been victorious at Stalingrad, the Axis Powers had been driven from Africa. Swedish neutrality which, as my friends in Limerick might have said, had hitherto meant, more or less, neutrality on the side of the Germans, might now be expected to become more genuine as it became increasingly evident that the Germans were going to lose the war. This was a situation which should be exploited.

I should be posted to Stockholm as assistant Military

attaché, and drop a step in temporary rank—as if that mattered. It was soon regained, anyhow. My work in the Middle East had been concerned entirely with propaganda in support of operations, never with operations themselves. I was therefore quite untrained in the most important aspect of S.O.E.'s functions, and this would be to some extent remedied by a series of intensive courses which I would attend before I left for Sweden. I should be treated as though I were an agent who was being dispatched to an occupied country, instead of to a snug, neutral capital. If I made an idiot of myself on the three long courses on which I should be sent I might as well abandon any hope of Stockholm.

"Then I could get into the French Section," I said, hopefully.

"Like hell you could," the major replied. "You know too much."

To-day Beaulieu Abbey, in Hampshire, is famous not only because it is one of the finest old houses in England, but as the home of a unique museum of ancient motor-cars, and once the venue of an annual jazz festival. During the war it was a name which one did not mention, because the estate gave cover, in every sense of that word, for the most important of our "schools."

The railway warrant with which I had been provided gave no more clue to my ultimate destination than that I was expected to alight at Brockenhurst. There transport would await me. It did, and that evening I was installed in a comfortable little house, very modern, inside and out. A young major welcomed me in. For the better part of a month, he told me, we should be constantly in each other's company. We should live together alone in the little house, and he would instruct me continuously. Sometimes one or two other students would join us, but often we should see nobody but one another for days on end.

The major showed me over the house. He mentioned that mushrooms could be picked in the early morning from the trim lawn beneath my bedroom window, a thing which, in early summer, struck me as being unusual. It seemed to add to the atmosphere of unreality which enfolded Beaulieu.

Over supper, served by an excellent batman-cook, Major Smith, as we might as well call him, told me something about the " school."

The place might have been designed for the purpose which it was now serving. In the years before the war the Beaulieu Estate had allowed people of some means to build themselves houses on its land. Many of those who had taken advantage of this opportunity were retired officers or civil servants, some were yachtsmen. They had been attracted to Beaulieu, it may be assumed, because they placed a high value on seclusion and privacy, and the size of the estate protected them from the encroachments of neighbours.

As a result, anybody who strolled round the estate—a practice which was sternly discouraged during the war years— would have seen a number of pleasant houses of varying size, each standing in a garden which, as a rule, was well screened by hedges or banks of rhododendron. Nothing could have better suited the purposes of S.O.E. In one house it was possible to train, in complete isolation, a party which was preparing to blow up an aqueduct in Northern Italy, while a quarter of a mile away another group was making ready to drop into Normandy, and a third, tucked away in an unobtrusive red-brick villa, was being trained to go into Holland.

As far as possible, the students never saw anybody except the members of their own group and the instructors assigned to it. " Togetherness " was the last thing that they sought at Beaulieu, and the unreal atmosphere which had struck me as soon as I set foot on the estate was easily accounted for. Most of the students in Beaulieu were living there under false names or cover-names—sometimes the staff themselves were ignorant of the real identity of their pupils. All of them were being trained to become new people, to lose their real personalities, and to assume those of men and women who were either dead or who had never existed.

Training was intensive and thorough. Police methods,

and in particular the methods employed by the Gestapo, were exhaustively dissected and discussed. We were taught codes, and one code in particular which I defy any cryptographer, however patient, to break, yet which is simplicity itself, and can be carried in the head with the certainty that it will not be forgotten.

We were instructed in poaching by an officer who, until he found himself in uniform, had been a gamekeeper on a great estate. Although, in my particular case, it was unlikely that I should be obliged to fend for myself in a hostile country, many students who were bound for areas more dangerous than Sweden found these lessons in woodcraft invaluable. It must have gone against the grain for our instructor to initiate us into the technique of stunning fish by throwing home-made bombs of quicklime and water into a stream, or of snaring rabbits and pheasants.

Methods of disguise were also the subject of several lectures by experts, and here emphasis was laid on simplicity. In an emergency, we were told, a little cigarette ash, properly applied, can transform a man's appearance as effectively as a false moustache. We practised altering our manner of walking and of carrying ourselves—the most difficult of all personal traits to conceal—and we were taught how to obtain and use various simple articles of make-up.

Burglary was another branch of knowledge to which much time was devoted. Our instructor was a highly respected professional. He had, it seemed, been responsible for a very large number of successful 'jobs,' to the certain knowledge of Scotland Yard, but had only once been obliging enough to provide them with any evidence which could justify a charge. As our teacher himself said, it did seem a little odd that his particular skill should have led to a commission, and to his " becoming a bloody schoolmaster."

The burglar was a delightful man and an excellent in-structor. Under his guidance we took impressions of keys in " Plasticine " and soap and from them cut duplicates, most of which, in the early stages of the course, were failures.

But practice brought success. If householders who rely upon spring locks for the protection of their homes realized how simple it is to make a false key from a sliver of metal cut from a tobacco tin, the sale of mortice locks would be very much larger than it is. Often a strip of celluloid or a piece of piano wire is all the equipment which the housebreaker needs.

Having learned the theory of burglary, we were called upon to put our knowledge to the test. A house was chosen, and the ' burglar ' and his mate—for we always worked in couples—were sent to ' case ' the place. This involved gaining admittance on some plausible pretext, which we were left to devise for ourselves, securing an idea of the general lay-out of the house, and obtaining the impression of a suitable key. The two students then filed up a duplicate key and were ready to go to work.

" An envelope containing vital documents has been hidden in the drawing-room of the house," the instructor might say. " Go and get it."

When my mate and I made our first assault on a house the home-made key failed to open the door which we had chosen for our entrance. The time was about 1 A.M., and it was raining steadily. Cursing under our breath, we tiptoed to a coach-house, where we had noticed that several ladders were stored. We had also, on our reconnaissance, observed an upper window which had been closed, but not secured. Perhaps it would still be unlatched. As the rain trickled steadily down our necks, we carried the heavy ladder and silently put it in position. The window was still unfastened. We entered the house, found the " vital documents," clambered out, replaced the ladder, did what we could to obscure footprints, and vanished gratefully into the night.

I would not, in any circumstances, adopt burglary as a profession. Fortified though we were by the consciousness of innocence, that ' job ' and another which followed it were nerve-racking affairs. We both suspected that somebody had changed the lock of the door which we had sought to

open, and I still believe that this was done. It was typical of
the kind of trick which one learned to expect at Beaulieu.
But then, as our instructors never tired of pointing out, the
Gestapo were quite an ingenious and alert body of men, too.

Towards the end of the course we were called upon to
put our training to the test. The first ordeal was known
as a " 36-hour scheme," and as far as I was concerned the
battle-ground was Portsmouth, where the police and security
authorities were particularly active, since the dockyard
was an obvious target for enemy agents. I was to make my
way into the dockyard and carry out a piece of simple
" sabotage." I should stay overnight in Portsmouth, and on
the following afternoon I was to have tea in the lounge of
the hotel in which I had spent the night. I was to assume
that my presence in Portsmouth had been notified to the
police, and that I should be followed.

I certainly was followed. Hardly had I registered at my
hotel and strolled out into the street, when a cyclist who,
on his form at that moment would certainly have won the
slow bicycling race at any village fête, came creeping along
behind me, and a pedestrian began to take the same intense
interest in the shop-windows as I was myself displaying.
I entered a branch of Woolworths, which occupied the entire
ground floor of a block, with entrances on two streets, but
by the time I had pushed my way through the crowds and
passed through the alternative exit, the cyclist, who was
obviously capable of a nice turn of speed when necessary, was
dawdling along behind me again, and another pedestrian
was earnestly inspecting a display of utility clothing in a
tailor's shop.

At last, after a long and tiring walk, I satisfied myself that
I had thrown off my pursuers, though I was never certain
that I had actually done so. At all events, I carried out my
mission, and, on the following afternoon, I sat, sipping tea,
in the lounge of my hotel. Every table around me was
occupied, for the most part by ladies seeking to revive themselves after the frustrations of war-time shopping. They all

looked up when two large and very obvious policemen in plain clothes approached my table. In loud, clear voices they informed me that I was under arrest, and produced their warrant cards. The sensation in that quiet lounge was tremendous. I demanded angrily to know on what grounds I was being arrested, and was curtly told that this would be explained at the police-station. I was then led away, amid a buzz of excited chatter in which I thought I heard the word " spy " mentioned several times.

Four hours later I was sitting in a bleak, chilly room. I had answered countless questions, I had been subjected to a " body search," which is a very humiliating business indeed. I had not, I thought, given anything away. Then the atmosphere changed completely, and I was informed that the exercise was over. I told my two interrogators that the only reparation which they could make to me was to return with me to the hotel and have dinner with me, an invitation which was cheerfully accepted. I shall long remember the look of mingled incredulity and relief upon the face of the manager when he saw us enter the bar and order drinks.

The " 96-hour scheme," which was the culmination of the course, was a very much more elaborate affair. Now the student was sent to a town of which he had no previous knowledge whatever. He was allowed three days in which to work up a ' cover story ' of his own invention, and to collect evidence to support it, and he then went to the city to which he had been assigned. He was given certain targets to ' attack,' but the methods which he employed were left to his imagination. During the exercise, which lasted for about a week, the fledgling saboteur was required to make certain contacts, as a rule one each day. He might be ordered, for instance, to be in a certain pew in a certain church at such and such a time, when somebody would give him further instructions.

The city chosen for my test was Bristol. The town had been heavily bombed, and when I arrived there I thought that it was a sorrowful place. London is so vast that it was possible, even in 1943, to walk quite long distances without seeing any signs of the Luftwaffe's attentions, but in Bristol they were everywhere. I took up my quarters in a small public-house which offered bed and breakfast. This modest lodging fitted in with my cover story, which I had spent three busy days in London preparing. I had all the right letters and documents, as I thought, in my pocket, I had established a background which I knew well from previous experience. If necessary I could give the police the names and telephone numbers of people who would support my story, although they had no idea that they might be called upon to do so. I had actually lived in the London lodgings which were my ostensible address for two nights. I knew the colour and pattern of the counterpane on the very uncomfortable bed, the entire family history of the landlady, the name of the local pub.

My first contact in Bristol was with a nondescript man whom I met, by appointment, in a public-house. The orders which he gave daunted me a good deal. I was to go to the cocktail bar of the Grand Hotel, on the following evening, and there I should meet somebody who would give me further orders.

Now, the Grand Hotel was not the kind of place which fitted in with my professed identity. It is a four-star establishment, exclusive and expensive. I was supposed to be a man of very modest means, spending a cheap and solitary holiday in Bristol, where I was pursuing a harmless hobby. I had neither the right clothes nor the right amount of money for the Grand Hotel.

My doubts were fully confirmed next evening when a charming young woman, beautifully dressed, her fair hair looking as though it had just been arranged by a good coiffeur, as it doubtless had, asked me to buy her a very expensive cocktail. I did so, explaining at the same time that I very rarely went into such places as the American Bar of the Grand Hotel. We fell into conversation, and it was soon apparent that my companion knew far too much about my past and future movements. Did I, she asked, know such and such a pub—naming the hostelry in which I had met the nondescript man. There were some wonderful old churches in Bristol, weren't there ? Had I been to a particular church, at which, in point of fact, I had a rendezvous for the following day ?

I bought another drink and decided that this delightful person was an *agent provocateur*. She knew a great deal about me, and was determined to know even more. I evaded an invitation to dinner with difficulty and hurried back to my pub.

If the encounter from which I had just come had taken place in enemy-occupied territory—as, for the purposes of the exercise, it had—I decided that my first step would be to cover my tracks as thoroughly as possible. I paid the bill at my pub, packed my bag, and took a bus to Bath. Even during the war the bus service between Bath and Bristol was excellent, and this made it possible for me to work in Bristol during the day and to return to the secrecy of Bath each evening.

As things turned out, this simple ruse was only too successful. When I had duly, as I thought, completed my mission, I telephoned to a certain number in London and reported the fact.

" Yes, I dare say," said the voice at the other end of the line, " but the point is that our friends " (by which he meant the police) " have lost track of you. You must meet them, you know. Go back to the place where you originally stayed."

Feeling rather pleased with myself, I returned to the little pub in Bristol. I was less pleased to be hauled out of bed at three o'clock in the morning and introduced to the superintendent.

The superintendent's office was more comfortable than the barren room in Portsmouth which had been the scene of my previous interrogation, but the atmosphere was no less chilly. The interrogation went on for hours, and I was congratulating myself on the enduring qualities of my cover story, when the whole carefully constructed lie collapsed under me.

Somehow the conversation turned on post-war credits. I had heard of these, of course, but in the Middle East we had never seen the claims forms which all residents of this country received. Had I been the man whom I pretended to be, though, I could not have failed to know all about those awkward little slips of paper. I did not know about them, and I felt the ground quaking beneath my feet. After that it did not take the superintendent long to demolish a story which was plausible enough, but false from start to finish.

That session at the headquarters of the Somerset County Police taught me one or two basic lessons from which, I hope, others profited later. The superintendent and I ate a large " brunch " and parted on the best of terms.

Within a few days I was in the Western Highlands of Scotland. At Arisaig S.O.E. had taken over a large sporting estate on the shores of Loch Morar. The headquarters was a typical Scottish shooting-lodge, now rather dilapidated, but comfortable. About it lay desolate, hilly country; almost uninhabited. This was the terrain chosen for a programme which combined training in the use of explosives with a battle course.

Of all the weapons, and they were extremely varied, with which S.O.E. equipped its personnel, plastic explosive was probably the most valuable. This substance, which looks like an innocent block of grey " Plasticine," and of which the French O.A.S. have since made such use, can, like " Plasticine," be moulded into almost any shape. It can be cut with a copper or even with a steel knife without fear of explosion, and it remains remarkably stable for long periods, which enables it to be stored with relative safety. Only when a primer and detonator are fitted is the stuff lethal, and then it is very lethal indeed.

For days on end we exploded charges of this stuff in every condition which was likely to be encountered in the field. We wrapped the plastic as lovingly as any embalmer ever bandaged a mummy, in layers of oiled silk and waterproof tape, and lashed magnets to the package. The finished product was known as a "limpet," its purpose to blow holes in ships. When we had done our homework we paddled out on Loch Morar in canvas canoes, and clamped the limpets on to boiler-plates which had been sunk in the loch. A few minutes later a gratifying explosion proved that the charge had been correctly made up, and that the time-delay fuse had not failed. Sometimes there was no explosion, and then we began again.

We must have destroyed tons of steel girders, which represented the supports of bridges, and dozens of fir-trees. One day we were taken to Mallaig, and there introduced to a large locomotive which stood on the sidings. Under the censorious eye of an elderly driver we piloted the monster up and down a quarter of a mile or so of track, until we were all confident that we knew enough to get any engine moving. Nothing, said our instructor, was more disconcerting than a rogue locomotive, careering, unmanned, along a busy line, and we should lose no opportunity of loosing such a monster upon the enemy when occasion offered.

Then we were shown the sensitive spots of a locomotive's anatomy, on which a charge of explosive could be relied upon to do the most damage. We should concentrate, we were told, on cylinders and valve-gear.

One of the more spectacular features of Arisaig was the pistol-range. Those who are accustomed to watching the remarkable shooting of such heroes as Gunslinger and Wyatt Earp on the television-screen may be surprised to learn that the effective range of a pistol, at which even quite a large target can be hit with some certainty, is not more than twenty or thirty feet. Expert marksmen who compete in the pistol-shooting events at Bisley stand sideways to their target with the arm rigidly extended before them, and in these leisurely conditions considerable accuracy can be achieved.

But an active enemy, keenly anxious not to be shot, does not often give the gunman a chance to aim at leisure. This fact was appreciated by an officer of the Hongkong police, Captain Sykes, who devised a method of pistol-shooting which combined a relatively high degree of precision with speed. This system, taught at Arisaig, involved what was called the " battle crouch position." The gunman, crouching slightly, held the pistol in line with the centre of his body. Soon it became a second forefinger to him.

After several periods on a more or less orthodox range, the students were shown quite an elaborate little village, which lay at the foot of a steep bluff. At the top of the cliff a soldier stood beside a set of levers which looked somewhat like those in a railway signal-box.

The village, we were informed, was full of Germans. It was our business to kill them all. We were given two Colt ·45 automatics, already loaded, and two spare clips of ammunition apiece. Then, one by one, we were to attack each house in turn.

The door of the first house sprang open in response to a brisk kick, and the signalman on the top of the bluff went into action. The houses were fully furnished and fully occupied. No sooner had a dummy, impelled by wires, leaped out of bed to tackle the intruder and been shot for his pains, than a trapdoor opened, " men " emerged from beneath tables, bottles and chairs came hurtling disconcertingly at the gunman's head. Pistols blazing, one dispatched, as one hoped, all the occupants of the first house, and dashed to the second, where a fresh set of hazards presented itself. Blackpool Pier was nothing to this, as one of my brother-officers observed. By the time I had gone through five houses in a matter of forty-five seconds or so, and had been told that I had scored a creditable number of hits, I was inclined to feel quite pleased with myself. Then came the chilling thought that the dummies, however lifelike their movements, had not been armed. If they had been . . .

From Arisaig the pursuit of knowledge led to Hertfordshire— to a place, in fact, within five miles of my home, although I could not reveal my presence in the neighbourhood. Here we were lodged in a small country house, which stood close to a large sandpit. The purpose of this juxtaposition became clear when we learned that we were to be taught how to make our own explosives and delay fuses, and that we should test them in the sandpit. Often, it was explained, supply drops of explosives were held up, for one reason or another, yet there might be occasions when it was essential that a target should be attacked at once. In that event, excellent explosive could be made with ingredients which were either readily available or which could be bought without any suspicion being aroused. Chemical fertilizer, which can be found on all farms, was a basic ingredient, and the other components could be purchased either from a chemist or from a grain-merchant. An excellent time-delay fuse can be improvised with water and dried peas.

Every morning saw us engaged in a strange cookery lesson. In a Nissen hut whose atmosphere, as lunch-time approached, became almost too thick to breathe, we bent over saucepans which bubbled malodorously on " Primus " stoves. The finished brew was taken, in the afternoon, to the sandpit, which shook with the detonations which our cooking had provoked.

Some time ago *The New Yorker* published a drawing by Charles Addams, in which that brilliant artist depicted an episode in the life of the fiendish family which his macabre sense of humour has made celebrated. The cartoon showed Dad with two or three devilish offspring about him, surveying with satisfaction a small rack which they had constructed together in their home workshop, and which was obviously a most efficient instrument of torture. " You see, kiddies," the father is remarking, complacently, " half the fun comes from doing it yourself." We felt this about our explosives. Their use was far more satisfying than playing with ready-made plastic, and no bride, taking her first cake from the oven and seeing that it had risen properly, could have been happier than we were when our maiden batch of explosives sent showers of sand over quite a considerable area of Hertfordshire.

As the time to leave for Stockholm approached, I was taken to visit several small but highly secret establishments which lurked, discreetly, in some of the less frequented parts of the Home Counties. At one of them it was surprising to see grown men playing with model boats on a large swimming-pool. Their activities began to make sense when it was revealed that the little launches which slipped to and fro in the glassy water were designed to ferry a heavy charge of explosive and to carry a detonating mechanism in their bows. If only the right electric motor could be devised these would provide a cheap and demoralizing method of attacking small enemy craft as they lay in harbour. For the present, the motors, supplied by a well-known firm of model-makers, had not proved entirely satisfactory, and the experiments which we were witnessing were designed to test what might be a more reliable type.

Another visit, to a small laboratory, was somewhat reminiscent of Christmas shopping in a department store.

" Now, I expect you'll be needing quite a supply of these," said a white-coated chemist, holding up a little gelatine capsule identical with those in which lighter-fuel is sold.

" Why ? " I asked in my innocence. " Are they short of lighter-petrol in Sweden ? "

" Oh, this isn't for lighters," the chemist said. With a pin he pierced the nozzle of the capsule and squirted a drop of oily fluid on to a piece of paper. The room was filled with a horrible, pungent odour, which seemed to be the concentrated essence of hundreds of pairs of very dirty socks.

" Hangs about for weeks," said the chemist complacently. " One of these applied, say, to a German greatcoat would make the thing quite unwearable for a long time to come. Now, considering how cold the winters are in Norway, I should say that these little toys would be ideal there. A child can use them, and I don't suppose that the German quarter-masters have any too many greatcoats to spare. The Russian front must fairly eat them up."

I ordered a generous consignment of these useful weapons.

" Itching powder, now," the chemist went on. " This is much better than the old chopped horsehair. More lasting. Difficult to get rid of once it's on the skin. I expect you could think of several uses for that."

I could, and I ordered a number of tins of the stuff.

My final posting came through at last. In my bulky luggage I packed several items of uniform to which I had supposed that I had said good-bye, at least for the duration of the war, and probably for ever—strapped trews, parade and dress wellingtons, a green patrol-jacket. I decided to leave my sword behind. If my formal duties ever required that I should wear one I could probably borrow a sword locally.

After three days of intensive ' briefing ' I took a train for St Andrews. From near-by Leuchars an extremely irregular air service, operated by B.O.A.C., who flew unarmed Dakotas, maintained a tenuous link between the United Kingdom and Sweden.

Captain Nigel Pelley, the skipper of the aircraft which would take me to Stockholm, was one of the most experienced civil pilots in the country. He had been captain of the air-craft in which Mr Neville Chamberlain had made his ill-fated trips to Germany, in 1938, and he was now furious that he was denied the opportunity of bombing the Fatherland.

" Still," Nigel said, " it isn't always a piece of cake, even on this run. We get Boche night-fighters over Norway and sometimes a bit of flak. So we have to fly at about 15,000 feet or more, which is pretty high for a DC3. For God's sake keep your oxygen mask on until we get across the Swedish frontier. We've had chaps pass out several times. Oh, and remember to dehydrate yourself."

" Eh ? "

" It's damned cold at fifteen thousand," Pelley explained, " and you'll be wearing two flying-suits and parachute harness. So no pennies can be spent for seven hours, which is about the time it will take to reach Stockholm. Still, let's have a beer now. The flight's scrubbed for to-night. Weather's much too good. We like ten-tenths cloud cover, if possible, for this trip."

The weather remained maddeningly good for several days. Every evening, so dehydrated that we felt we must rustle like sheaves of corn, we dutifully zipped ourselves into our flying-suits, and waited in the little airport building, only to undress again an hour later.

Then, on an evening of low cloud and driving rain, the weather was bad enough even for Pelley. The Dakota took off, and headed eastward.

5. NORTH OF HITLER

It is not very difficult to imagine the feelings of an agent as he lands for the first time in enemy-occupied territory. Whether he arrives by parachute or by light aircraft, as some of our agents in France did, there will be a pattern of lights on the ground beneath, the uncertainties of landing, a " reception committee " of strangers. The parachute must be buried, perhaps a wireless-set hidden, and then the newcomer may find himself faced with a long tramp to the " safe house " across a darkened countryside from which at any moment an enemy patrol might surge up out of the blackness.

As our Dakota landed at Bromma Airport, a few miles from the centre of Stockholm, I could not help contrasting my own soft job with some of the missions on which other members of S.O.E. were now engaged all over Europe. The flight to Sweden had not been quite uneventful. German night-fighters had been active over Norway, and Pelley had thrown the aircraft all over the sky before we managed to shake them off. At 15,000 feet (or more) it had been very cold, notwithstanding the two flying-suits, and the cabin was in darkness, but after we crossed the Swedish frontier the lights in the aircraft were switched on, and now here we were landing, like respectable tourists in an airport which, even at 3 A.M., was brilliantly lighted. My reception committee was a customs officer, who saluted politely when he saw the diplomatic visa on my passport—I was now no longer a " Government Official " but a major, which means a good deal more in Sweden than it does in this country. A large car drove me to a comfortable hotel. As I fell asleep, I felt thoroughly ashamed of myself.

Stockholm is one of the world's most beautiful cities, and it was looking at its best on the sunny morning in August 1943 when I first set eyes on it. As one gets to know Stockholm well it loses much of its appeal. Beneath the bright, modern surface of the capital of Europe's oldest and still most advanced Welfare State there is an almost antiseptic coldness which somehow put me in mind of a very modern hospital. Apart from the fact that the actual climate is bitterly chill for many months of the year, there is in Stockholm a strange lack of spiritual warmth which many foreigners find daunting.

But on that first morning none of that was apparent. The water, which is Stockholm's chief beauty, since arms of Lake Mälar constantly intersect the city, sparkled in the brightness of late summer. The little white steamers, which ply between the capital and the hundreds of small islands and scattered homesteads and villages which lie about it, had not yet entered upon the long hibernation which would begin with the end of September. Pretty girls in light dresses sat on the steps of the Dramatiska Teater, or " Dramaten," as it is usually known, gazing at the water, and nibbling their luncheon sandwiches in the sunshine. The bakers' shops were full of cream pastries, the department stores offered Swiss watches, German cameras, and even Scotch tweeds. Neutrality had become a tangible reality.

By the time I reached Stockholm the tide of war had turned with a vengeance. In Italy, Mussolini had been arrested and the Government of Marshal Badoglio was on the point of capitulating to the Allies. In Russia, the German Sixth Army had been utterly destroyed at Stalingrad, the siege of Leningrad had been raised, and the German Forces in the Caucasus had fallen back.

These great events had naturally had their impact upon Sweden. At the beginning of the war the general feeling of the nation had been that Sweden must at any cost avoid becoming involved in the conflict. Since Germany was a great deal closer to Sweden than either France or Great Britain, and since she clearly intended to stop at nothing in order to ensure the supplies of high-grade Swedish iron ore upon which her armaments factories largely depended, Swedish neutrality meant in fact neutrality in favour of the Germans. The luckless Norwegians discovered this when, after the invasion and occupation of their country, the Swedish Government allowed the Germans to run supply trains for their forces in Norway through Swedish territory.

It was this fact that had brought to a standstill the activities of the German Section of S.O.E. in Stockholm, which I was under orders to revive. My predecessor had organized an operation whose purpose was to blow up a German ammunition train during its passage through Sweden to Norway. The Swedes got wind of the plan, raised a mighty, if discreetly muffled, hullabaloo with the British Government, and expelled its author from Sweden. The German Section had lain low for many months thereafter, and now I had the most formal orders that no operations whatever were to be undertaken on Swedish soil.

But if neutrality which favoured Germany seemed politically expedient to the Government it also accorded with the views and wishes of people in positions of influence and, for that matter, with those of many working-class men and women. The links between Sweden and Germany had always been close. There had been much intermarriage between the two countries, both among the aristocracy and in less august circles. Sweden had not been through the embittering agony of the First World War. Germany's, or rather Prussia's, shameful attack on Denmark in 1864 was now forgotten, and if it was not many Swedes felt that the Danes had only got what they deserved, since there is no love lost between the two countries, even to-day.

There were, of course, enclaves of pro-British feeling. The great seaport of Gothenburg, which looks out towards the Atlantic, never wavered in its attachment to the Allied cause. Stockholmers were wont to say, with a sneer, that if it rained in London the people of Gothenburg could be relied upon to put up their umbrellas as a demonstration of sympathy.

Certainly the moral climate there was very different from that of Stockholm. The city's great newspaper, *Göteborgs Handels-och-Sjöfartstidning*, which has a European reputation, never ceased its attacks on the Nazis and on everything for which they stood, nor did it flinch when King Gustav V of Sweden threatened to take action against the paper for its anti-German attitude. Its editor, Torgny Segerstedt, continued to stump around the streets of Gothenburg leading his bulldog Winston on a leash, and caring nothing for the threats against his life which Goebbels's propagandists constantly made.

In Stockholm, almost landlocked, matters were very different, and the German attack upon Russia made them worse rather than better from the Allied point of view. For although many Swedes might not approve very warmly of Hitler, no Swede at all, with the exception of the members of the tiny Communist Party, approved of Stalin. Nor was their detestation confined to the Communist regime. Its roots lay far back in history. Many times Swedish and Russian soldiers had faced one another on the battlefield. Once a Russian Army had actually come to within a few miles of Stockholm itself, and had been halted by the very last troops which Sweden could muster, at the Battle of Stäket. Hitler, almost all Swedes were ready to agree, was not a very admirable person, nor were his followers much to boast of, but any German was, in principle, preferable to any Russian, and if the Germans were fighting the Russians, good luck to them.

The author, Cairo 1943

Leaflet dropped by the Germans on the Maginot Line during the "Phoney War." At first sight it appeared to show only French troops in action under the caption "What's happened to the Tommies?" When held to the light, as the second photograph shows, it depicted British soldiers in a brothel. The transparency consisted of two separate pictures, glued together.

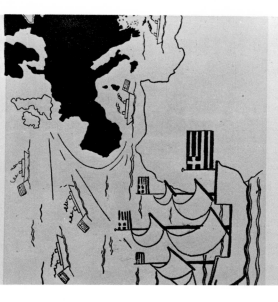

Η ΣΥΜΜΑΧΙΚΗ
«ΤΑΞΙΣ ΤΗΣ ΕΛΕΥΘΕΡΙΑΣ»

Ἡ Γαλανόλευκη κυματίζει ὑπερήφανη παντοῦ ὅπου τήν φέρουν τά Ἑλληνικά πλοῖα ποὺ ἐλεύθερα ταξιδεύουν σὲ ὅλα τά μέρη τῆς γῆς !

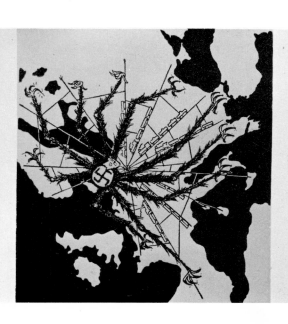

ἡ
Η ΓΕΡΜΑΝΙΚΗ ΑΡΑΧΝΗ ΑΠΟΜΥΖΩΣΑ ΤΟ ΑΙΜΑ ΥΠΟΔΟΥΛΩΝ ΛΑΩΝ!

Μπορεῖ ποτέ ἡ Ἑλλάς, χώρα τῆς ὁποίας ἡ ναυτιλία κατέχει ἐξέχουσαν θέσιν εἰς τόν Εὔξεινον, τήν Μεσόγειον καί τούς Εὐρωπαϊκούς λιμένας τοῦ Ἀτλαντικοῦ, νά ἐσημείρωσῃ μέ νικήτριαν τήν Γερμανίαν ;

Leaflet printed by us in Cairo and dropped on Greece by the R.A.F. The original was in three colours. The Nazi spider is shown as drawing the wealth of the subject countries to Germany, the centre of his web. The reverse shows that when the Nazis are defeated Greece will resume her true rôle as a maritime trading nation, with the seas of the world open to her. The headings contrast "The Hitlerian 'New Order'" with "The Allied 'Order of Freedom.'"

The first studio of
" Sharq el Adna "

The building in which the studio was concealed

Captain John Robertson (John Connell), one of the founders of
"Sharq el Adna"

By courtesy of John Connell
Robertson

Sheik Muzaffar,
" Sharq el Adna's "
dynamic commentator

Срби! Ваши непозвани гости оних дана не осећају се најбоље. Прошли су дани када су њихове војске побе-доносно марширале и када су били заузети цртањем грани-ца свог животног простора. Свуда око њих је небо мрака — и сада уместо да шаљу пакете, пуне хране и одеће, својим дебелим женама и се-страма, чекају на писма да сазнају последње вести о на-падима Р.А.Ф.-а.

Ви видите промену на њи-ховим лицима и у њиховом држању. Немачка висока ко-манда опажа ту промену. Они раде све могуће да сузбију зле вести о хлађавама оних које је Хитлер осудио да по-стану ухапшеници или лешеви. На вама је да ови увиде те чињенице један је начин, да дотурите овај лист немачком или италијанском окупатору.

Оно ће помоћи да уједате дан сад их нетерe више ви-дети.

TOTALER KRIEG...

Jeder Deutsche Soldat weiss: Der Totale Krieg ist eine Deutsche Erfindung. Solange das Kriegs-glueck auf Seite der Deutschen stand, bewunderten sie den To-talen Krieg. Sie waren ueber-zeugt, dass nur sie allein den totalen Krieg fuehren koennen. Wenn die westlichen Demokratien ihren Abscheu vor den Schrecken des totalen Krieges zeigten, legten ihnen die Deutschen dies als Schwaeche aus.

Die Bewohner von Essen, Koeln, Dortmund, Duisburg, Rostock, Luebeck wissen heute, dass der totale Krieg auch eine Kehrseite hat. Churchill sagte in seiner Rede am 10. Mai 1942: "Wir haben eine lange Liste von deutschen Staedten, in denen die kriegswichtigen Industrien liegen. Es ist fuer uns eine zwingende Notwendigkeit, diese Staedte ebenso zu behandeln, wie wir Luebeck, Rostock und ein halbes Duzend anderer wichtiger Deut-scher Staedte behandelt haben."

Wir haben jetzt Juni 1943: Jeder Deutsche kann heute sehen, dass es Churchill mit dieser Erklaerung ernst war. Und das ist erst der Anfang.

Ihr seid fern von zu Hause und fragt Euch, was mit Eurem Heim und mit Eurer Familie geschieht. Erinnert Euch, dass es Deutsch-land war, das den totalen Krieg erfand und zuerst gegen War-schau, Rotterdam und Belgrad anwandte. Erinnert Euch, dass es Goebbels war, der den aufreiz-enden Film : "Sieg im Osten" mit den Bildern der Verwuestung in Polen drehen liess. Wenn Ihr etwas nachdenkt, werdet Ihr ent-decken, wer fuer das Elend in Deutschland verantwortlich ist.

LA GUERRA TOTALE

è un invenzione tedesca. In breve essa significa non esitare di fronte a nulla che ta della guerra. Se un trat-tato firmato solennemente sia a vantaggio della condot-tieri ostacola il corso dei piani di guerra, esso viene strac-ciato. Se il bombardamento dei profughi sulle strade con-tribuisce a far vincere una battaglia, questi profughi vengono massacrati c o l l e bombe.

Se l'impiccagione di inno-centi sulla pubblica piazza contribuisce a terrorizzare la popolazione civile, uomini e donne, preti e suore sono trascinati sulla pubblica piaz-za ed impiccati.

I tedeschi hanno fatto in-numerevoli dichiarazioni per giustificare la guerra totale. Essi la praticano con zelo e ne magnificano i risultati. Solo quando le cose vanno male cominciano a strepitare ed a protestare.

Benito Mussolini aveva tanto a cuore la guerra totale che, dimenticando il secolare antagonismo fra Italia e Ger-mania e l'interesse evidente del suo paese dichiarò guerra ai fedeli amici dell'Italia. Egli ignorava talmente i sistemi impiegati da Hitler in Norve-gia, Belgio, ed Olanda che cercò d'applicarli in Grecia.

Egli penso, che il bombar-damento di Londra fosse un'idea così geniale che chiese al Fuehrer il permes-so di parteciparvi.

Слике са ове је веома ретке изгледа; које су приказа-вале воених генерала з, триумфалну] позе. Овде је слика фон Арнима који маршира у заробљеништу.

Он ноје на прву не изоставио.

Hier ist eine Bild von General v. Arnim, wie er im Gefangenenlager marschiert. Es ist nicht der Erste- und nicht der letzte.

Ecco una fotografie di con Arnim mentre va in prigionia. Non è il primo, e neanche l'ultimo.

Leaflet in Serbo-Croat, German, and Italian, produced in Cairo and dropped on Yugoslavia by the Allies, June 1943. The Yugoslavs are urged to resist, the German troops are warned that total war will be carried into their homes in Germany, the Italian forces are told that Mussolini has dragged them into total war against their real friends. The picture shows General von Arnim, German C.-in-C., in Tunisia, after capture.

The Residence, British Legation, Stockholm

Photo Pressens Bild Ab, Stockholm

Stockholm, Christmas, 1943. While London was blacked out, this was the spectacle that confronted me in Stockholm—the virtue of neutrality. This is the old town.

By courtesy of the Swedish Institute for Cultural Relations

The guarantee of Swedish neutrality. The great iron-ore field at Kiruna, which was essential to the German war-effort. As long as Sweden was prepared to deliver to Germany she was safe from invasion, and deliver ore she accordingly did, until the end of the war.

By courtesy of the Swedish Institute for Cultural Relations

Selv i denne Europas Skæbnetime, hvor alene de sidste 1¾er har kostet mere end Fœrerhovedkvarterets geniale og uforglemmelige Pindsvinestilling Stalingrad, selv i denne Stund har Tyskland Raad til en saa storslaaet Gestus som at invitere alle Norges Studenter og Professorer til et Ophold i Tyskland, en Invitation, som blev modtaget i meget stor Udstrækning, hvad der er et værdigt Svar til alle dem, der tror at kunne sætte Splid mellem de blodbesmittede Folk!

I denne afgørende Skæbnetime tilraader vi dig et

Slut op og fyld ud i Rækkerne! (Det haster).

Følg
Fritz Clausens
Eksempel!

Bliv
Frikorpsmand!

Ved Offre skabtes Danmarks Ære!

Meld dig til Førerskolen paa Ebberodgaard eller til Ersatzkontorerne ved Hospitalernes respektive Psykiatriske Afdelinger.

P. S.

Vore Modstandere har ikke undset sig for at eftergøre vore Blade og Skrivelser, men vore intelligente Læsere vil altid gennemskue disse platte Falsknerier og vide, at denne lille Tryksag er ægte.

Sieg Heil!!

SS-Ersatz.

„Forrædderlandets Trykkeri.

Front and back pages of a four-page leaflet produced in Stockholm in 1944 and distributed by the Danish Resistance. The text overleaf At first sight this is an appeal to Danes to join the S.S. and to fight " for Denmark against Bolshevism." makes ironic fun of German claims to defend " European Culture." The back page shows Fritz Clausen, the Danish Nazi leader, tramping through the Russian winter in S.S. uniform, and says, in part, " Fill the ranks ! (Urgent). Follow Fritz Clausen's example ! Report to the S.S. Officers' School or to the psychiatric wing of any hospital !" The name of the press is given as " Traitors' Printing Works."

Dette er historien om
DE NORSKE
HJEMMESTYRKENES
deltakelse i
SLAGET OM RHINEN

DEN 24. mars 1945 gikk britiske og amerikanske hærstyrker over Rhinen og innledet dermed det siste og avgjørende slag mot Tyskland og det tyske voldsherredømme i Europa.

Visste du at de norske Hjemmestyrkene deltok i dette slaget ? Det er rimelig at du ikke gjorde det, for Hjemmestyrkene visste det ikke selv før etterpå. *Nu* vet de det, og de vet at den øverste allierte krigsledelse har tillagt deres andel i slaget om Rhinen stor betydning. De vet at den samme krigsledelse betrakter Hjemmestyrkenes innsats ved dette høve som et av de mest vellykte slag som har vært levert av de undertrykte nasjoners skjulte hærstyrker i løpet av denne krigen.

De norske hjemmestyrkene visste bare en eneste ting, nemlig at de hadde fått en ordre og at ordren måtte følges.

Her er historien :

I løpet av kvelden 14. mars og natten til 15. mars 1945 lød det noen hundre eksplosjoner langs alle jernbanestrekninger i hva vi kan kalle Oslofjords-området, fra Halden i sydøst og nesten ned til Arendal i sydvest. De lød som tordnende sleggeslag utført av usynlige armer. Broer fløy i luften, pensesystemer gikk op i kaos, lagre av reparasjonsmateriale ble ødelagt.

Dagen etterpå forelå følgende situasjon: Alle de jernbanene i Sør-Norge som i de siste månedene hadde arbeidet i et feberaktig

Set Europe Ablaze ! " Leaflet dropped on Norway by the R.A.F. towards the end of the war to show the part played by the Norwegian Resistance in the Battle for the Rhine crossing. By sabotage, they prevented the Germans from moving reinforcements from Norway to Germany.

The author (fifth from left), with the American Assistant Naval, Military, and Air attachés, admiring a model locomotive. It was made by an American airman interned in Sweden.

By the late summer of 1943, however, when I came to Stockholm, it was pretty clear that the Germans were not having much luck either against the Russians or against their other enemies. Slowly Swedish policy and Swedish opinion began, however reluctantly, to veer towards the Allies, tainted though they were in Swedish eyes by the Russian connexion. If the Allies, including Russia, were going to win the war Sweden must not appear, at the end of hostilities, to have been too favourable to the Germans.

It is easy to condemn this reasoning as cowardly. Yet it is true, as Mr Günther, Sweden's able Foreign Minister, never ceased to point out to the British, and, later, to the American Government, that armed resistance by Sweden to Germany's demands for iron ore could have resulted only in the occupation of the country. Germany would still have had full access to the iron ore, and, in addition, complete control over Swedish industry. A neutral Sweden, the Government argued, was at least more useful to the Allies than a Sweden under full German occupation, and there is a good deal to be said for this view.

The British Legation, in fashionable Strandvägen, consisted of the Chancery, a pleasant but undistinguished building of red brick, and the Minister's residence, a fair example of the Office-of-Works Georgian style of architecture, which stood some distance away. The Chancery building had been more than adequate for the modest staff which the British Government had maintained in Stockholm until 1939, but now it was hopelessly overcrowded. The Military attaché, Brigadier Reginald Sutton-Pratt, to whom I reported, as my formal commanding officer, was squeezed, with his clerks, into two very small rooms. The Air attaché had two assistants, and so did the Naval attaché. The Commercial department was swollen, as if stricken with elephantiasis, and as for the Press attaché's large staff, there was no room for them in the Chancery at all.

In the courtyard of the legation prefabricated offices, adequate, well designed, but unsightly, had been hurriedly run up, and still the legation was overcrowded. After I had formally paid my respects to the Minister, Sir Victor Mallet, who was an old acquaintance from the days when I had served *The Times* in Washington, and to the other service attachés, I was led down to an office in a permanent annexe of the legation.

It was a smallish room, whose windows gave on to the forecourt of the legation. There was space for two desks, a massive safe, filing-cabinets, and for little else, except a large coloured print which depicted Hitler, armed *cap-à-pie* in plate armour and still contriving, in spite of the loyal efforts of the artist, to look ridiculous and insignificant— which he was not. Evidently Janet Gow, who was seated beneath this monstrosity, believed in keeping a sharp eye on the enemy.

Janet was a person who inspired immediate confidence. Aged about thirty, attractive, witty, very well dressed, she had, within the very strict limits imposed upon her, kept the German Section of S.O.E. in a state of very efficiently suspended animation. Her contacts in Stockholm were wide and highly diversified. She had seen to it that a regular flow of information from and about Germany reached the little basement office. Her sources were German, Austrian, and Sudeten German refugees in Stockholm, who maintained contact with home, and the correspondents of Allied news-papers, numerous and able, among whom Janet had many friends. She was also extremely well informed about the Swedish scene, and I learned more from her in those first days than from anybody else in the legation.

If we were to operate agents in Germany it was clear that we should have to start from scratch, and try to make up for lost time by building up an organization in a hurry. This is not, as a general rule, a wise thing to do in intelligence work of any kind, but we had no alternative. Yet Janet's files showed clearly enough that to recruit the men we needed would be very difficult indeed.

In the meantime I must take care not to forget that although

my principal duties in Stockholm were dictated by my membership of S.O.E., I was still a Military attaché, and must behave
as such. The world at large, as I earnestly hoped, would
accept me at my face value as a young officer sent to help
Reggie Sutton-Pratt in his very exacting job.

6. PINPRICKS AND PRISONERS

WE OFTEN ENVIED our colleagues in the Danish and Norwegian sections. They were able to call upon an almost limitless number of recruits, and, within the countries towards which their efforts were directed, active, patriotic resistance movements stood ready to give them every assistance in their power. Moreover, it was possible for our colleagues to ship their most promising recruits to the United Kingdom for extensive training. A steady flow of refugees, some of them of the highest quality, trickled across the long, desolate frontier which separates Norway from Sweden, or crossed Öresund, the narrow strait which lies between the Danish and Swedish coasts.

It can hardly be said that they received a very hearty welcome from the Swedes. The Utlänningskommission, or Aliens Department, granted them temporary residence papers but did little to help the refugees to earn a reasonable living. Although Sweden was maintaining some 500,000 men under arms, in the Army alone, which represents a high proportion of manpower in a population of 7,000,000, and despite an actual shortage of skilled workers, the power of the trade unions inhibited the Government from putting the skills of their guests to proper use. They were allowed to fell timber in the vast northern forests which, as the war dragged on, were called upon to provide more and more of the country's basic needs, from motor-fuel to aquavit, the potent liquor without which no Swedish meal can be said to have properly begun. Sometimes the Danes and Norwegians were permitted to fill a few of the less rewarding and harder jobs in industry, but they had not come to Sweden to do work of that kind. Hitler could provide plenty of very similar jobs in Germany, and was indeed eager to do so. The more supine of the Danes and a very few Norwegians accepted the bait offered by Hitler's recruiting-officers, and allowed themselves to be shipped to Düsseldorf or Essen, where they proved themselves to be rather doubtful assets to the Nazi war effort. The German Section of S.O.E. had good reason to be thankful for these " voluntary workers," since it was thanks to them that we were eventually able to move our own men in and out of Germany.

But the younger Danes and Norwegians who came to Sweden did so either because they simply wanted to continue to fight against the invaders of their countries or because their resistance activities at home had already made them obnoxious to the Gestapo and a price had been set on their heads by the Germans. These men were potentially admirable recruits, and they established in Stockholm organizations manned by trained officers, journalists, and politicians, which maintained close and constant liaison with the resistance movements at home.

As far as the Norwegians were concerned, one of the most active workers in Stockholm was a young officer who had left Norway hurriedly for the excellent reason that he had been born a German. In Sweden he carried on his original profession, as a journalist, worked tirelessly for the Norwegian resistance, and maintained contact with the various groups of German émigrés in whom we were also interested. The world now knows him as Willy Brandt (which is not the name under which he was born), and as Lord Mayor of West Berlin, the leader of the West German Social-Democrat Party, and the Party's candidate for the Chancellorship of the Federal Republic.

The Danish and Norwegian sections possessed another advantage which we lacked. Since they were dealing with proved patriots and allies, it was possible for the British officers of the two sections to have personal contact with their Norwegian and Danish colleagues. This was not practical in the case of the Germans, apart from a few exceptions. One or two of our collaborators—for example, Dr Bruno Kreisky, who is now Foreign Minister of Austria, and Ernst Paul, the distinguished Sudeten-German Socialist—were absolutely reliable. But it would have damaged their position with the Swedish authorities had they been known to frequent the British Legation or even to meet British subjects too often, and so our direct contacts even with these well-attested allies were reduced to a minimum.

Our other informers were kept even more at a distance. I never met any of them until the war had ended. When it was absolutely necessary Janet Gow conducted a brief conversation with one or other of our contacts in one of the 'neutral' flats to which we had access. Our private homes were never entered by anybody except those whose visits would arouse no particular suspicion in the minds either of the Swedish secret police or the Gestapo. Only one exception was ever made to this rule.

Soon after my arrival in Stockholm one of the legation messengers came to my office to report that a German was sitting in the lobby demanding to see somebody on the staff of the Military attaché, and claiming sanctuary of British soil.

" What sort of a German is he ? " I asked.

The messenger was contemptuous.

" He's a shabby little fellow, sir. Almost in rags, one might say. Says he's escaped from a concentration camp."

The messenger sniffed, incredulously.

" All right, bring him up," I said. This might be interesting, in one way or another.

The person who came into the room a few moments later did not, at first sight, inspire much confidence. I could see what the messenger had meant. A lined, haggard face was joined by a stringy neck to a very dirty, collarless shirt. A pair of deplorable trousers sagged over broken shoes and were partly covered by one of the filthiest raincoats I have ever seen. The man was trembling, violently.

" Well, what can I do for you ? " I asked.

" Herr Major, ich bitte um Asylrecht "—" I ask for asylum."

" Germans can't come here for protection."

" Aber, Herr Major—I have escaped from Papenburg Military Concentration Camp."

On the face of it this was very interesting indeed. Militär K.Z. Papenburg, near Hamburg, was a notorious establishment, into which only the very hardest cases in the German Forces found their way. The regime there, by all accounts, made a British ' glasshouse ' seem like a holiday camp by comparison. If this man had really been in Papenburg he must be a very tough fellow indeed. Of course, he might also be an *agent provocateur*, and his answer to my next question tended to confirm that suspicion.

" What did they put you in Papenburg for ? "

" Sabotage," said the visitor.

We had become more than leery of German professions of sabotage. The mythical " resistance movement " among the workers, in which many people in England still persisted in believing, made large claims to wrecking activities which were never substantiated. I therefore greeted this claim with scepticism.

" Why don't you go to the Swedish police ? " I asked.

" Because, Herr Major, I have a criminal record. Nothing important—picking pockets, petty larceny, and so on. But the German Government would ask for my extradition on an ordinary criminal charge—they could always trump one up against somebody with my previous convictions—and then they'd cut my head off."

" They would," I agreed. " Now. Name, rank, number, unit ! "

The little man gave the information.

" Where did you serve ? "

He told me. Poland, France, Greece, France again. That could be checked.

" All right. Now before I start wasting my time, had you any reason for coming to Sweden—and I'd like to know how you got here—apart from wanting to get as far away from Papenburg as possible, which I quite understand ? "

" Yes, Herr Major. I want to kill Hitler. I hoped the British might help me to do so."

" I think you'd better come home with me," I said.

" And then . . . ? "

" We'll see."

We smuggled the man out of the legation. The Swedish secret police, who kept patient vigil from a roadmenders' caravan, permanently parked opposite our front entrance, may not have recognized the man who accompanied me to a taxi, since we had fitted him up with a hat and an overcoat. At my flat in Banérgatan my maid, a sour-faced old woman, welcomed the visitor without enthusiasm, and was even less co-operative when she was told to make up a bed in the spare room.

Private Haas stayed with me for a week. Once I had convinced myself that the story of his escape was true, as I did after an evening's conversation, I felt that it was quite safe to leave Haas alone in the flat. As long as he remained indoors my own diplomatic immunity protected him, and he could therefore be relied upon to do so. As for petty larceny, he, professional though he was, could hardly hope to compete with my maid in that line of endeavour, and there was nothing in the flat worth stealing, anyhow.

Haas talked and talked, and I made notes. It was fairly clear that he had indulged in a certain amount of minor sabotage, out of sheer " bloody mindedness," and there was no doubt that his hatred of Hitler was perfectly genuine. The little man had a certain fanatical courage, and would gladly have sacrificed his own life if he could have taken his Führer with him.

We felt that Haas was at least a reasonable risk, and I suggested to London that Haas should be flown over for further interrogation with a view to his possible employment on a very dangerous mission indeed.

By 1943 the death of Hitler by the hand of a German might have altered the whole course of the war and of history. Baker Street agreed that Haas should come to England, and one night, to his passionate relief, he clambered aboard one of our comparatively rare Dakotas.

In England Haas was lodged in what was known as the " patriotic school." This was a somewhat ironical title, since those who were sent to this establishment found their way there precisely because their patriotism was in question. Dutchmen who came drifting into English harbours in stolen fishing-smacks, newly arrived Norwegians who could find nobody to vouch for them in London, nondescript allies and pseudo-allies of all kinds and nationalities, were interrogated patiently and at length at the " patriotic school," until their good faith was established, if it ever was.

The name " patriotic school " was not, incidentally, devised by a security officer with a cynical sense of humour. The place to which Haas was taken was, in fact, the Royal Victoria Patriotic School, situated on Wandsworth Heath, conveniently adjacent to Wandsworth prison, on whose scaffold some of the school's inmates who failed to make the grade perished, without any member of the British public ever even knowing their names.

Here Haas was interrogated for many days on end, and at last we received a signal which gave us the bare bones of the result.

Haas, as London later told us, was perfectly genuine. His story stood up to the closest questioning, and of his obsessive hatred of Hitler there could be no doubt whatever. But the man's criminal record, the experts felt, told against him. Not that we were particularly squeamish about a mere matter of petty thieving—S.O.E. numbered in its ranks some really serious criminals who were now applying their special talents to the common cause. But it was thought that for the immensely important job, which was the only one with which it would have been worth while to entrust Haas, the moral weakness which was obviously a part of the man's character presented a risk which could not be taken.

It is perhaps worth mentioning that about a year before Haas's arrival at the " patriotic school " a certain George Behar had been an inmate there for some days, having arrived, with excellent credentials, from Holland, via Spain. Unlike Haas, he passed out with flying colours, joined the Royal Navy, and, after the war, the Foreign Service. Now, as George Blake, he is serving a sentence of forty-two years for espionage, the longest sentence, I believe, ever imposed by a British court in the past 150 years—that is to say, since imprisonment rather than hanging became the normal punishment imposed under our penal code. Blake was sentenced on May 3, 1961. My poor Haas, who failed where Blake succeeded, was, I hope, more fortunate, and I hope that he has managed to keep out of gaol since he returned to Germany. Certainly we were not unkind to him.

Haas was sent to comfortable internment in the Isle of Man. Months after he had left Stockholm I received a letter from him. He was enjoying himself very much. Life in the Isle of Man was paradise, after Papenburg (as one might well imagine), and Haas expressed his gratitude for this satisfactory conclusion to his war. " But," he added, " I respectfully assure the Herr Major that I should gladly have made any sacrifice which might have been required to rid the world of the so-called Führer." And I, for one, believe that he would.

Our first recruit was, even by the most sanguine reckoning, rather a long shot. All the same, it was disappointing that Haas had not been used. Wearily Janet and I went, once again, through the files which Janet had so carefully kept up to date during the months of inaction. They gave little comfort, since they contained nothing but the names of people whom we had already proved to be unreliable.

Everybody who has ever had any connexion with intelligence

work knows these people—indeed, they are common enough in any walk of life. They are the opportunists who are ready to be all things to any man who will give them a few hundred kronor or francs or pounds, who are perfectly prepared to be double, treble, or even quadruple agents if they can find two, three, or four masters each of whom is prepared to pay them for the kind of information which he would like to hear. Men of this kind buzzed round the Allied and Axis legations like flies round a series of honey-pots, and my predecessor and Janet, between them, had sorted them out very thoroughly indeed. Not one of them could be trusted to give a straight piece of news, far less to risk his neck by going into Germany. Our regular and reliable informants all had ties in Stockholm, and were in any case too well known to the Gestapo to be safe in Germany for more than a few days at the most. They were also too valuable, potentially, to be risked even had they been willing to hazard their lives, which they were never asked to do. In any case, politicians, which most of our German contacts were, are apt to make very poor intelligence officers or agents because few of them are able to evaluate information. If this had not been so we might have been spared the wars of 1914 and of 1939, which seemed to take the politicians, at least on the Allied side, by surprise, but which came as no surprise at all to the French Deuxième Bureau and to the War Office.

In the meanwhile the many rejects whose names cluttered our files had discovered a new and succulent honey-pot. Hardly had the smoke of the slaughter at Pearl Harbour drifted away across the Pacific, when America, straining every sinew to make up for lost time, decided to establish a counterpart of S.O.E. British officers were seconded to help in the building of the Office of Strategic Services, and in London American officers laid the foundations of a relationship with S.O.E. which, at first tentative and charged with a certain amount of suspicion on both sides, soon became very intimate indeed.

By 1943 an O.S.S. mission had appeared in Stockholm,

under the command of George Brewer junior, who seemed to most of us to have just about every quality that one would hope for in an American gentleman, if the use of an old-fashioned word may be allowed. Brewer was also a playwright of distinction. Those who did not see his *Dark Victory* on the stage in New York, where it was immensely successful, may remember the moving performance of Bette Davis in the film version.

Brewer had no difficulties where Norway and Denmark were concerned. Although at first O.S.S. showed a natural tendency to wish to go its own way, the solid Danish and Norwegian resistance movements which S.O.E. had nurtured for the past three years could not be ignored and must be used. Germany was a very different affair, since it was virtually virgin soil for both organizations, and O.S.S. lost no time in seeking to recruit agents for work in that country.

They did not go about the job as discreetly as they might have done, since it was not long before we began to get reports from our own trustworthy sources that members of the American Legation's staff had been observed in the company of a number of doubtful and more than doubtful people about whom we possessed a good deal of information, little of it to their advantage. In particular, our report said, Americans were apt to go to the Regnbågen (Rainbow) Restaurant, in Stureplan, one of the central points of Stockholm, and there to meet, with the best intentions in the world, a fairly unsavoury collection of hangers-on.

That the Americans should have resorted to Regnbågen was understandable, if unwise. The restaurant, expensive, garish, decorated, as might have been expected from its name, in all the colours of the spectrum, was a favourite resort of the German Legation. Its owner made no secret of his Nazi sympathies, and we strongly suspected that the place was heavily, though discreetly, wired for sound by the Gestapo.

It was not easy to decide how to warn O.S.S. without giving offence. Finally we commissioned a contact, who was an expert with very small miniature cameras, to take some snapshots of our American colleagues in the company of one or two of their less desirable acquaintances. The pictures were taken and sent to George Brewer, accompanied by a brief biography of the people who were shown in them to be making the most of American hospitality. George was horrified, and we suggested that it might make things easier all round if we showed him our files of worthless but predatory and dangerous would-be agents.

When he had studied the file George was more disconsolate than ever.

" But look," he said, " these names here are just about all the contacts we've got, on the German side. We haven't been in touch with some of them yet, but we had hopes of them."

" Abandon hope," we counselled, " and if it is any consolation we may say that we have been here for three years and have so far failed to find a single really reliable man to go into Germany. We're both in the same boat, and if we can do anything to help, just let us know."

This was the beginning of a close and fruitful collaboration.

At all events, O.S.S. went to work with a will. The cover which they provided for some of the members of the mission might seem, to us hidebound British, sometimes a little bizarre, but it worked.

One of our most charming colleagues, for example, was Miss Mab Wilson-Wright. She had been an associate editor of *Vogue*, and her ostensible job in Stockholm was that of " Fashion attaché." This job she filled admirably. She had the looks and the knowledge to sell American fashions, via the couturiers and the large stores of Stockholm, and she did so. What she did, apart from that, I do not know, but she was an acknowledged member of O.S.S., and an officially recognized colleague within the small circle of the two organizations.

In any case, I would be ready to bet that Mab did whatever she was required to do with the utmost efficiency and aplomb. I judge that her work somehow brought her into contact with Denmark, since, as the war ended, she married Bobby Moltke, an extremely aristocratic member of the Danish Resistance Movement. I can only say that the Danish *noblesse* thereby acquired, in their American countess, a very considerable asset indeed.

The American Minister, Herschel Johnson, may have been a little bemused by some of the additions to his staff which he was required to accept. If so he did not, as a career diplomat, give any indication of his alarm, any more than did our own Minister.

Mr Herschel Johnson was an eighteenth-century figure, in the best sense of that term. Immensely well-read, a lover of music and wine and good food, extremely astute, he seemed, at least to an outsider, to preside with great firmness and dignity over his bloated legation. I dined with him quite often, and these were memorable occasions, which the passage of years has not dimmed.

We should have been less than human if we had not fretted at our apparent inability to strike, in however modest a fashion, at our chief target. Patience, though, is one of the virtues which anybody who has anything to do with intelligence work must, at all costs, cultivate. I had been told in London that on no account must the German Section undertake any rash operations. It would be far better to wait until the right chance presented itself than to try to create opportunities before they really existed. Our sources of more or less reliable information increased week by week, and both Janet and I were confident that sooner or later we should make a strike which would reward our patience. In the meanwhile we made ourselves as useful as possible.

One of our first acquisitions, made soon after I arrived in Stockholm, was a small printing-press. This machine was able to reproduce any document or photograph by the offset process in large quantities and at great speed. We were flattered to learn that Baker Street had, yielding to our importunity, snatched this press from under the very nose of Mr Winston Churchill, who had had his own designs on it, since it was the only machine of its kind in the country. We felt a little guilty at having deprived the Prime Minister of a new toy, but our need was very great.

We already had, in the basement of the legation, a small hand-press, a very varied selection of type, and a young printer, Mr Clarke, whose cheerfulness and willingness was never impaired by the mole-like existence which he was obliged to lead. Now, assuming that we could match our paper with that of the original, we should be able to produce, at very short notice, a plausible facsimile of any document of which we possessed one genuine copy. Fortunately Sweden makes paper in almost infinite variety, and matching never presented any great difficulty. The propaganda potentialities of the little press seemed almost limitless.

Our new equipment had hardly been delivered when an opportunity of testing its effectiveness in a modest but entertaining manner presented itself. The German Legation in Stockholm published a monthly magazine called *Der Deutsche in Schweden* (*The German in Sweden*). This periodical was intended to circulate only within the large German colony, but we were among its most devoted readers. Often the social gossip and carefully censored news of arrivals and departures provided us with clues which were extremely useful.

It is worth remarking, incidentally, that the study of newspapers, and particularly of local newspapers, is an important part of routine intelligence work. I recall a case, which was only one among thousands such, in which an advertisement offering a reward for the return of a lost dog, which appeared in an obscure North German weekly newspaper, enabled our " order of battle " experts to locate an enemy division which had apparently vanished from the earth, and whose whereabouts was a matter of some concern to the War Office.

On this occasion *The German in Sweden* gave us a chance of combining amusement with instruction. A half-page advertisement announced that a company of actors, fresh from a successful season in Berlin and led by the notable light comedian, Georg Alexander, would present in Stockholm the comedy *Der Elfte an der Reihe*, or, to employ a very loose translation, *The Eleventh Man*, an entertainment which had no connexion

with the film, *The Third Man*, later made by Sir Carol Reed.
The company sponsored by the Organization of Germans
Abroad, of which Bradford-born Gauleiter Bohle was the
titular head, was to play for three performances only, and
admission would be limited strictly to members of the German
community in Stockholm. Tickets might be obtained from
the German Legation.

We tried very hard to get a ticket, but all our sources failed
us. So we were driven to imagining what a ticket might look
like, and we finally produced a design which seemed to us
extremely convincing. Three thousand rectangles of white
pasteboard were printed, and, in order that they might look
the more impressive, were serially numbered. We then
composed a letter, purporting to be signed by the German
Press attaché, and sent a copy, with two tickets attached, to
1500 of the prominent Swedish Nazis and Nazi supporters
whose names we kept in one of our dossiers.

The covering letter warmly invited the recipient, in the
name of the German Minister, to attend a gala performance
of *Der Elfte an der Reihe*, to which the enclosed tickets would
secure admission. White tie and tails, with decorations,
would be the order of the day for those who owned such
garments, but a dinner-jacket or dark suit was a permissible
alternative. It was quite unnecessary, the Press attaché
assured his guests, to acknowledge his communication. Anyone
who was unable to make use of the tickets, which were for the
first of the three performances, was urged to pass them on to a
friend whose devotion to Hitler's cause was equal to his own.

The first snow of winter was, fortunately, falling as Janet
took up her post in the window of a flat which overlooked the
entrance to Borgarskolan, in whose auditorium Herr Alexander
and his company were to perform.

The scene, as the time for " curtain-up " approached, was
gratifyingly chaotic. The German colony had turned out in
full force to support their Minister, Hans Thomsen, and to
applaud the talented visitors from Berlin. They found themselves forced to fight their way through a dense crowd of in-

furiated Swedes, many of the men in top-hats, their wives in
sumptuous fur coats. Distracted ushers were trying to explain
to the angry gathering that the white tickets which they had
confidently proffered were worthless. The genuine tickets,
although almost identical in design with the forgeries (a
tribute to our powers of imagination), were printed on light-
blue pasteboard.

It took a long time to sort out the muddle, while the German
Minister fumed in his front-row stall and the actors fretted
in their dressing-rooms. Many of the deluded Swedes had
come, as we hoped that they would, from distant parts of the
country, anxious not to miss an opportunity of basking in the
sunshine of Nazi favour. Janet enjoyed her evening very much.

Next day the Stockholm newspapers made a good deal of
the incident. Facsimiles of the forged tickets were published,
and leading articles were written. The German Legation
issued an official statement which attributed the hoax to a
" despicable clique of Jewish émigrés," but many Swedes
laughed heartily, and applauded the unknown practical
jokers.

The art of what might be called subversive forgery has,
since those distant days of 1943, been considerably developed.
The Germans never proved themselves very adept at it.
Apart from the celebrated £5 notes with which Himmler
planned to ruin the British currency, such German forgeries
as I saw were feeble, clumsy productions. To-day the Russians
make great use of the technique, particularly in Western
Germany and in Africa. If the West German authorities are
to be believed, no fewer than eight thousand separate items—
propaganda booklets, leaflets, and forged documents of all
kinds—pour into the German Federal Republic every *month*
in large quantities. This massive output makes the efforts
which we made in Stockholm look puny indeed, and perhaps
one should feel no satisfaction at having been among the
originators of a practice which is now being turned against
us. But it is also not unreasonable to hope that if the Com-
munists are attacking the West by these means, we, on our

side, are not inhibited from counter-attacking in kind. Certainly we were not inhibited in 1943.

Many of the victims of this hoax were members of the Swedish Nazi Party which stood under the leadership of a fanatic named Lindholm. It published a daily newspaper, held public meetings, and maintained close touch with the German Legation. One day Peter Tennant, our Press attaché, told me that Lindholm was coming to his flat for a drink that evening, and suggested that I should join the party.

" You might help me to put the fear of God into the man," Tennant said.

Lindholm, whose appearance was as insignificant as that of most of the German Nazi leaders, was understandably nervous when he entered Tennant's drawing-room. Peter did most of the talking, since his Swedish was perfect, which could not, and cannot, be said for mine. I had, however, got a sufficient grasp of the language to be able to interject suitably menacing remarks at proper intervals.

" Well, Mr Lindholm," Peter said, " I do hope that you are not contemplating any foreign travel after the war."

Lindholm bridled.

" Certainly I mean to travel. Why shouldn't I travel ? "

" I doubt if it would be safe," Peter said, solemnly.

" And why not ? "

" After we have won the war—and even you must see that we are bound to do so—the Allied Governments intend to take proceedings against war criminals. That covers a multitude of sins, Mr Lindholm."

" I am a Swedish subject," Lindholm protested. " This is a free country. It is my country, and as long as I do not transgress Swedish law you cannot touch me."

Peter nodded.

" Exactly. That is why you would do well to stay in Sweden. You will be perfectly safe here. But the Danish and Norwegian Governments have ample evidence that you have abused your position in order to give active support, in Denmark and Norway, to the German oppressors. From the Danish and Norwegian point of view that might very well make you a war criminal. At any rate, I don't think that I should put the matter to the test, if I were you. You stay where you are and you'll be all right. Do have another drink ! ''

Lindholm denied that he had ever given aid and comfort to the Germans, but his protestations lacked assurance. One of the purposes of the interview had been to confirm our suspicions that the Swedish Nazi Party was actively helping the enemy outside Sweden. Lindholm's denials, which became less and less convincing as the conversation went on, persuaded us that our suspicions were well founded, and Lindholm was a frightened man when he took leave of us.

My day might begin with an hour's routine staff work of one kind or another, carried out in Reggie Sutton-Pratt's sunny office on the first floor of the legation. I had ridden to the embassy on a bicycle, since Sweden had virtually no petrol. Cars and taxis drove on motyl, a wood alcohol compound, but even that was rationed. An alternative source of power was gengas. This involved mounting a formidable furnace on the back of the car and stoking it with bags of charcoal. The process called for gauntlets which covered the arm from hand to elbow, pokers and shovels. As I later discovered, when I had the use of a car driven by this system, it was not ideal when one was dressed for a dinner-party. For most of my time in Stockholm I used my legs, either as a cyclist or as a pedestrian.

After an hour with Reggie I would go down to our room on the ground floor of the legation annexe. The morning might be spent in a little forgery, in laying out a leaflet, in working out a cover story, or in packing a subversive consignment of one kind or another for dispatch to Norway or Denmark.

Lunch might be eaten at one of our " cover flats," in the company of somebody with whom I did not wish to be seen abroad. Then home and into uniform for a Swedish military occasion at which the service attachés were expected to appear in full force. By 4.30 P.M. the saluting and standing to attention would be ended. We should have saluted politely General von Uthmann, the German Military attaché, a fine old soldier whom we always greeted with respect when we passed him in the street, although we never spoke.

Still in uniform, I might go down to our little printing-press and help Clarke to run off the last batches of a booklet for Norway. It might combine, as some of our productions did, photographs of girls with few, if any, clothes, and a text which bore no relation whatever to the illustrations, but which painted the future of the Third Reich and of the German Army in the gloomiest terms.

Home, and change for a dinner-party. In Stockholm, at any rate in those days, no dinner-party counted unless there were at least twenty-four guests. The formality was daunting. Six-thirty was the dinner hour, and guests were expected to arrive on the minute—not a second late, not a second early. Hot baths were a rare luxury—Sweden had practically no coke or coal—but an electric heater provided enough hot water to scrub the printer's ink off one's hands and to wash down.

Then a taxi and a skelter through dark streets to a large flat, where twenty-three guests, as a rule, impatiently awaited the belated foreigner.

One glanced at the table plan. All too often I found that as a lieutenant-colonel and a diplomat, by courtesy, I was placed on the left of my hostess. This, oddly enough, is the place of honour, and its occupant is required to make a speech of thanks on behalf of all the guests at the end of the meal. This prospect at first ruined many an excellent dinner for me, but, as my Swedish improved and I learned the formula, the speech became a matter of routine.

Brännvin. Skål! Skål!... Smörgåsbord—smoked salmon, herring, pâté, smoked reindeer meat, anchovies, sardines, smoked ham. Roast woodcock. An ice. White wine, red wine, champagne. A speech at the beginning from the host, one from me at the end. Then all the guests file out and shake their hostess by the hand. " Tack för maten, snälla Grevinna " —" Thank you for the meal, my dear Countess." Coffee, brandy, conversation. Later more canapés and Swedish

punch. " God natt, god natt ! Det var så hemskt trevligt !
Jag har aldrig haft det så roligt ! "—" I couldn't have enjoyed
myself more ! " And often that was true.

There might be some shy night-bird to be seen before going
to bed—one made appointments with helpers at strange hours,
but with luck I could go straight home. I would go to sleep
feeling that I had earned my pay.

And then, before sleep came, as the woodcock and the pâté
settled down comfortably in my stomach, I thought of British
rations—of tiny scrapings of margarine, of infinitesimal allow-
ances of meat, of dried eggs, of soya-bean sausages. And I
was thoroughly ashamed of myself.

It is now an accepted fact that Communist Military attachés
spy against the country to which they are accredited. Almost
all the recent spy cases which have been brought before the
British and American courts have involved the service personnel
of Iron Curtain embassies.

They, of course, are professionals. I was an amateur. The
professional must be ruthless. He must be able to sit next
to a charming young woman at dinner, to draw her out, and
subsequently to blackmail her without a qualm of conscience.
He must sparkle at the dinner-tables of those whom he is
conspiring to destroy, accept their hospitality, speak them
fair, while well aware that he is working for their downfall.

I did not have to do this, thank God, in Sweden. I liked
the country and the people, and I wished them well. My
target was the Germans, who were the enemies of my country,
if not of Sweden. And so I could drink my brännvin and eat
my dinner at a Swedish table with a clear conscience.

Social obligations, then, which a person in my position was
expected to fulfil could not be avoided, nor could official
receptions. As far as the Swedes were concerned, there were
very few of these. Occasionally a party to which attachés of
the Allied Powers were invited was held, immediately preceded, or followed, by an identical gathering to which our
colleagues—if that is the right term—of the Axis Powers were
invited. We were allowed to see very little of the Swedish

Army. With the exception of a comparatively small area around Stockholm and similar enclaves round Gothenburg, Malmö, and Hälsingborg, the port which faces Denmark on the West Coast, the whole of Sweden was a prohibited area for foreigners, and particularly for foreign soldiers.

This restriction was irritating, chiefly because it prevented us from making the most of what little leisure we had. In summer we were forbidden to sail in the Skärgården, that entrancing sprinkling of tiny islands which lies scattered off Sweden's Baltic Coast, within easy cruising distance of the capital. Since everybody in Stockholm spends each spare minute of the summer on and in the water, it was galling to hear Swedish friends describe the splendid week-ends which they had enjoyed among the islands while we ourselves were confined to the admittedly spacious but almost land-locked waters of Lake Mälar.

Nor were matters easier in winter. Bydalen was the only skiing resort which foreigners were allowed to visit, and there it was quite impossible to avoid clashing with the enemy. Britons, Americans, Germans, Japanese, Vichy French, and Free French skied together by day and ignored one another elaborately in the evenings. Since it was impossible to go home on leave, the British and Americans were left with no alternative but Bydalen in winter and such ' permitted ' resorts on the West Coast as Fälsterbo or Viken in the summer. There one met again all the people whose faces had become a tedium in Stockholm during the past year.

The Swedish General Staff were, however, perfectly justified in imposing these restrictions. The Germans were not particularly interested in spying on the Swedes, and in any case we knew that they had Swedish friends who were more than willing to give them any information which they required. The British and Americans, concentrating strictly upon the immediate prosecution of the war, were not much interested either. But the Russians, who, as their post-war policy has shown, take a strictly long-term view in political and military matters, were very interested indeed.

Whenever our Russian colleagues, Colonel Nikitouchev and
Major Pinyugin, paid us a visit, which was quite frequently—
we were never encouraged to visit *them*—the conversation
always turned to the Swedish Army.

Nikitouchev was a genial, stocky tank specialist, his assistant
a taciturn gunner. To our great regret, Nikitouchev suddenly
disappeared, without even bidding farewell to his foreign
colleagues, all of whom were his friends. Indeed, we had
good reason to suspect that his sudden recall to Moscow was
prompted by a fear that " Niki " had too many foreign friends.
Stalin did not encourage intimacy, even between fighting allies.

These visits from our Russian opposite numbers always
ended in an interrogation on Swedish military dispositions.
Had we confirmed that the 7th Tank Regiment was in Umeå ?
Somebody had reported to them that troops of Smålands
Infantry Regiment had been seen in Lappland. Did we
suppose that the whole division, of which that regiment
formed a part, had been moved to the North ?

To these probing questions we presented a façade of bland
ignorance, which was usually perfectly genuine. We were
not, we explained, very much concerned with the Swedish
Army, which seemed unlikely to play any very decisive rôle
in the war. We were deeply concerned with the war itself.
If the Russians would like to learn London's latest estimate
of troop movements to Germany, or to know how things were
going in Italy, we should be delighted to tell them all we
knew. But it was evident that the Russians were not interested
in these matters, and their anxiety to learn about the Swedish
Armed Forces was one of the chief reasons which led the
General Staff to brandish its flaming sword and banish us
from the paradise of the Skärgarden and the northern ski-
slopes. And if the Swedes had ever suspected us of giving
information to the Russians . . .

But, goodness knows, we had no cause to complain of any
restrictions imposed upon us, and most of us, while we hoped
that we were doing a useful job in Sweden, often felt that we
were no more than *embusqués*. Contact with prisoners of war

was a salutary corrective to the pervasively smug atmosphere of Sweden, which sometimes affected us all and caused us to lose a sense of proportion.

As far as I was concerned, these contacts with escaped prisoners of war were a relief and a solace. We were liable to receive at any time a telephone call from the police of some remote seaport to let us know that they were holding a man, or perhaps two or three men, who, they were satisfied, were escaped British prisoners of war. What should be done? Our answer was always the same. The escapers were to be put on the first train to Stockholm, and the legation would refund the cost of the fare. We would also repay a small sum which the local police were asked to advance as pocket-money.

It generally fell to Mr Wright, the Military attaché's confidential clerk, an old soldier with many years service behind him, to meet the new arrivals. Many men who passed through Sweden to freedom have good cause to remember him, his wife, and his very pretty daughters, for their flat was always open to them, and sometimes every available bed and sofa was occupied by former prisoners of war, who used the place as a hotel while awaiting the flight which would take them home.

The newcomers had to be fitted out with clothes, since they usually arrived in a filthy condition. This was natural enough, because the normal escape route to Sweden led through the holds of small colliers which carried Polish coal from Stettin. If an escaped prisoner managed to get as far as one of the jetties at which these little ships loaded—and many escapers were captured in Stettin after successfully evading their captors for weeks and even months—there was a good chance that a friendly member of the crew would smuggle him aboard and almost bury him in a grave of coal. Appeals to officers, and in particular to skippers, were less likely to succeed. Indeed, we had cases on record of skippers returning escaped prisoners of war to the Germans, and one monster actually turned back, after his ship had left German territorial waters, in order to deliver into the hands of the enemy an R.A.F. officer, who had declared himself, as he was entitled to do, on the high seas. This officer was shot by the Germans, and we went to some pains to ensure that the name of the captain in question was put on an Allied black list, where I trust it still remains if the man is alive.

A voyage in a coal-bunker can be relied upon to play havoc with clothes, and most of our guests, who had often spent weeks on the road, would not have won a *concours d'élégance* at the best of times. We therefore used to take them to the Nordiska Kompaniet, or N.K., Stockholm's largest department store. Their eyes nearly started out of their heads, as mine had when I first came to Sweden, at the display of goods which to British civilians, let alone to men who had spent some years in a prison camp, were no more than a memory. Sometimes the very lavishness of the display was a source of potential trouble. A man who has been on the run in Germany, stealing to keep alive, and indeed regarding theft from the enemy as a patriotic act, may be forgiven if, after a few hours in a neutral country, he forgets where he is and stretches a cautious hand towards a tray of foodstuffs or a display of watches. We had to keep a sharp eye on our charges, and when we caught them pilfering their embarrassment was pitiful. As one of them explained, stealing had, in a way, become second nature to him, though had he remembered that he was now in Sweden he would never have thought of shoplifting. This was certainly true, and it did not take our guests long to revert to their normal habits of honesty.

On the whole, it might be true to say that the " other ranks " were more successful escapers than the officers. Since the war we have read many books about escapes, all of them written by officers and concerned with the doings in Oflags—that is to say, with camps in which officers were confined. The " other ranks " from the Stalags, many of whom escaped successfully after adventures which they were hardly able to describe verbally, much less in writing, have left no record of what must have been some of the most exciting stories of the war.

But the British soldier was accustomed to take things as they

came, and to be surprised at nothing.   Unless he could be at
home—and that meant in his own home town, and not merely
in the British Isles—he did not greatly mind where he was.
Iraq was much the same as Egypt, as far as he was concerned ;
Italy was very similar to Iraq, except that it was a trifle less
warm ; Austria, Czechoslovakia, Poland, Germany were to
him indistinguishable from one another—none of the languages
made sense anyhow, so why bother ?

This simple attitude, I am sure, resulted in many successful
escapes, whereas officers often failed through trying to be too
clever.

I remember a sergeant and two private soldiers who came
to lunch with me after they had been in Sweden for a matter
of fifteen hours or so.   They drank a lot of thin Swedish beer
and ate a great deal of steak-and-kidney pudding, but the
story of their escape came out in fragments, and I am sure that
nine-tenths of it still remains untold, to anybody except,
perhaps, their families.

The men had been in camp somewhere in the depths of
Silesia, and had escaped with roughly forged papers—they
showed them to me, and, as something of a forger myself, I
was amazed that such miserable counterfeits could have
passed muster.   But pass they did, for eight months, during
which the three companions wandered through a large part of
Germany, Czechoslovakia, and Poland in the rather improbable
guise of Czech workmen.   Since they spoke no language but
English, this pose was as good as any other.   For a time they
had joined a small band of Slovak partisans, who were engaged
in guerilla warfare against the Germans.   This, they said, had
been most enjoyable, and they had been really sorry to leave
their Slovak friends.   They had spent the previous Christmas
in a Silesian farmhouse.

" D'you know, sir," the sergeant said, " the old girl there—
nice old girl she was, too—had never even *heard* of Christmas
pudding !   Of course we taught her how to make it—she had
all the doings there.   Very nice Christmas we had, didn't we,
lads ? "

The lads agreed that it had been a splendid Christmas.

" But what did you do about language ? " I asked. " After all, you were on the road for eight months."

One of the private soldiers indicated the sergeant.

" No difficulty there, sir. Old Nobby here speaks German very good."

I addressed Nobby in German, and a look of blank incomprehension came over his face.

" I don't speak German *that* good," he said.

Cleverness did sometimes almost pay dividends, though, as the case of Lieutenant James goes to show.

When it came to escaped prisoners of war, our Naval attaché, Captain Henry Denham, R.N., fared less well than did we and the Air attaché. Comparatively few sailors found their way to prisoner-of-war camps, since submarine commanders rarely had the time, the inclination, or the accommodation to pick up survivors when they sank a warship. James, an Old Etonian officer of the R.N.V.R., was an exception to the general rule. He was in command of a motor torpedo-boat in the English Channel, and when it had been sunk close to the French coast the Germans had rescued him, and he was eventually sent to an Oflag in southern Germany.

This camp had a remarkable " escape committee," headed by a man who, possessing an extensive knowledge of Europe and of European languages, had been bound on a highly secret mission, disguised in uniform, when the aircraft in which he was a passenger had been shot down. His plan for James's escape was based on a sound knowledge of German psychology.

Instead of seeking to camouflage himself, James escaped in the full uniform of a Lieutenant R.N.V.R. His buttons shone, his trousers were beautifully creased, his shoes gleamed with polish, and he carried a smart suitcase. He carried also a really beautiful set of documents, all forged in the camp, of which the most impressive read, roughly, as follows :

ROYAL BULGARIAN LEGATION. BERLIN. W.
To whom it may concern :
The bearer of this letter, Lieutenant I. Buggeroff [this was

the name which was actually used], Royal Bulgarian Navy, is in Germany on special duty. All naval and military authorities are requested to afford him any assistance which he may require. Lieutenant Buggeroff speaks little German.

(Signed) ————

Minister Plenipotentiary and Extraordinary.

The only true statement in this disingenuous document was that the bearer spoke little German. James spoke practically none at all, but he hoped, justifiably as it turned out, that he would not have the misfortune to encounter a German who spoke Bulgarian.

Unlike most escapers, James travelled through Germany in comfort. Whenever he needed a bed or a meal or a railway warrant he reported to the nearest headquarters, saluted smartly, produced his credentials, and asked for what he wanted in fractured German. His array of documents, liberally and impressively stamped, never failed to create the right impression. Fortunately the crown and foul anchor has been almost universally adopted as a badge by the navies of countries which still possess a monarch, and although the Bulgarian crown is of rather different design to the British one, which adorned James's cap, no German noticed the discrepancy.

The Germans simply could not take too much trouble on behalf of an officer of an allied Power, and James went through Germany, in his own words, " like a dose of salts."

Disaster awaited him at Stettin, however. There the naval authorities had had some experience of escaped prisoners of war, and they were suspicious. When James presented his credentials and said that his orders required him to inspect certain jetties, which happened to be those from which the Swedish colliers sailed, nobody could have been more obliging than the German naval officer who interviewed him. But certainly Lieutenant Buggeroff would be given every facility. In fact, an officer would be detailed to accompany him on his little tour of inspection.

No, really, " Lieutenant Buggeroff " assured them, that would be carrying kindness too far. He could easily find his own way to the jetties. It was quite unnecessary to waste the time of a German officer. So vehement were the visitor's protests that the Germans allowed him to leave on his own, speeding him with expressions of good will, but putting a spy on his tracks. James reached the jetty and approached a Swedish seaman. As so often happened, the man said that he would get the fugitive aboard his ship, but that he dared not do so until the skipper had gone ashore. James was forced to kill time, and it was while he was doing this that the Germans pounced. A day or two later he was behind barbed wire again.

A second escape, which did bring James to Sweden, was less ambitiously planned, and perhaps that is why it succeeded where the ambitious journey of " Lieutenant I. Buggeroff " had failed.

The story of Eric Williams, Oliver Philpot, and Michael Codner, who successfully escaped from captivity with the help of a vaulting-horse, is probably the best-known episode of its kind to have come out of the war. Both Williams and Philpot have written books about the " Wooden Horse," which has also provided the theme for a film. Williams is now a well-known writer, and Philpot a successful businessman. Poor Codner was killed not long after the war by Malayan terrorists, while serving as a policeman.

The " Wooden Horse " party were even more fêted by the British colony in Stockholm than other escapers, which is saying a good deal. Group Captain Maycock, our Air attaché, was extremely proud of his protégés, as he was entitled to be, and when they finally left for London we said good-bye to them with real regret. Although it is a comparatively large city, Stockholm can be a boring place, particularly in wartime. The " Wooden Horse " party provided us, thanks to their charm and modesty, with a very welcome distraction.

One escaped prisoner, whom I shall call Wells, although that was not his name, presented a very much less pleasant problem. He arrived in Sweden by the usual route, and his account of his escape was suspiciously circumstantial. For a private soldier he was remarkably articulate. Every question was answered pat, and this was extremely unusual, at least where " other ranks " were concerned.

Wells was a gipsy, and in civilian life had worked in a circus. He was an excellent conjurer, and he had all the glib patter which is the stock-in-trade of the magician. We could not pick a single hole in his story from the incomplete background information which was available to us in Stockholm, yet we were not happy about Wells, and the War Office received from us a rather fuller account of his adventures than we usually devoted to the reports of our escapers.

Our vague doubts were more than justified. Wells, London told us, was strongly suspected of being a traitor, who had been allowed to escape by the Germans in order that he might serve them in England as an agent. Prisoners of war who had been repatriated under exchange arrangements, and who had been imprisoned with Wells, had already reported on the close relationship which he had established with the Germans, and the authorities had been keeping an eye out for him for some time past. We were to give Wells no indication that he was under suspicion. When he reached London he would be arrested.

Unfortunately Wells's stay in Stockholm was prolonged by the fact that for several days after we received this ominous signal no aircraft was available to fly him to Scotland. For more than a week those who knew the man's secret were forced to treat him with a show of hollow friendship and approbation which it was very difficult and unpleasant to maintain. It was particularly difficult for Mr Wright, with whom Wells stayed, and who had, of course, seen the sinister telegram from London. As it happened, Mrs Wright was at that time producing a little entertainment in aid of one of the many war charities in which she was interested. Wells offered to do a conjuring act, and Mrs Wright, who knew nothing of the shadow which hung over him, accepted the offer with gratitude. It was really horrible to see Wells, arrayed in a hired dress suit, take the stage and give a polished performance of standard conjuring tricks. One felt rather like a prison officer on duty in the condemned cell. We were deeply relieved when we could at last put the man aboard an aircraft and wish him good luck. He would need it.

I never knew what happened to " Wells," and I rather imagined that he had been hanged. However, he was not, perhaps unluckily for him. In November 1961, after the first draft of this book had been written, I happened to read in a newspaper that he had been sentenced to fifteen years preventitive detention. The judge, in passing sentence, had some very harsh things to say to the prisoner, and I have no doubt that they were thoroughly deserved. It would be interesting to know the story of the eighteen years of Wells's life which intervened between the moment when the Scotland-bound Dakota took off from Bromma Airport, with Wells aboard, and the moment in 1961 when prison officers tapped him on the shoulder and led him from the dock to face a sentence which he will not complete until he is aged more than sixty.

7. INTO GERMANY

In THE EARLY months of 1944 we had virtually given up hope of recruiting any reliable agents in Stockholm for work in Germany, and we were at a loss. Then O.S.S. told us that they had discovered a hopeful recruit, and that they proposed to dispatch him through a route of which they had heard good reports. The man was a German, and he was unknown to us. Our own German contacts had never heard of him, so that at least we had nothing positive against the man, although equally we knew nothing in his favour, except that O.S.S. believed in his integrity.

The Americans intended to mount this operation themselves, but we offered any help that we could give. About ten days after the first news of the impending venture reached our ears O.S.S. sent across the agent's documents for checking They looked very good indeed—identity card, ration cards, military discharge papers, membership card of the German Labour Front, and so on. Indeed, it seemed to us that the documents were almost too perfect. Even in Germany, whose officials have a passion for Ausweise, or identity cards, of every kind, a man who habitually carried in his pocket an absolutely complete set of documents would be something of a paragon, and an alert policeman might ask himself the reason for this meticulous respect for regulations.

Incidentally, it is ironical to reflect that our chief enemy in Germany, Heinrich Himmler, himself fell into this very trap. After the German capitulation, Himmler, equipped, as might have been expected, with a very convincing set of papers— towards the end of the war the S.S. set up a special department to supply members of the organization with such forgeries— was making his way through Northern Germany in disguise. An intelligent British N.C.O., who had demanded to see the papers of this refugee, decided that they were just a little too good to be true, and detained Himmler for interrogation. A little later the once dreaded Reichsführer S.S. und Chef der Deutschen Polizei had taken his own life by poison.

Although at the time we did not have this useful example to guide us, we advised that they should tell their man not to carry all the documents with which they had provided him on his person. Otherwise the papers themselves seemed to be unexceptionable, and we were particularly impressed by the speed with which they were produced. When we asked London for identity cards or for rubber stamps of almost infinite variety, with which to embellish them, we could reckon with a delay of at least three weeks before the diplomatic bag disgorged them in Stockholm. Washington, we told our American colleagues, taking care to give no more than a hint of the envy we felt, were much more expeditious in fulfilling orders than were our own people.

" Oh, but these didn't come from Washington," my American opposite number, in charge of the German Section of O.S.S., explained. " There's a little printer and blockmaker, up in the Old Town here. He's a reliable guy. He did the work for us."

I drew a long breath.

" Unless you want to sentence your man to death," I said, earnestly, " you'll burn those documents and all the rubber stamps and start all over again. We'll check on your ' little printer,' and I'm prepared to bet that you'll find that he has some connexion with the German Legation."

" And in the meantime ? "

" In the meantime postpone the operation, alter the man's whole cover story, and get the papers and stamps made in Washington. It's only fair to your agent to take every possible precaution for his safety."

My American colleague looked glum.

" But Washington will take even longer than your outfit in London to get the stuff ready."

" I don't want to interfere, or to know more about your operation than you care to tell me," I said, " but if it would help you, and you'll let me know what you need, I'll get London to do the job for you. It would certainly save time."

" And we won't tell Washington," said the American.

In the event it did save time, and an investigation of the " little printer in the Old Town " confirmed that he had given full details of the job which he had done to the enemy. But that agent was still unlucky. The route through which he was dispatched proved to be unreliable. He was arrested, and, one morning, in the chill of dawn, an executioner, ceremoniously attired in top-hat, frock coat, and white cotton gloves, lopped off the poor man's head in the courtyard of a German prison. At least his fate served to warn us that one possible route into Germany must never be used again. This was not much consolation either to O.S.S. or ourselves, but it was something.

No active German Resistance Movement, or at least none with which we could make contact, seemed to exist. We knew, of course, that a group of senior Army officers, diplomats, and civil servants were exploring the possibilities of overthrowing Hitler. Adam von Trott zu Solz, a former Rhodes Scholar, whose name now stands on the war memorial of Balliol College, Oxford, since he died horribly at the hands of Hitler's tormentors after the plot of July 20, 1944, came to Stockholm in February of that year with the specific purpose of getting in touch with us. Knowing a very little of what was in the wind, and suspecting a great deal more, we asked London's permission to meet von Trott. It was refused. Roosevelt and Churchill had enunciated the doctrine of unconditional surrender at the Casablanca Conference, and any contact with Germans who might seek, as von Trott and his associates did, to get rid of the Nazis and shorten the war was forbidden. The young German went back to Berlin and to a shameful death, and the Allies, as I am still convinced, missed a great opportunity.

The first five months of 1944, though busy enough, were very unsatisfying. The collection of information from Germany, Denmark, and Norway had become a reasonably efficient routine, and the lines through which we distributed subversive material of all kinds, at least in Norway and Denmark, improved with every week that passed.

As has already been explained, the German Section undertook no independent operations in those countries. These were left entirely to our Norwegian and Danish sections, and very busy they were. But so savagely anti-German was almost the whole population, particularly of Norway, that even the children wanted to play some part in harassing the enemy, and elderly people were no less eager to help. Anything which served to maintain civilian morale was very welcome to the resistance, and so we did what we could to supply them in increasing measure with devices which would embarrass the enemy and, while encouraging those who used them, would not involve any serious risk.

The capsules of evil-smelling fluid, of which I had ordered a consignment before leaving England, were very useful indeed. Two or three of them, which could be carried in a waistcoat pocket, were enough to put the contents of an entire cloakroom out of commission. German officers and soldiers in Norway took to wearing their outer garments indoors, whatever the room temperature, rather than risk being deprived of the use of their greatcoats for weeks.

We sent over, also, powerful catapults complete with packets of small leaflets packed and wrapped in such a manner as to burst and scatter on impact. These could be fired at the closed windows of establishments frequented by German troops. Since there was a shortage of glass, as of most other things, in

Norway, a broken window was a serious matter, considering the severity of the northern winter, and the leaflets may have done some good. At least they cheered a lot of Norwegians.

We shipped other supplies to Norway and to Denmark in bulk. In particular, admirably simulated packets of German cocoa, pudding-powder, pea-soup powder, and other foodstuffs were dispatched from Sweden in comparatively large numbers. The aim was not to supplement German Army rations, since the containers held no food. Instead, they concealed a number of little phials and capsules and a booklet, printed on India paper, which instructed the German soldier how to use them.

The phials contained chemicals which, if used in accordance with the detailed instructions enclosed with them, would enable a soldier who wanted a rest to produce convincing symptoms of various illnesses, ranging from a swollen knee to jaundice and tuberculosis. The T.B. kit even included a tiny capsule of dried blood, which the patient was instructed to carry in his mouth and to bite if the medical officer ordered a sputum test. By taking one other precaution, which need not be described here, the ' sufferer ' could produce a gobbet of phlegm which would look convincing even under a microscope.

The booklet also gave full details of the symptoms of each illness concerned, and careful coaching on what must be said by the patient when he confronted the doctor.

We were always nervous lest the enemy should try to turn this weapon against us—there are tired soldiers in every army. But he never did so successfully, and the havoc which these little packages played towards the end of the war was very serious indeed. Identical kits to those which we were sending from Sweden were dispatched from other neutral capitals, and the situation finally became so serious that many German M.O.'s refused to pass a man as being sick no matter how genuine his illness. The effect of this upon morale need hardly be emphasized.

Another duty which we undertook was that of Scandinavian correspondents of the three ' black ' British radio stations, broadcasting to the German Forces under the names " Gustav

Siegfried I," "Radio Atlantic," and "Soldatensender
Calais." British thinking in propaganda had advanced a good
deal since the "Programme for the German Forces" had been
hamstrung four years previously. Now a powerful transmitter,
situated in the South Midlands of England, broadcast regularly
to the German Forces on two frequencies, and what the
stations had to say was often taken very seriously indeed,
particularly by neutrals. It was sometimes amusing to hear a
Swede quote as coming from a "secret German station" a
news item which had just been broadcast by "G.S.I.," and
which we had sent back only a few hours before. In the
television programme, "This is Your Life," my old friend
Tom Delmer, the former Chief Foreign Correspondent of the
Daily Express, admitted to millions of viewers that he had been
responsible for these two stations. There may therefore be no
harm in my paying him the tribute here which he richly
deserves. "G.S.I." and "Soldatensender Calais," not to
mention other stations in the same network, if that is the right
word, were brilliantly run, and their effect on the enemy and
upon neutrals was certainly very considerable.

The preparation and dispatch of 'toys' of various kinds,
the printing and distribution of propaganda, the gathering of
information and its transmission to London, made up a more
than fair day's work, when combined with my more legitimate
duties as a Military attaché. But we longed to begin operations
in Germany, and as the invasion of "Fortress, Europe" became
even more imminent our sense of frustration increased.

Fortunately we were not the only people in Sweden who
were galled by comparative inactivity while great events
were taking place six hundred miles or so to the south. In a
remote camp in the southern province of Skåne a young officer
of the Danish Army was packing his suitcase for a visit to
Stockholm which was to prove momentous for him and
for us.

Some people will remember that on the night of April 8–9,
1940, while the German Minister in Oslo was showing the
ghastly film *Baptism of Fire*, which glorified the murder of

Poland, to a party of awed Norwegian politicians, Dr Wilhelm
Furtwängler was conducting the Berlin Philharmonic Orchestra in Copenhagen.   The film show and the concert were both
arranged to distract the attention of the people who mattered
in Norway and Denmark for an hour or two, while Germany
took the final steps to her plan for subjugation of both countries.
Norway, with some help from Great Britain and France, was
able to resist the assault of seven German divisions for a little
time.   Denmark, even less ready for war than her northern
neighbour, was, in the words of Sir Winston Churchill, " easily
overrun after a resistance in which a few faithful soldiers were
killed."

The Danish Army suffered bitterly from the humiliation of
an almost bloodless defeat.   Some officers and men were able
to make their way direct to the United Kingdom in small
craft, but many more crossed the Öresund to Sweden, believing
that the Swedish Government, neutral though it might be,
would still make it possible for them to reach an Allied country,
where they might redeem what they regarded as their failure
by taking up arms again for the liberation of their country.

These hopes were disappointed.   The Danish soldiers, to
their fierce indignation, were interned when they reached
Sweden.   The Danish Government in London, with the active
support of Great Britain, brought pressure to bear on the
Swedish authorities, and at last a small concession was made.
The Danes were allowed to form a Danish Legion on Swedish
soil.   They were somewhat sketchily equipped with light
weapons, and permitted to train on the assumption that, one
day, they would return to Denmark and play their part in
driving out the invader.

For a time the two thousand Danes in the legion were
reasonably content to train as hard and as effectively as their
Swedish hosts would allow, sustained by the belief that they
would one day recross the Öresund as liberators.   But as the
months wore on it became increasingly obvious that while the
Swedes were allowing them to play at being soldiers they had
no intention whatever of giving the Danish Legion a chance

to fire a shot in anger. The imminence of an Allied landing in France brought to a head the dissatisfaction which many of the younger officers felt at the supine existence to which they were condemned.

One of the most discontented of these officers was Captain Johan Mackeprang Bøge. Aged about thirty, a dedicated patriot, and a man whose whole background and training led him to abhor everything for which National Socialism stood, Bøge decided, in the spring of 1944, that he must, at all costs, take an active part in the war before it was too late. It should not be said of him, at least, that he had allowed the British and the Americans to free Denmark while he sat safe and sound in Sweden. These views were shared by a dozen other officers, who were Bøge's close friends in the legion, and they deputed the captain to travel to Stockholm and there to prospect for some form of active employment which would enable them to inflict the utmost possible damage upon the enemy.

As might have been expected, Bøge reported to the British Legation, and there he was taken in hand by the Danish Section of S.O.E. But membership of the Danish Resistance Movement was not quite what the captain thought. He regarded that as a civilian affair, whereas he was a soldier. He did not see himself spending the rest of the war rubbing shoulders with German soldiers on Strøget, Copenhagen's Bond Street, even as one of the leaders of the Danish Home Front. Captain Bøge wanted to serve on a still more active and dangerous front.

Bøge explained this to the Danish section. As it happened, I had, that very morning, as far as I recall, been telling the head of the section, Ronald Turnbull, who was also head of the whole S.O.E. mission, that he did not realize how lucky he was in having a large pool of keen and patriotic recruits upon which to draw—a whole nation, in fact. I had contrasted his fortunate situation with my own dismal plight, and Ronald had been kind enough to say that at least the German Section had never tried to lure away any of his good men. As a matter of fact, I had often been tempted to try this, but " body snatching " is not a sport which endears those who practise it to their colleagues, and I had refrained.

Now Ronald remembered our conversation.

" I think there's a friend of mine downstairs who might like to see you," he said to Bøge.   " I'll just go down and see if he's there."

In three minutes Ronald Turnbull explained the position to me, and Bøge came into my office.

I saw a man of medium height, slim, but obviously athletic and wiry.   Cold blue eyes were set deep in a face that looked almost emaciated, the cheeks hollow, the nose thin and bony. Darkish-blond hair curled crisply but not abundantly above a high forehead.   It was the kind of face which would have looked entirely in place had it been framed by a monk's cowl, but it was not, at first glance, a face that would stamp itself upon the memory—and that is the kind of face which an agent should have.

The captain explained his predicament.   He added that he had been given to understand that I was interested in German affairs, and so was he.   He knew North Germany well, particularly South Schleswig, once a Danish province, which had been snatched from Denmark by Prussia after the war of 1864, and was now a part of Schleswig-Holstein.   He had an intimate knowledge of Flensburg, Kiel, Lübeck, and Hamburg, and he knew people, in all those towns, upon whom he believed we could rely for help.   They were, for the most part, of Danish extraction, but some of them were of pure German blood.

I began to feel the kind of thrill which, I imagine, is experienced by a gun-dog when it makes its point.   It was just possible that we might now, at long last, get to work.

The conversation had not yet reached the stage when a direct approach should be made.   Indeed, an approach would come better from Bøge than from me.

" How would you get in touch with these friends of yours ? " I asked.

" I should think the best idea would be to go and see them," Bøge answered, casually.

" Would you be ready to do that ? "

" Of course. There'd be no particular difficulty that I can foresee."

" You wouldn't mind working in Germany ? "

" Certainly not. There's a mild risk, of course, but it would be better fun than skulking about Sweden."

" Yes, it would. What do you think these contacts could do for us ? "

Bøge refused a cigarette. He neither smoked nor drank.

" Well," he said—his English was good, though not entirely fluent—" down at the camp I've got a dozen friends—Danish officers like myself. They're as fed up as I am. I'm sure they'd jump at the chance of going into Germany and causing a bit of trouble."

" I live in Grev Turegatan," I said, and gave Bøge the number of my flat. " The flat is empty at the moment. It's in a block, on the third floor. I'll go ahead. Follow me in twenty minutes and ring twice when you reach my front door. See that you are alone in the lift when you come up to the flat, and if by any chance there happens to be somebody on my landing—one of the neighbours or a tradesman—press the lift button to the next floor and carry on upward. Then come down when the coast is clear. All right ? "

Bøge's eyes gleamed in their deep sockets.

" It sounds interesting," he said.

When I got home I made myself a drink. I was very excited indeed. Twenty minutes later the door bell rang twice.

When he entered the drawing-room the captain looked about him attentively. His eyes lingered on the picture above the mantelpiece and on the plaster moulding on the high ceiling, from which a candelabrum had once hung. I guessed what he was thinking.

" No microphones," I said. " Our security officer checked the place the other day. You seem to have the right reactions for this kind of job."

The captain smiled, something that he rarely did.

" One gets to hear about things," he said.

I settled him on the sofa.

" Now, tell me about yourself," I said.

Bøge was the son of a clergyman. He was not a regular officer, but held a commission in the reserve-list of an infantry regiment. In civilian life he was a bank officer. He had been brought up in a village not far from Kolding, in Jutland, some thirty miles from the German frontier, where his father was pastor. Memories of the war of 1864 were still very lively in that region, and hatred of the Prussians, who had stolen South Schleswig from Denmark after what was surely one of the most shameful little wars in history, was deeply rooted in the minds of the people.

Bøge had been a member of a patriotic society whose aim was to restore South Schleswig to the Danish Crown. Since he was a man who liked to be precise in everything that he did, he made it his business, in the years before the war, to learn as much as he could about the lost province at first hand. He had accordingly spent holidays wandering about South Schleswig, and had made many friends. His travels had taken him to Hamburg and to Kiel, and as far south as Bremen and Hanover.

If Bøge had ever chosen to be a journalist he would have been a good one, for he was full of the spirit of inquiry, and he had a passion for exact facts. He also had a photographic memory and excellent powers of recognizing and remembering faces and names. He had only six or seven contacts in North Germany, but for these he was prepared to vouch absolutely. As we had never, until that moment, been able to establish a single " safe house " in Germany, Bøge's offer, if he could justify it, represented a great step forward.

We talked at length, but it was not yet time to get down to business. First I wanted to check Bøge's credentials with the Danish Section, to make quite sure, or, at least, as sure as possible, that he was a man to be trusted absolutely. We arranged to meet two days later at a neutral address.

The Danish Section were prepared to certify Captain Bøge's

good faith. His record with the Danish Legion was excellent, and his past history had been thoroughly checked by the resistance movement, which, for its own protection, was bound to have an efficient organization for ' screening ' would-be members. I went to my second meeting with Captain Bøge ready at last to place my full trust in him.

Together we worked out a plan. Bøge must first go to Germany and make a thorough reconnaissance of the territory which he knew. He would ensure that the contacts whom he had known before the war were still alive and on the spot, and find out how many of them were able and willing to help us. These people must provide shelter for our agents when required to do so, and act as " letter boxes." They must also be willing to furnish, or, at least, to indicate, places where small supplies of stores of one kind or another could be hidden. The last thing we sought was to burden the men whom we should, as we hoped, send into Germany, with incriminating contraband whose discovery by frontier guards or police would automatically ensure the arrest and execution of the traveller. A charge of plastic would be a difficult thing for an innocent Danish worker to explain away if it were discovered in his rucksack. It would be far better to deliver all compromising material in one consignment, and to cache it well inside Germany at convenient spots, where our men could collect what they needed more or less at their leisure.

During his stay in Germany, which would last, as we reckoned, about a fortnight, Bøge also undertook to reconnoitre suitable targets for sabotage. Here again we were in a very different position from that of the other " country sections " of S.O.E. Agents who were sent into France, say, or Holland or Denmark from the United Kingdom were always met by a local " reception committee " whose members knew every inch of the area in which the newcomer would operate. Only in exceptional cases involving demolitions of real importance were targets designated by London. The normal practice was to assume that the local people who were working with us knew far better than anybody in London could hope to do what installations in their district could be most profitably attacked. It was left to the discretion of the agent from London to sanction these attacks or to veto them.

But in Germany, though we might, if we were lucky, find " safe houses," there would be no reception committee, and it would be too much to expect much local help in choosing targets. Bøge would have to do what he could to select two or three suitable points for attack by our first agents. Thereafter we might hope that our men would themselves be able to suggest targets for those who were to follow them. In any case, we agreed that Bøge himself would take no part in actual operations. He would be the organizer of what we hoped would become a little network, travelling between Germany and Stockholm, ensuring that our men in Germany got their orders and the supplies which they required, building up our communications, and, in general, maintaining contact with the men on the spot.

In the ordinary way, agents sent from England by S.O.E. were provided with a wireless operator, and were thus able to keep in daily touch with headquarters. To adopt this system in Germany was out of the question. However willing Bøge's friends might be to give shelter to our men, the hiding of a W/T set was a very much more perilous undertaking. It might be assumed that the Germans, whose methods of detecting illegal transmitters in occupied countries were efficient enough, had brought the technique to an even higher point of perfection inside their own frontiers. In any case, we had no hope of being able to train wireless operators in Stockholm, and London would have no men to spare for us. We must rely, in communicating with our agents, on codes and personal contact.

The route into Germany presented no particular difficulties. By now the Danish Resistance Movement had organized what amounted to a regular ferry service between Sweden and Denmark. In September 1943, indeed, soon after my arrival in Stockholm, these illegal routes had safely brought no fewer than ten thousand refugees to Sweden, most of them

Jews escaping from Hitler's " final solution " of what he chose
to regard as the Jewish problem. Bøge would have no difficulty
in reaching Denmark with the help of the Danish Section, and,
once there, the resistance would speed him on his way to the
German frontier.

We devised a simple cover story which, like all good cover
stories, was tailored to fit, as far as possible, Bøge's actual
background and past career. His documents would show him
to be a Danish volunteer, working in a factory in Hamburg
which Bøge happened to know, and which he would have been
able to describe in detail if he had been called upon to do so.
His work would, however, oblige him to travel about the district from time to time, and the captain would thus be able to
make his way round his diocese, as we hoped, without arousing
suspicion. In fact, Bøge did look upon his job rather as that
of a missionary bishop *in partibus infidelium*.

I undertook to put the whole scheme to London for approval.
While they were brooding over it Bøge would return to his
camp and recruit four trusted officers. If Baker Street agreed
to our plan these men would be brought to Stockholm and
given an intensive course of training. I should ask that a
training-officer might be posted to us, and we would establish
a tiny school, where the methods taught at Beaulieu would be
instilled under the very noses of the Swedish Secret Police and
the Gestapo.

I returned to the legation to draft a very long memorandum,
while Captain Bøge took a train for the south.

London wasted little time. Within ten days we were told
that our project had been approved in principle. The forged
papers which we had requisitioned for Bøge's journey arrived
a few days later. A training-officer, headquarters said, would
be warned to stand by to fly to Stockholm as soon as his first
pupils were ready to begin their course.

In the meantime Bøge had returned from the south. He had
enlisted four keen candidates, and we made arrangements,
through Danish military authorities, for their posting to
Stockholm when we gave the word. Bøge's own training was

a comparatively simple affair. He had a thorough knowledge of the country in which he was to work, his journey would, with luck, be completed in two weeks. We equipped him with codes and secret inks, and I went over the cover story again and again.

The yacht *Valkyrian* proved her value during the days which preceded Captain Bøge's departure. Nothing could have been more innocent than the little white cutter which, on several warm spring afternoons, put out from Smedslätten with a man and a girl aboard. Neither Janet nor I was a very experienced sailor, but if there was no wind or too much of it the outboard motor could generally be relied upon to bring us to some lonely jetty, conveniently close to a bus route, where Bøge awaited us. Then we would drop anchor in a sheltered cove, and lessons would begin, while in the cabin, the tea-kettle hissed over a " Primus " stove. Here, in the wide expanse of Lake Mälar, we could not be overheard or watched.

8. "...YOUR WAR IS ENDED"

As a neutral country close to Germany and not too far from Great Britain, and one which had access to the sea, Sweden naturally found herself involved in the exchange of wounded prisoners of war which are provided for by the Geneva Convention. This treaty stipulates that belligerent countries which are signatories to the convention, as the United States, Great Britain, Germany, and Italy were, and Russia was not, may, under the auspices of the International Red Cross, exchange prisoners of war who are judged to be medically unfit for further war service. Those exchanges may also include interned civilians whose age or state of health makes them incapable of taking any active part in the war. Military personnel are exchanged irrespective of the numbers involved on each side, but civilians are swapped head for head—say fifty old German men and women for fifty British, neither more nor less on either side.

In Count Folke Bernadotte, whose murder in Israel after the war was a sad loss to humanity, the Swedish Red Cross had an excellent chief and we a good colleague. Not that Count Bernadotte ever departed from the strict impartiality without which international Red Cross work could not continue. But he was a brilliant and fearless negotiator in the service of suffering people, and the success of the two exchanges of prisoners of war which took place while I was in Sweden may be largely ascribed to his influence.

I was not much concerned with the first exchange, which took place very soon after my arrival in Stockholm, except as a matter of routine. In the second, I was deeply involved. Soon after Bøge's departure for Germany my work for S.O.E. had to be put aside for some days while the preliminary negotiations were under way, and during the actual exchange I spent the better part of a week in South Sweden, since I was in charge, on the British side, of the disembarkation and onward transport of our prisoners.

The route by which hundreds of maimed and crippled prisoners from Great Britain and the Commonwealth made their way to freedom, while the war still raged, lay through the German Baltic port of Sassnitz, to which prisoners who had been certified as unfit for further service by a medical board were brought by train from the camps. There the Swedish train-ferry *Drottning Victoria* awaited them, and, a few hours after leaving Germany, the men were landed at Trälleborg, on the southern tip of Sweden. German hospital coaches, in which the lying cases travelled, were shipped to Sweden in the ferry, and coupled to the trains of the Swedish State Railways, which carried the jubilant prisoners to Gothenburg, where they embarked in the transatlantic liner *Drottningholm* for Newcastle. In the meantime German prisoners had been landed from the *Arundel Castle*, which had brought them from England, and were sent back to Germany by the same route, in reverse.

All this sounds a perfectly simple and straightforward arrangement, and, on paper, it was. But, as always happens in affairs of this kind, snags of all sorts, some predictable, some utterly unexpected, kept cropping up.

The Swedish Royal family took a keen interest in these exchanges. Perhaps it was fortunate that their sympathies were sharply divided between the belligerents, since this ensured that both the British and the Germans could count upon being greeted by a sympathetic princess.

The Crown Princess, now Queen Louise of Sweden, made no secret of the fact that she favoured the Allies, as might have been expected of a sister of Lord Louis Mountbatten. Whenever, in the Anglican Church in Stockholm, we held a service of thanksgiving for a victory or of intercession, as we did, for example, on D-day, a middle-aged lady, usually dressed in a quiet tweed suit and felt hat, would slip silently into the church after the service had begun, and sit alone in one of the back pews. When the Blessing had been pronounced by the chaplain the Crown Princess stole away as quietly as she had come. It was she who welcomed the British prisoners to her country.

Princess Sybilla, the mother of the present Crown Prince of Sweden, on the other hand, was ardently pro-German. This was understandable enough, since her father was the Duke of Saxe-Coburg-Gotha, who, rather implausibly, managed to combine the holding of high rank in the S.S. with the Presidency of the German Red Cross. After the war the British arrested the Duke on suspicion of being a war criminal, an occurrence which led to a slight tiff between King Gustav V, whose private sympathies were also with the Germans, and Lord Tedder, our deputy supreme commander, who visited Stockholm soon after VE Day. While the Crown Princess was welcoming the British, therefore, Princess Sybilla was greeting the Germans, and nothing could have been fairer than that, although the Germans regretted that it should have been the junior of the two princesses who elected to meet them. Questions of prestige and precedence are looked upon by the Germans, or at least were looked upon by the Nazis, as matters of great importance, and many of the disputes which arose during the exchanges turned upon some quite trivial point of etiquette. Since the Allied representatives could never meet their German opposite numbers in person, Count Bernadotte and his staff were condemned to a wearisome round of diplomatic compromise before both sides professed themselves satisfied.

When the exchange was in full swing the headquarters of

the operation was in Gothenburg. Here a staff from the British Legation, led by George Labouchere, at that time a First Secretary and now Sir George and Her Majesty's Ambassador to Spain, confronted, at a distance, a contingent of German diplomats, while Count Bernadotte held the ring and maintained contact with both sides. Down at Trälleborg we worked on purely military lines. Colonel Carl Carlsson von Horn, who is now a general, and was, in 1960, the first commander-in-chief of the United Nations Force in the Congo, represented Sweden. I was supposed to watch British interests, and the German assistant Military attaché, whom I never saw, performed the same duty for Germany.

Colonel von Horn was, at that time, Director of Movements and Transportation, Swedish General Staff. He is an officer of great ability, a dark, saturnine man of immense charm and fiery temper. I had a taste of this when, owing to some muddle in Gothenburg, he and I received orders which directly contradicted one another. Backed by a platoon of Swedish troops with fixed bayonets, the colonel faced me on the platform of Trälleborg station, and for a moment or two we both feared that an international incident might ensue. Not only did this not happen, but the clash caused us to respect one another, and led to a friendship which has long survived the war. We all had reason to be very grateful to the colonel in the days and months which followed.

An exchange of prisoners of war is an extraordinarily moving experience for those who witness, as I did, the men's first contact with friendly soil. As the big ferry pulled in, I stood on the dock in tartan trews and glengarry, my Sam Browne belt as glossy as I could make it. It was interesting to watch the faces of the men who stood clustered along the rail. Many of them had not yet grasped the fact that they were again among friends. To see a British lieutenant-colonel turned out as if he were on a peace-time parade-ground was to them astonishing and inexplicable. When the gangway was lowered, and two Swedish sentries took up their posts at the foot of it, some of the ex-prisoners still mistook them for

Germans, and shouted insults at the poor men. I myself stood at the bottom of the gangway and repeated the words "Welcome to Sweden!" until I was hoarse.

A few of those who came ashore, on stretchers, on crutches, limping with sticks, rewarded me with a look of concentrated loathing, believing that this was simply another German trap. Others smiled, half-heartedly. A few, who had already begun to accustom themselves to the idea of being free, returned my greeting with a smart salute—unless they happened to be on crutches—and with a rapturous grin.

It was only when they reached the platform of the railway-station that many of the men realized that they were almost free. They were overwhelmed with kindness by their hosts. Nurses, most of whom would have seemed attractive at any time, but who looked positively angelic to men who had not seen a woman for years, took charge of the serious cases. A contingent of "Lottas," usually young, fresh, and smiling, members of a very fine corps of women, who in a sense combined the functions of the nursing-reserve and the Women's Voluntary Service, hurried forward with supplies of sandwiches, beer, fruit, and coffee.

I kept a watchful eye everywhere. One had, for instance, to discourage a charming Swedish girl from trying to force a ham sandwich on a bearded Pathan warrior, who, extended on a stretcher, strove to smile politely while at the same time clenching his teeth lest the unclean food should pass his lips.

"I'm afraid you mustn't give him ham. He's not allowed to eat it."

"But it's very good ham—quite fresh."

"Yes, but he's a Moslem, you see, and Moslems mustn't eat pigs. It's a part of their religion."

"What a silly religion," the girl said, but since she said it in Swedish this insult to Islam did not interfere with the beaming smile which the Pathan now felt safe in assuming.

As I moved through the train, men kept putting out their hands to stop me. "Are we really free, sir?" "Is it true we'll be going home now?" To all these men, with their empty sleeves and their ill-fitting wooden legs, the notion of freedom was still too good to be true. Some of them wept, particularly when the band of the Skåne Infantry Regiment on the station platform played *Tipperary, There'll Always be an England, Pack up your Troubles*, and other songs, old and new, which our soldiers have made particularly their own. We had gone over the programme carefully with the regiment's director of music. A few hours earlier his musicians had been bidding farewell to the Germans with *Muss i' denn* and *Erika*.

Out on the platform an extremely dirty soldier, who seemed to be in the best of good health, came up and saluted smartly.

" Excuse me, sir. I've escaped. Ought I to tell anyone ? "

" Good God, no ! How did you do it ? "

The man jerked a thumb towards one of the German hospital coaches.

" Hung on underneath that coach, sir. All the way from Silesia. Wasn't half a rough ride."

" Now look," I said, " get into the train, sit down, have a bottle of beer, and if you open your mouth about this before you get home I'll see that you're court-martialled. If the Germans find that we have an escaped prisoner of war in the party they'll halt the whole exchange."

" Sir ! " said the grubby man, turned about, and clambered into the train.

It need hardly be said that the escaper did not keep his mouth shut, and one can hardly blame him. But the result was, as I had foreseen, that the *Drottningholm* received a signal to heave-to before she had left Swedish territorial waters. A launch came out to pick up the escaper, and brought him ashore. There was no court-martial, though. In fact, the odd man out got home before his comrades, since an aircraft happened to be leaving for Leuchars on the following evening, and we managed to put him aboard it.

The train was almost ready to pull out, and I went through it once again, giving out a few essential orders, answering questions. One of the orders was inspired by an experience which I had had on the previous exchange. On that occasion

I had travelled to Gothenburg with a trainload of prisoners, and had been told that the train would stop at Oldskroken, a junction just outside Gothenburg. There the Crown Princess would be waiting to greet Sweden's temporary guests. It was impossible to move through the train, since, although there was a comfortable seat for every man, the corridors were permanently jammed with jubilant soldiers. So, at one of the stops, I walked down the platform and singled out an officer in each coach.

" In about an hour we'll reach a place called Oldskroken. A lady will be waiting there, and you'll see me get out and salute her. Now, that will be the Crown Princess of Sweden, the sister of Louis Mountbatten, and I don't want any dirty jokes or wolf-whistles. I rely on you to see to it that this news gets around, and that people in your coach behave themselves."

We reached Oldskroken. The Crown Princess, looking like the nicest kind of English country lady, in beautifully cut tweeds, was waiting on a siding, beside a line of goods wagons. I marched towards her across the railway-lines as smartly as I could, saluted, reported the arrival of the train, saluted again, and fell in behind her. The Crown Princess began to walk down the train. A young officer, to whom my message had obviously not penetrated, was leaning out of a window with a very pretty Swedish nurse. The officer's right arm was missing, but the left was clasped firmly round the nurse's waist, and it was quite clear that the girl had not recognized the Crown Princess.

" Good afternoon," said the Crown Princess, " and how do you like Sweden ? "

" Oh, absolutely wizard ! " the officer replied. " And I must say they have the most marvellous popsies here, don't they ? " and he slapped the nurse affectionately upon her behind.

The Crown Princess was forced to turn her back on the train for the better part of a minute, while she laughed.

This time I took care that every man on the train received proper warning of the Royal visitor.

The first train pulled out, but the second was delayed. This arose from the fact that it carried civilian internees, and the Germans claimed that they were being cheated because more British civilians had been released, as they maintained, than German.

" I'm afraid you'll have to go through the coach and make a count with the German escort," one of the Swedish Red Cross representatives said to me, " and I might as well tell you that the man who'll be doing the count with you is an S.S. man and a member of the Gestapo."

The German was waiting for me. It was difficult to imagine this man, who was dressed in a rather shabby raincoat and a cheap grey trilby hat, in black S.S. uniform. No greetings were exchanged, and we clambered aboard the coach.

There were about sixty civilians in the party, most of them elderly men and women who had been swept into the German net in 1940 in Northern France or the Channel Islands. They were retired officers and their wives, superannuated jockeys picked up at Longchamps or Chantilly, elderly men who had been employed by the War Graves Commission to tend the cemeteries in Northern France in which our dead of the Kaiser's war are buried, businessmen, shopkeepers. The German and I stood in the doorway of the first compartment. " Ein—zwei—drei—vier—fünf—sechs—sieben—acht.   Acht Personen.   Richtig ? "

" Richtig ! " the S.S. man agreed, and we both wrote down " 8 " in our notebooks and moved to the next compartment.

The faces of the old people, as we went through this formality, were a pathetic mixture of bewilderment and disappointment. Here was what purported to be a British officer, in uniform, consorting with some one whom they knew to be an S.S. man, and talking German to him into the bargain.

" Look here, sir, are you British ? " cried an old man who looked as though he might be a retired colonel, his voice filled with indignation.

" As British as you are, sir. Don't worry. You'll be on your way home in a few minutes."

Our passage through the train led us into an empty guard's van, and here the German turned to me and held out his hand, clicking his heels as he did so.

" Müller ! " he said, introducing himself.

I ignored the proffered hand, and did not give him my name. Doubtless he already knew it, anyway.

" I have many friends in England," Müller said, in English.

" I'm glad to hear it. I should think you're going to need them after the war."

The count was concluded in silence, and a quarter of an hour later the train rolled away northward.

As I returned to leave the station, my job for the day ended, a Swedish soldier came up and handed me a message form. It was a signal from von Horn, who was now at sea in the *Drottning Victoria*, on his way back to Sweden. The ferry was empty, except for von Horn's troops. On the following morning he would embark a party of German civilians, take them to Sassnitz, and finally return empty to Sweden. The exchange would then be over.

But the signal which had just been given to me presented a new complication. It was written in English :

> Dirty work at the crossroads. Eight British civilians locked in goods shed at Sassnitz. Germans refuse to release and say they will be returned to camps. I must have orders to deal with position by time I arrive Trälleborg about 2300 hours tonight.

I telephoned headquarters in Gothenburg. George Labouchere and Count Bernadotte went into action at once. The niceties of diplomatic protocol in war-time were ignored, in this emergency, and the British and German representatives met, face to face. We learned afterwards that it had been a hard struggle, but, thanks largely to Count Bernadotte, the orders for which we had asked came through to Trälleborg just as the *Drottning Victoria* was edging her way into dock. Colonel von Horn was authorized to insist on the release of the British civilians, and the German officials in Sassnitz were told to open the goods shed and let the men go.

Von Horn was delighted. He foresaw the prospect of a pleasant altercation with the Germans next day, and in this hope he was not disappointed.

I had intended to return to Gothenburg early on the following morning, but now I decided to remain in Trälleborg for a further day. It seemed only fair that the last forlorn remnants of that exchange should have somebody from their own country to welcome them to freedom.

Drottning Victoria sailed next morning with a cheerful cargo of German civilians. At Trälleborg the day passed very slowly. The station was deserted now. I killed a few hours by watching one of those earthy films about rural life which seem to be a speciality of Swedish producers, but the antics of the rustic lovers and the jealousies of close-fisted peasants had no power to grip me. I kept wondering what had happened at Sassnitz. It was quite illogical that, after superintending the homeward journey of hundreds of soldiers, one should feel emotionally involved in the fate of eight obscure civilians, but so it was. The ferry was due to dock at about 5 P.M.

At six o'clock there was still no sign of the ferry. Standing alone on the jetty, I began to be anxious. Perhaps the Germans had refused to release the men. It was strange that von Horn had made me no signal.

The signal and the *Drottning Victoria* arrived almost at the same moment. As the ship approached, a little group of people in plain clothes could be seen leaning over the bow rail. The signal announcing success was unnecessary.

There was no band to welcome the rearguard, but von Horn did his best to atone for any absence of ceremonial. After I had shaken hands with each of the jubilant passengers a dozen times the colonel came ashore.

" It's strictly against regulations," he said, " but these chaps have had a pretty rough time, and I don't think anybody would mind if we took them into the town and bought them a decent dinner. The train doesn't leave until nine."

The best hotel in Trälleborg—and Swedish provincial hotels are often very good indeed—made a special effort that night. The men who, a few hours earlier had been trying to reconcile themselves to the prospect of indefinite imprisonment, after freedom had been dangled before their eyes, goggled as the dishes of Smörgåsbord were brought on—smoked salmon, smoked eel, fish in all kinds of delectable guises, ham, tongue, smoked reindeer meat.

"Only one glass of schnapps each, I think," von Horn said. "They're not used to drink yet."

One of our guests confirmed this.

"Do you know, sir," he said to me, "when we got aboard that Swedish ship to-day the colonel took us up to the saloon, and there was a bar, all laid specially for us, with sandwiches and beer and "—his voice took on a note of reverence— "*whisky*. Well, I mean, we all had a couple, and they went straight to our heads."

"My dear," said a young man who somehow managed to look elegant even in the filthy clothes which he was wearing, "I was *absolutely* pixillated."

As dinner went on, the story of the day's events came out. The Germans had arranged a special welcome for their civilians. Trumpeters of the Hitler Youth stood ready to sound a fanfare on the quay, while girls from the League of German Maidens waited with bunches of wild flowers to greet the homecomers. The crowning moment of the ceremony was to be a speech by the Gauleiter himself, and that potentate was already on the jetty as the *Drottning Victoria* came alongside. The gangways were lowered, and two stolid Swedish sentries took up their positions at the head of each of them, with rifles and fixed bayonets. The German representatives came aboard and were met by von Horn.

"Now, I want this clearly understood," the colonel said. "This is a Swedish ship and I am a Swedish officer in command of the troops aboard. You have eight Englishmen locked in that goods shed over there."

He produced the orders which he had been given at Trälleborg.

"Here are your orders to release these men, and to let them

come aboard this ship. Until they are aboard, my sentries
have orders that no Germans will be allowed ashore. Is that
clear ? "

It was not yet clear to the Germans, because they could not
believe that this arrogant Swede really meant what he said.
They pointed to the jetty, where the boys and girls were
patiently waiting to play their part in the ceremony, and the
Gauleiter was beginning to show signs of impatience. It
would not, the German envoys explained, be at all a good idea
to keep the Gauleiter waiting. Von Horn replied blandly
that there was no need whatever to keep him waiting. As
soon as the British prisoners were aboard the ferry the ceremony
could proceed.

The baffled Germans went ashore and conferred with the
Gauleiter. Two hours passed. Some of the German passengers
appeared on the deck of the *Drottning Victoria* and approached
the gangways, but they were turned back by the bayonets of
the sentries. The German officials came aboard again and
tried to argue, but without avail. At last the doors of the
goods shed opened, and eight weary, haggard men walked up
the gangway. By the time the ferry's passengers went ashore
the Gauleiter had departed in a huff and the wild flowers
which the girls still clutched were sadly wilted. As the last
German set foot on the soil of the Reich, the ropes were cast
off, gangways brought in, and the eight happy Britons were
on their way to Sweden.

After dinner we returned to the station. Von Horn and I
were travelling to Gothenburg by the ordinary night train, as
were our eight charges. I was surprised to see two of the very
luxurious sleeping-cars of the Swedish State Railways attached
to the train.

" I didn't know there were sleepers on this train," I said, to
von Horn.

" There aren't normally," he replied. " But you see your
chaps told me in the ship that when it looked as though they
had no hope of getting to Sweden, because the Germans were
going to send them back, the S.S. who were guarding them had

said that no doubt if they ever *did* get to Sweden, the soft, silly Swedes would have sleeping-cars waiting for them, with sheets and pillows. So I thought, being a soft, silly Swede myself, that we *would* give them sleepers, and I made a signal laying them on."

The eight men were almost in tears when they saw where they were to spend the night—a snug compartment for each man, with a spotless berth, hot and cold water, towels, soap. They felt the sheets gingerly with reverent fingers, as though they were too good to be true, which, in a way, they were.

Von Horn and I sat up all night. We were very happy.

9. EIGHT TROJAN HORSES

I GOT BACK to Stockholm from the exchange of prisoners of war to find that Bøge had returned from Germany. He made light of his journey, which, according to him, had been a pleasure-trip. Most of his contacts in Northern Germany were still on the spot, and willing to help, at least to the extent of sheltering our men. One " safe house " was already waiting to receive visitors.

Bøge did not think highly of the prospects of effective sabotage at this stage of the war. The British and American Air Forces were by now doing such a massive job in that respect that it seemed hardly worth while for amateurs to pit their puny efforts against them. There were, however, a few small but important targets—generator-boxes in country districts, water mains, isolated sets of points on rural stretches of railway, which would be worth attacking, if only to maintain the morale of our men.

The real job, Bøge maintained, was one of intelligence rather than of sabotage. It was by now pretty clear that within a few months, at the worst, Allied troops, and probably British troops at that, would overrun the Hamburg-Bremen-Schleswig area, in which our men would be operating. They would have no knowledge of local conditions. Every German would profess an ardent hatred of the Nazis. Denunciation and talebearing, to which Germans are particularly addicted, would be rife. Everybody would try to pay off old scores, and it would be too much to expect that any Allied commander, senior or junior, would be able to make sense of what he found.

Might it not be valuable, Bøge suggested, to have on the ground a small corps of Allied observers, who had spent months in learning every detail of the area in which they lived. They would know every local personality, all important localities, the intricacies of local government. When Allied troops arrived our men would give an agreed recognition-signal, and, putting on the uniform of their rank, place themselves at the disposal of the Allied Forces.

This seemed to be a sensible and practical proposal, and Baker Street fell in with it gladly. Our first recruits were almost ready for dispatch, and while they went through the last stages of our training we checked and rechecked the equipment, documents, and cover stories with Bøge. On his advice we bought, through intermediaries, thirty " Longines " and " Omega " wrist-watches of the highest quality. Although every agent would carry twenty-five gold sovereigns as a provision against emergencies, and, of course, a large amount of German paper money, Bøge reported that small, easily portable articles of permanent value were often more useful as bribes than almost any quantity of Reichsmarks. Watches were specially prized, and a man might do things for a " Longines " which he could not be induced to attempt for any amount of German money.

Among the smaller items of equipment which each man took with him was a sheet of postage-stamps of 20-pfennig denomination. These were sewn into the collar of a shirt or the lining of a jacket, and their discovery by the Gestapo would have had deadly consequences for their bearer. For these stamps, although at first glance identical with those which could be bought at any German post-office, differed from any others in Germany in one important respect. They bore an effigy of Himmler, instead of Hitler's portrait.

These beautiful forgeries had been sent from London to all

neutral posts which operated lines into Germany. It was known that since the plot of July 20, 1944, the deterioration in Hitler's health was giving rise to such grave anxiety among his immediate entourage that Himmler was under pressure from some of his close collaborators to take over the reins of Government. We suspected that Hitler might be suffering from the onset of paralysis, induced by long-standing syphilis, and Himmler's masseur, Dr Felix Kersten, who was probably closer to the Reichsführer S.S. than any other member of his court, has, since the war, confirmed the accuracy of this belief.

As far as we knew—and this also proved to be the case—Himmler had so far resisted these suggestions, but the fact that they were being made must have been known to Kaltenbrunner, who had succeeded Heydrich as head of the Gestapo, and who loathed Himmler.

The forged stamps would, it was hoped, do something to confirm Hitler and Kaltenbrunner in any suspicions which they might have that Himmler meant to seize power. Our agents were told to use the stamps in the ordinary way, and to send letters franked with them through the open post. At the same time, rumours were set afoot in Germany that Himmler was so confident of being able to overthrow his master that he had even had stamps printed to celebrate the event. The assumption which we hoped the Gestapo would make—and which, as we afterwards learned, they did make—was that a block of these subversive stamps had somehow found its way into one or two post-offices by mistake. There is reason to believe that the stamps caused Himmler a great deal of trouble.

When the war ended American collectors were offering $10,000 for a single cancelled cover bearing one of these stamps. As we had, in our safe in Stockholm, several hundred stamps and an excellent selection of German cancellation stamps, the temptation to earn $10,000 for one minute's work was a strong one. We were, however, required to send to London a certificate guaranteeing that all surplus stamps had been destroyed by fire, and so, with some reluctance, we burned what might have been a cosy little fortune.

After the failure of the plot against Hitler's life, on July 20, 1944, and the subsequent execution, by slow hanging, of the principal conspirators, London provided us with another set of forged stamps. These bore the head of Field-Marshal von Witzleben, who had headed the military element in the plot, recorded the date of his execution, and a slogan originally devised by the Nazis to honour those who fell in the Munich Putsch of November 1923. " Und Ihr habt doch gesiegt "— " And you were victorious in spite of all," the slogan ran. We may look back now upon fifteen years of cold war and wish, from the bottom of our hearts, that this had indeed been true.

Now that operations into Germany had actually begun, the unreality of life in Stockholm became more and more painful to us. On September 6, London, which had manfully withstood the assaults of the V.1 missiles, in whose detection and destruction we in Stockholm had played a modest part, first came under the fire of the V.2. Swedish newspapers, even those whose sympathies lay with the Allies, wrote in the gloomiest terms of the effects of this terrible weapon, while their Germanophile contemporaries gloated openly at the success of the missile, and predicted that Great Britain could hardly survive its impact. London newspapers and the B.B.C., hampered by censorship, gave little reassurance. We felt very isolated in a make-believe world.

The Swedes, now that Christmas was once more approaching, were worried about the food situation. Thick cream fit for whipping was already a thing of the past, and housewives could be heard lamenting this fact in every dairy. But would there be enough ham, traditional centrepiece of every Swedish Christmas dinner, to go round ? The newspapers were reassuring. Large consignments of ham, they assured the anxious population, were on their way from Argentina, from Portugal, from every corner of the neutral world. Towards the end of October several papers carried banner headlines : JUL-SKINKAN ÄR SÄKRAD (THE CHRISTMAS HAM IS ASSURED). Sweden breathed a sigh of relief and we a sigh of exasperation. And if such things were infuriating to people from Great Britain, where food, however wretched and monotonous, was adequate, the feelings of the Norwegian exiles, whose people were more or less starving only a couple of hundred miles away, can easily be imagined.

However, we planned a Christmas surprise for the people of Oslo which would, we felt, help to make life a little brighter for them. In Scandinavian countries the place of our Christmas-tree is taken by a wreath of evergreen, decorated with scarlet ribbon and fat red candles, which is hung from the ceiling of the principal room in each dwelling. It occurred to us that it would be a pleasant gesture of friendship and solidarity if the " Hird," the force of Norwegian traitors led by Vidkun Quisling, whose name is now a synonym of treachery, sent a Christmas tribute to their friends at the S.S. headquarters in Oslo. This token of goodwill would take the form of an enormous wreath, six feet in diameter, lavishly decorated with greenery and ribbon. In fact, the more lavish the decoration the better, since the embellishments would conceal the fact that the core of the wreath would consist of a ring-charge of plastic, fired by a fuse concealed in one of the candles, and powerful enough to bring down the roof on the heads of the black-uniformed revellers. A delay fuse would also be included, in accordance with the excellent principle that a wise man wears both a belt and braces.

This was precisely the kind of plan which appealed to the Norwegian resistance. They had plenty of " Hird " uniforms, they assured us, and would guarantee to deliver the gift in an impressive manner on Christmas Eve. They would also ensure that if any inquiries were made by the S.S. at the headquarters of Quisling's gang of cut-throats a reassuring answer would be given, for the resistance movement had its own men in Quisling's ranks. If we would furnish the explosive charge, and the ribbon and the candles, which were in short supply in Norway, our friends across the frontier would do the rest.

Unfortunately the German Section in London did not agree with the scheme. It was, they thought, contrary to the spirit of the Christmas season, which was true enough, of course, and it might reflect adversely on the Norwegian Resistance Movement. The head of the German Section at that time was General (now Field-Marshal Sir) Gerald Templer, who was doing a temporary desk job, most reluctantly, while he recovered from injuries received on the Italian front. Since the war he has earned a reputation for ruthlessness, a knight-hood, and a field-marshal's baton, all of which are well deserved. But General Templer's refusal to violate Christmas is typical of him, and very much to his credit. We, however, were deeply disappointed, and the Norwegians even more so. In the meantime, our little press was printing material specially designed for Norway.

We founded an organization which we called the " League of German Officers." This enterprising body, of which Janet and I were actually the only members, specialized in issuing leaflets which reproduced, in facsimile, top-secret military documents which had allegedly come into the possession of the dissident officers, and which, they felt, should have a wider circulation. As the Allied and Russian armies approached the frontiers of the Reich, these patriots were more and more worried, as might have been expected, and their views of the prospects of the troops in Norway became increasingly bleak.

Finally they obtained possession of an order, ostensibly issued by General von Falkenhorst, G.O.C., Norway, whose circulation was confined to regimental commanders or their equivalent, and which, as the stamps on the head of the document (made with a toy printing-set which had a good assortment of rubber type) plainly showed, was to go " By Hand of Officer Only." We enjoyed forging this particular order, and took a great deal of trouble over its composition. The results, we felt, justified our pains.

The Führer had decided, von Falkenhorst revealed to his senior officers, that Norway was to be the last redoubt of National Socialism. If the Reich collapsed, resistance would continue there to the last man and the last round of ammunition. There would be no evacuation in any circumstances. On receipt of a code word, commanding officers were to take their

junior officers down to company commander into their
confidence, and to tell them the worst. They, in turn, would
pass on the bad news to the troops.

General von Falkenhorst admitted, with soldierly frankness,
that the consequences of the Führer's decision would be unpleasant for the forces under his command. If the Allies
occupied the Reich, mail from home would, of course, cease
to arrive, and rations were more than likely to be quite inadequate. The general was confident, however, that the
privilege of being the last soldiers to fight for the Führer would
in itself be sufficient recompense for any hardship.

We printed about 100,000 copies of this leaflet, which also
carried some gloomy comments from the " League of German
Officers," and packed them off to Norway, where they were
distributed by the resistance movement. The effect on the
troops was all that we could have hoped, and copies of the
leaflet found their way back into Sweden. Here they were
seized upon by the military experts of the principal newspapers.
Our document was reproduced, and military commentators
went on to base their appreciation of the general situation in
Germany upon von Falkenhorst's order. The ripples which
we had caused took a long time to subside.

By now, all that we could think of had been done to equip
our first agents for their journey to Germany. Bøge had
returned to Hamburg and was waiting for his protégés there.
Small supplies of explosives and other equipment had been
hidden on German soil, ready for collection. For the twentieth
time we went through the cover stories. Chaytor, who, as
training-officer, bore a major share of the responsibility, was
as nervous as I was, and certainly far more nervous than the
two young Danes who were to make the perilous journey. We
dined together for the last time.

" Look here," I said, " whatever happens, the war will be
over by August 5, 1945. Your orders are that when you have
done your job you are to go to ground and learn everything
you can about your district. You are Danish workers and you
will live up to your cover, taking advantage of any oppor-

tunities for minor sabotage which present themselves, and which you can carry out without risk. Your real value will be to the Allies, when they overrun you, and you know the recognition-signal which you are to give to Allied troops as soon as they arrive. On the first Saturday in August 1945, we shall all meet, at noon sharp, on the terrace of the Hotel d'Angleterre, in Copenhagen. Somehow you must get leave and keep the appointment—it's an order. And be prepared for a pretty cheerful party."

Jenssen and Poulsen grinned and shook hands. We had dined in a nondescript flat, one of the many temporary dwellings which we used for our own purposes. The dinner had been brought in, ready cooked, from a restaurant. We heard the booted feet of two brave men go clattering down the stone staircase, and Chaytor and I looked at one another solemnly. Then we separated, taking care not to leave the flat together, and went home to a restless night.

10. OPERATION "EMETIC" AND JULY 20

When it went to war in 1940 the position of the German Army may, in some degree, be compared with that to which Gulliver awoke upon the shores of Lilliput. While he slept, it may be remembered, scores of tiny men, any ten of whom Gulliver could have crushed underfoot, had bound him with threads of gossamer, each in itself almost without substance, yet together sufficient to render the giant helpless. Between 1933, when Hitler came to power, and 1939, the Army had slept. The awakening began in 1938, but by then the threads were firmly fastened, and the pygmies were in control. It was the duty of S.O.E.'s German Section to encourage the fettered giant to break his bonds, and it is, perhaps, not presumptuous to believe that we had some success in that direction.

At all events, Hitler had no reason to be pleased with his soldiers by 1944, or, at least, he seemed little disposed to give them credit for the valour and tenacity with which they had fought for nearly five years. In the summer of that year even the last outward appearances of the independence of the Armed Forces from the Nazi Party were swept away. By order of the Führer and Commander-in-Chief, the military salute was abolished, and its place was taken by the " German Greeting," a form of salutation which looked ridiculous enough at any time but which was positively grotesque when delivered by soldiers.

In 1918 Lord Northcliffe, a propagandist of genius, devised a slogan for the German Army which had a deadly effect, not only upon the fighting troops, but also upon civilians. At first sight the simple sentence of five words, which could be conveniently chalked on any wall or hoarding, sounded quite encouraging : *Hindenburg is like the Sun.* To illustrate the phrase it was only necessary to draw a straight line, to represent the horizon, and a semicircle, with a few rays darting from it. At first, when Germans saw this slogan they took fresh heart. Then it occurred to them that perhaps the crude drawing did not represent the rising sun after all. Might it not portray sunset ? Hindenburg's sun had risen at Tannenberg, in 1914. The more the Germans thought about the matter the more it seemed that twilight was now falling.

In 1944 twilight was falling again over Germany, but this time the enemy was obliged to contend with media of communication more formidable than the odd malcontent armed with a scrap of chalk. Radio assailed the ears of the German people from every point of the compass. In the heady days of victory, which now seemed so far distant, it had been easy enough to obey the prohibition which made it a capital offence to listen to enemy wireless-stations. But by the autumn of 1944 fighting was taking place on German soil, and news had become a vital necessity. The forged order of General von Falkenhorst which the " League of German Officers " had, thanks to us, distributed to the troops in Norway, was hardly more dismal than the genuine order which Field-Marshal von Rundstedt saw fit to issue on September 21, 1944 :

As fighting is now taking place over large areas of German soil and since German towns and villages are becoming battle-grounds the Führer has ordered that our conduct of the war must be more fanatical than ever. In the battle areas . . . every pillbox, every block of flats, in every German city and each German village must become a fortress in which either the enemy will bleed to death or will be buried beneath the bodies of the garrison, who have fallen in hand-to-hand fighting. There is no choice between holding fast or destruction. I request Gauleiters to impress upon the population in a suitable manner the fact that this battle is essential and to stress the implications which it holds for each individual. The bitterness of the struggle may enforce not merely the sacrifice of property but even its destruction for military reasons or its loss in battle . . .

Orders of this kind, the total subordination of the Army to the Party, the growing certainty that the war would be lost by Germany, were meat and drink to the propagandists, including ourselves. Our signals to the quiet midland village which housed " Gustav Siegfried I " and " Soldatensender Calais " became longer and more frequent as each week passed, and the news began to pour out of Germany, like rotgut from a leaky and overfilled wineskin. But the traffic in news was not entirely in one direction. Each week we received from London a list of rumours, or " sibs," which, for one reason or another, the Allies wished disseminated either in Sweden or in Germany or in both countries. Many of them had a purely operational purpose, and many were extremely obscure. It was difficult for an outsider to appreciate, for instance, the significance of the report to which we were asked to give publicity, that a certain Frau So-and-so had been admitted to hospital suffering from nervous exhaustion, and that special precautions had been taken to ensure that the patient received the repose and attention which her condition required. This sad intelligence, our orders might add, was to be circulated in Mecklenburg.

Trustingly we would see that the story got all the prominence which we could give it in the right quarter, and occasionally we had the satisfaction of learning, much later, that we had scored a bull's-eye. This Frau So-and-so might prove to be the mother-in-law of the local Gauleiter, and the hospital, to which, allegedly, she had been so comfortably consigned by her solicitous son-in-law, was one which had refused to admit less exalted patients, victims of bombing or of the battlefield though they might be. In that case, and provided our rumour had achieved the circulation which we hoped, we might see denials of it in local newspapers, and even achieve a reference to it in an official speech.

Our own agents in Germany were assiduous in spreading the news which we sent them. By this time they had got to know the areas in which they operated very well indeed, which in fact was one of the chief purposes of their presence in the Reich. They knew who could be trusted to pass on a really fruity item of gossip without revealing its original narrator, and I am afraid that we were guilty of spreading quite a network of damaging lies and half-truths throughout Northern Germany.

In this work the representatives of the British Press in Stockholm were also extremely helpful, sometimes consciously, sometimes without knowing that they were actively assisting the war effort.

In his autobiography [1] Mr Arthur Christiansen, for many years Editor of the *Daily Express*, tells of an approach which was made to him in the early days of the war by Colonel Dallas Brooks, who, as I have already mentioned, was my first commanding officer in Fitzmaurice Place. A member of the *Daily Express* staff had, it seemed, done good intelligence work before the war, and Colonel Brooks now asked that he might be allowed to continue to do so. Mr Christiansen declined to grant this request, and soon afterwards parted company with the journalist concerned, on the general principle that newspaper work and intelligence duties consort ill together.

The principle is, I am sure, a sound one. It is one thing for a correspondent to pass on to his embassy any unusual or interesting information which he may gather in the course of his work, and which, he feels, deserves rather more discreet handling than it might expect to receive in Fleet Street. During the time which I spent in Berlin from 1937 until 1939 I made a practice of doing this, as did many of my colleagues, as a matter of patriotic duty. In return *The Times*, at least, was

[1] *Headlines All My Life* (Heinemann, 1961).

sometimes able to receive, by a confidential route, reports from me on the background situation in Germany which could have been sent by no channel less discreet.

But this is a very different matter from intelligence work in its proper sense, which involves receiving orders to collect specific information and becoming, in a greater or lesser degree, a conscious member of an intelligence organization. It has always seemed to me that to invite a journalist to do this is unfair to the man himself and to his newspaper. The normal job of a correspondent in a police state is quite trying enough, without any added complication.

It did not, however, seem unfair to suggest from time to time that our journalists in Stockholm might care, in conversation with one of the many *soi-disant* ' neutral ' travellers from Germany, whom they spent much of their time in tracking down, to drop one or two of the carefully selected seeds which we received each week from London, although we never told our helpers the origin of the titbits of news which we gave them. Sometimes these found their way back to the British newspapers, and that was all to the good, since there was no more certain method of bringing something to the attention of the German authorities.

Not that the Press Corps in Stockholm did not indulge in some subversive activities on their own account. For one thing, they made life a burden to Dr Theodore Boettiger, the Stockholm correspondent of Hitler's official Party newspaper, the *Voelkischer Beobachter*.

I must confess that I was rather pleased about this campaign, in which I had no hand, because Dr Boettiger had, before his transfer to Stockholm, been the chief correspondent of his newspaper in London, and therefore my own opposite number, since I represented *The Times* in Berlin. Indeed, the fact that the Nazis placed *The Times* and the *Voelkischer Beobachter* on an equal footing (a proposition with which I could not be expected to agree) was made clear to me by Dr Josef Goebbels himself.

Displeased by a dispatch which I had written, the Reich Minister for Popular Enlightenment and Propaganda had summoned me to his office in the Wilhelmsplatz for a dressing-down.

" Do not suppose," the Minister had said, in the course of his admonition, " that I shall do you the pleasure of expelling you from Germany. For that we shall wait until the correspondent of the *Voelkischer Beobachter* is expelled from England."

" But Herr Reichsminister," I remember protesting, " Dr Boettiger is known to be Ortsgruppenleiter of the National Socialist Party in London. It is quite possible that the British Government might expel him for his political, as opposed to his journalistic, activities. Whereas I do not even belong to a British political party."

" That," said Dr Goebbels, " is a risk which you must accept."

And now here were my former colleagues in Stockholm hounding Dr Boettiger, day and night. Telephone calls in which the callers threatened horrible vengeance in a variety of languages brought the good doctor from his bed at all hours of the night. Letters, anonymous or signed by pseudonyms, but extremely explicit in their content, arrived by post and by hand. Dr Boettiger sought the protection of the Swedish police and got it, but the campaign continued.

As I remember that late summer and autumn, it was illuminated for us by one of those strokes of luck which elude many professional intelligence officers, even after they have spent years in their arduous and unrewarding profession, yet which sometimes, as was the case here, fall into the clumsy hands of the amateur.

For many months past, one of our most productive agents had been a man whom we knew as Potts. He was a strange and somewhat enigmatical person, whom I, of course, had never met, a Central European who provided a great deal of information, much of it valueless. But in every load of pay dirt which Potts produced—and was paid to produce—there was almost always at least one nugget, sometimes a nugget of some size. And so Potts continued to receive his little bundle of banknotes, and we continued to sieve through the sheets of information, closely typed with a purple ribbon, which he provided in exchange.

One day Potts demanded a personal interview with somebody who was empowered to accept or to reject a proposition which he would make. The matter was, Potts said, one of importance. We gave Potts a rendezvous, and Janet kept it.

The proposition which the agent put forward was this : Potts knew a woman who worked in a confidential capacity in the German Legation. One of her duties was the transmission, by teleprinter to Berlin, of reports sent to one of the service attachés from German agents working in Great Britain. The girl, who seems to have had a clearer premonition of coming events than most of her colleagues at the German Legation, was anxious to reinsure her future. In return for the promise of a British passport after the war, safe asylum in England, and enough money to enable her to find her feet in her new home, the teleprinter operator was willing to supply Potts with copies of messages within an hour or so of their having been sent to Berlin. Would we accept this proposal, Potts asked ?

The answer was, of course, that we should not buy a pig in a poke. The first step was to make sure that the goods offered were genuine and of real quality. The lady must produce a sample, and this Potts undertook that she would do.

In handling this affair at all I was going far beyond my terms of reference. If the teleprinter messages were actually what they were claimed to be they dealt with intelligence rather than with operations, and with counter-espionage at that. They were thus no concern of S.O.E. I therefore drove to an unpretentious office in the centre of the Stockholm business district, and told two friends of mine who worked there of the proposal which had been made.

They were highly sceptical, as people in their profession (and of necessity) are. Good if true, summarized their attitude. By all means let the man Potts produce his alleged messages, and my friends would be glad to look at the sample. IF—and the word was spoken in capital letters—there was any substance at all in the claim, then the question of British passports and so on might be considered. And, incidentally, how much extra money had this man Potts demanded for his part in the business? When I replied that Potts had made no additional demands for himself you could have cut the scepticism in that office with a fish-slice. Nevertheless, Potts was told to deliver his sample as soon as possible.

It arrived a week later, typed, as usual, in single spacing with a purple ribbon. Four full pages of flimsy paper. To me it was pure gibberish. "V-mann meldet aus gewöhnliche Stelle von Qu.27 . . ." Well "V-mann" was "Vertrauens-mann," or "agent," and "Qu.27" was presumably "Quelle," or "source," 27—an informer. But as to what this agent had reported I had no idea, and in any case it was not my business. I took the envelope down town to my unobtrusive friends in the business district.

London's reaction to our little present came with gratifying promptness. Potts and his friend were to be encouraged by all reasonable means. If subsequent deliveries proved to be up to the quality of the sample there might be no difficulty in meeting the terms of the lady who had placed this bonanza at our disposal.

Our personal and social relations with our colleagues had always been friendly and indeed cordial, but professionally they had tended to regard us as scarcely worthy of notice. Now Janet and I enjoyed the unusual sensation of basking in the professional esteem of the professionals, and we found it a pleasant and amusing experience. We asked whether they would like to handle Potts themselves in the future. "No, no," cried our friends, "perish the thought! You continue to deal with Potts," they said, "but whenever you get one of these particular envelopes, rush them down to us." "In future," said one of our colleagues, "I shall feel sick with excitement every time I see one of them." This remark led us to christen the whole affair "Operation Emetic."

Thereafter the envelopes arrived at intervals of about a week. They were whisked down town in my breast-pocket and handed over. No complaint as to quality was ever made. We were asked to assure the girl in the German Legation that she need have no fear for her future. Though the sky itself might fall on Germany—as indeed it was literally doing during the winter of 1944–45—she would be safe.

I have often wondered what consequences flowed from those sheets of cheap quarto paper, covered with purple characters. Perhaps men stood, pinioned, on the drop at Pentonville or Wandsworth, not knowing that they were to be launched to their death because I had made a journey of a couple of miles in Stockholm, to deliver an envelope to a quiet young man in a small office. When the war was over I sometimes speculated on whether men and women were still serving long terms in prison because of those flimsy sheets.

In the meantime, much encouraged by " Operation Emetic " and by the fact that the men whom we had already sent to Germany were safe and were soon to be joined by others, we continued to do what we could to snip the threads of loyalty and duty which kept the German armies in the field, even though their commanders had long been aware of the true nature of the masters in whose bondage they lay.

As war spilled over on to the sacred soil of the " Thousand Year Reich " itself, the Party made increasingly desperate efforts to retain the loyalty and esteem of the Army, upon whose continued resistance its whole future and that of its leaders depended. Earlier in 1944 " National Socialist Leadership Officers " had been foisted upon the Armed Forces by Hitler—he might just as well have called them " Political Commissars " and have had done with it. But the troops, as they pulled back doggedly towards the German heartland, could not, and did not, fail to observe that the conduct of many Nazis, on what had once been their lines of communication and had now become a fighting front, hardly lived up to the professions of ardent patriotism and sacrifice which were constantly being rammed home to them by their " Leadership Officers."

This was frankly recognized by the " Chief of the National

Socialist Leadership Staff of the Armed Forces," who, on October 24, 1944, issued an order which fell into our eager hands :

> The effectiveness of National Socialist indoctrination in the Armed Forces is hampered by the fact that in many cases troops are not fully convinced that the burdens which the war entails are fairly distributed. Incidents involving high-living in the lines of communication area, of which there have been many in recent weeks and which have had grave consequences, must be ruthlessly suppressed, since they are the most prolific possible source of political dissatisfaction. Unless we act brutally against those who are guilty in this respect National Socialist indoctrination is bound to be useless.

The Nazis, however, were lucky in having the ridiculous policy of " unconditional surrender " on their side. It would seem to call for a knowledge of psychology of only the most elementary kind to understand that if you invite men to turn against their lawful leaders, however monstrous they may be, it is only reasonable to offer them some reward for doing so. This the Allies consistently declined to do, in accordance with a decision taken at the Casablanca Conference of 1942. While urging German soldiers to overthrow Hitler and his gang, they would give no undertaking as to what they might expect when they had succeeded.

Naturally the Nazis made great play with this ominous silence from London and Washington, and, in the words of a post-war German historian :

> Many soldiers closed their minds to the terror of the National Socialist rule of force in order that they might still be able to fight against the external enemy. The quarrel between the Party and the S.S., they thought, was bound to come after the war. In the meanwhile they looked no further than the sector held by their own unit and allowed events to take their course.

Well aware as we were of this fatalistic attitude, largely engendered by the misconceived policy of the Allies, it was nevertheless our duty to do all that we could to break it down. The Heinrich Himmler Fund for Distressed Dependents of

Fallen S.S. men seemed to offer an opportunity, not only of sowing dissension between Army and Party, but also of further infuriating the Swedes against the Germans. This was one of the little projects upon which we set our printing-press to work in the last year of the war.

The Heinrich Himmler Fund launched its appeal to charitable Swedes with a long and heartrending letter signed, apparently, by Himmler himself, as Reichsführer S.S. The Schutzstaffel, Himmler explained, had for five years borne the chief burden of the war. On every front the Waffen S.S. had fought with exemplary gallantry, and their casualties had been correspondingly heavy. As the chief bearers of the Nordic Idea, to which the Swedes, as a pure Nordic race, might be expected to be particularly attached, members of the S.S. tended to have large families, and were encouraged to have them. Now, alas, many splendid Aryan women and children, deprived of their breadwinner, who had fallen in defence of principles which the Swedes, no doubt, endorsed as heartily as the Germans, were in dire want, and the resources of the Reich did not suffice to provide them with proper pensions. The Reichsführer S.S. was, however, confident that many Swedes, no less devoted to the ideals of racial purity than was Himmler himself, would gladly contribute towards the relief of these deserving families. Remittances might be sent to a Post Cheque Account which had been opened in Stockholm.

This guileless missive was sent, not only to all the Swedish Nazi sympathizers on our list, but also, as if by mistake, to one or two Swedes whose detestation of National Socialism was well known and vocal. The storm which broke within a few hours of the delivery of the letters was all that we could have hoped for. The anti-Nazis who had received our letter hurried from newspaper office to newspaper office, displaying the outrageous document to suitably horrified editors. Leaderwriters of liberal sympathies rolled up their sleeves and squared up gleefully to their typewriters. What, they inquired, did the butcher Himmler think that he was about? The atrocities committed throughout Europe by his S.S. were notorious. Did

Himmler seriously suppose that he could, with impunity, ask Swedes to finance the relics of his gang of assassins? The impudence of the Nazis was well known, but this was really too much to stomach.

Meanwhile, from the English Midlands, our old friends " Gustav Siegfried I " and " Soldatensender Calais " took up a different version of the same theme, addressing themselves to their audience of German soldiers. While the men of the Wehrmacht were bleeding and dying in defence of the Reich, these stations said, here was Himmler appealing to neutrals for special favours on behalf of a body of men whose chief contribution to the German war-effort had been to besmirch the honour and the good name of the fighting services. If the Reich had not enough money to pay decent pensions to the families of fallen S.S. men what hope could there be for the dependents of an ordinary soldier? And why should the S.S. have the benefit of special pleading?

As usual, it was impossible to gauge the effect of this operation, but we had some reason to believe that it was considerable. At all events, it did produce one strictly practical result. " Himmler " had not entirely underestimated the generosity of Nazi supporters in Sweden. A trickle of money flowed into the Post Cheque Account which we had opened. When, after the end of the war, the Swedish Red Cross arranged for the care and rehabilitation of a large number of Himmler's victims from concentration camps, the funds subscribed for the relief of the S.S. were sent, anonymously, to succour those who had suffered at their hands.

As the British, American, and French armies battered their way towards the Rhine, and the Russians, justifying at last the " steam roller " epithet which had given us much comfort in World War I, ground remorselessly westward into Germany, the hopes and expectations of our agents and informers in Stockholm rose to fever pitch. After years of exile they might soon be able to return home, and somehow few of these ageing men could imagine that when they did return things would not be once again much as they had been before Hitler had shattered their existence. In the meantime our " friends," as we called them collectively, persisted in coming forward with schemes each of which was more impractical than the last. The situation is summed up, with due allowance made for poetic licence, in some doggerel which I wrote at the time for Janet Gow, who was on a short spell of leave :

> Oh, desolate and weary week
> While Gow is up at Örnskjöldsvik !
> The days go solemnly and slow,
> While " Philip," Clarke, " Freund B " and " Po,"
> Deprived of Gow's restraining hand,
> Go crazy. " Po " thinks 'twould be grand
> To blow the Riksdag [1] up, while " B "
> Desires to send in poisoned tea,
> To every *Hausfrau* in the Reich.
> Young Clarke suggests that he would leich
> To print a twelve-page daily sheet
> In Hebrew. How am I to greet
> (Maintaining still my cover) " Tony " ?
> He thirsts to write and send a phoney
> Dispatch to Hitler, while " Apollo " . . .
> But all these joys are false and hollow
> Unless Miss Gow is also there
> Our varied pleasures for to share.
> So do come back ! But first, I pray,
> Enjoy a well-earned holiday.

One of our informers, however, was refreshingly free from illusions, because he had lived, not in Sweden, but in Germany, until July 1944. This was Herr Willi Jesse, perhaps the most influential and certainly the best informed of our " friends." Jesse had been a member of the select inner ring of conspirators which, under the leadership of Dr Karl Goerdeler, formerly Lord Mayor of Leipzig, planned to take over the civil government of Germany after the success of the plot to murder Hitler which was carried out on July 20, 1944. By an extraordinary mischance the plot failed, but for some hours both the soldiers and the civilians involved in it believed that it had succeeded.

[1] Riksdag—Swedish Houses of Parliament.

From the Bendlerstrasse, in Berlin, nerve centre of the German Armed Forces, at 7 P.M., Field-Marshal von Witzleben issued by teleprinter Document " HOKW 02165 " :

Adolf Hitler is dead !
An unscrupulous clique of Party leaders who have never been near the front line, has sought to exploit this situation by stabbing the struggling fighting troops in the back in order to seize power for their own ends. . . .

Willi Jesse, who had been appointed civil governor of the great province of Mecklenburg, lost no time in putting into execution all the carefully concerted measures which the military and civilian members of the conspiracy had devised between them. But he had, wise man, taken the precaution of ensuring that the tank of his car was full, and that it stood, half-hidden, behind his house.

That night the Gestapo came for Jesse while a Hitler, preserved by destiny to suffer a worse fate than murder within less than a year, was speaking on the radio of the " little gang of criminal elements which will now be pitilessly rooted out." The particular criminal element who had, for an hour or two, believed that he was to rule Mecklenburg, dived from his larder window while the Gestapo were thundering at the front door, and was making for the Danish frontier before the avengers realized what had happened.

By a series of lucky chances Jesse fell into the hands of the Danish Resistance Movement, who notified us of their distinguished guest. Gleefully we told the Danes to send Herr Jesse on to Sweden by one of their ' illegal ' routes, and when he reached Stockholm we welcomed him as an ally. Probably, in the light of the policy of unconditional surrender and the mutterings about " non-fraternization," which could already be heard in London and Washington, we were technically wrong to do this, but much Janet and I cared. As we greeted the large, calm man in the baggy, unpressed suit, who stepped from the train in Stockholm's Central Station, we felt that, for us at least, the moment was a climax. At long last we were

actually shaking hands with an active member of the German
Resistance Movement, with a man of education and influence
who had been prepared to risk his life to overthrow Hitler.

For the remaining months of the war Herr Jesse was of
great assistance to us. Without in any sense underestimating
the services of those Germans in Stockholm who had helped
us for years past, it is not unfair to say that they were all
' dated.' Their minds were conditioned by a past which had
vanished for ever, and by long exile. Jesse came fresh from
Germany, and he was of inestimable help. To-day, I believe,
Herr Jesse is an active politician in the Social Democratic Party.

But if most of our informants in Stockholm were out of date
in their notions of Germany, what were we ourselves ? It was
easy enough to sneer at exiles who had not seen their own homes
for many weary years, but I myself had left Germany on August
30, 1939, and, for obvious reasons, I had not been back since.
I had spent five years in reading reports about Germany, in
seeking to evaluate German feelings and attitudes, to put the
right construction on the news which came out of that sorrowful
country. There were times when I shared the feelings of Sam
Weller, as he expressed them in the witness-box during the
celebrated action " Bardell v. Pickwick " :

> Yes, I have a pair of eyes . . . and that's just it. If they wos a
> pair o' patent double million magnifyin' gas microscopes of
> hextra power, p'raps I might be able to see through a flight o'
> stairs and a deal door ; but bein' only eyes, you see my wision's
> limited.

Looking back now with all the clarity of hindsight, it does
not appear that our " wision " was as limited as we then
supposed. But at least we now had some eyes in Germany.
There were several quiet young Danish workers there who were
keeping their eyes very wide open on behalf of us all.

As Christmas approached, the German armies in the West,
which, but for the policy of unconditional surrender, would
probably by then have laid down their arms or disintegrated,
made a last desperate bid for victory. For the American and

British troops fighting in the Ardennes against ten Panzer and fourteen infantry divisions the situation seemed grim, but it was the last throw of the German Army, and they and we knew it, even though the troops, locked in battle, perhaps did not. During that Christmas our thoughts and hopes were far from Stockholm. Bastogne was closer to us then than Strandvägen.

But with the New Year came the final certainty of victory. Von Rundstedt's last effort—and a very gallant one it was—had failed, and we could now be quite sure that we should be able to keep our promise to our men in Germany. We should meet them in Copenhagen next August.

Conditions in Germany were now so chaotic that to send more men into the country would have been to risk lives uselessly. British and American forces were already on German soil, and the Russians were biting deep into Eastern Germany. Nothing that any saboteur could do could hope to compete with the pounding which was being inflicted upon the Master Race by Allied bombers and Allied guns. The eight men whom we had already sent to Germany were at their posts, waiting with growing impatience the arrival of Allied troops, to whom they might make themselves known and thus complete their dangerous mission.

So swiftly did events move that it became increasingly difficult to sift fact from fiction and wishful thinking. Even the most experienced diplomats were bemused by the speed with which the Third Reich was hurtling to destruction. For my birthday party, on February 7, 1945, at which the British Minister, Sir Victor Mallet, was a guest, as were many of his staff, I went to the trouble of making a record of a bogus B.B.C. news bulletin.

To listen to the news from London was, naturally, an act of ritual, and nobody noticed that I had turned on the radiogram instead of the radio. When I announced, in a voice which I hoped was reasonably like that of Stuart Hibberd, that the British Government had received from Hitler a request that the Isle of Wight should be given extra territorial status, so that the Führer and his colleagues might take refuge there, hardly an eyebrow was raised. So many strange things were happening that nothing was too bizarre to be believed, and it was some time before the party woke up to the hoax. After nearly twenty years it may be amusing to quote the actual text of this bogus ' broadcast,' which I have preserved. Read, and duly preceded by courtesy of the Swedish State Radio, who made the record, by the chimes of Big Ben, it ran :

In a communiqué issued simultaneously to-day in London, Washington, and Moscow, it is announced that all arrangements for the occupation of Germany are now complete, and that full agreement has been reached on plans for the treatment of the German people and their leaders after the end of hostilities. It is intended that Herr Hitler and prominent members of his Government shall be interned on a suitable island. The German delegation which has taken part in the three Power Conference, at the invitation of the Allies, suggested that Heligoland might form a suitable place of internment. The proximity of this island to the German coast was, however, thought to render it unsuitable for such a purpose. Instead it is suggested that the Isle of Wight should be leased to Germany for a period of twenty-five years following the conclusion of hostilities, and our correspondent in Moscow, Paul Winterton, reports to-night that it is generally believed that this proposal will be accepted. It is understood that preparations will immediately be put in hand to convert a suitable residence on the sunny side of the island for the comfort of new tenants.

In the sweeping advance which has carried the Germans to within three kilometres of Berlin, the enemy has succeeded in disengaging himself from the Russian Forces, who, according to a German High Command communiqué this evening, are now unable to find the German Army at all. This latest success of elastic warfare is hailed by Berlin military commentators as proof of the continued vigour of German resistance and the fertility of the German military mind. B.B.C. correspondent Paul Winterton cabled from Moscow to-night, that Marshal Sjukow has flown back to that city in order to ask Marshal Stalin where the Germans are. . . .

In a communiqué issued this evening from 10 Downing Street, the names of senior British officials who will administer Germany during the interregnum between the cessation of hostilities and the establishment of a full sovereign government in Germany, have been announced. The High Commissioner is to be Mr Roger Hinks, who will be responsible for the Allied civil administration of that part of Germany under British occupation. He will be assisted by Miss Janet Gow as Deputy Commissioner. Miss Gow has been created a Dame of the British Empire to signalize this appointment. Among the other names which appear on the list of senior British officials are : Mr James Knapp-Fisher, who has been appointed Controller of Propaganda in the British area, and the post of Chief of Police goes to Squadron Leader Sir Richard Boord, whose promotion to the rank of Air Vice Marshal is announced in to-day's *Gazette*. The fact that so many of these senior appointments have gone to officials of the British Legation in Stockholm has not escaped notice, but the communiqué explains that this is purely a coincidence which arises from the exceptional brilliance of the staff of this Legation.

The leaky wineskin, which had begun to spurt news some months earlier, now burst wide open, and a torrent of information came pouring out of the stricken Reich. So did a torrent of people. The British journalists who for years had prowled hopefully in search of " neutral travellers " now found that they had a positively embarrassing choice of willing informants on their hands, and not all of them neutral, either.

One newspaper man who, because he was the holder of an Irish passport, was able to pay occasional visits to Finland, technically a belligerent against Great Britain just as the journalist was technically a neutral, had an eerie experience during a brief stay in Helsinki at this time. The green passport in his pocket notwithstanding, this man was always glad when his visits to Finland ended. On this occasion a sharp knocking at the door of his hotel room at 7 A.M. convinced the journalist that the worst had at last happened. When he opened the door these fears were confirmed. A Sturmführer, or captain of the S.S., stood outside. My friend's jaw dropped.

" Heil Hitler ! " said the Sturmführer.

"Good morning," replied my friend, without much conviction.

" I may come in ? " said the Sturmführer politely, in English.
" By all means," the journalist answered.

The visitor entered the room and closed the door, while his host was mentally cursing the fact that his room was on the third floor of the hotel.

" I have worked for some time Lloyds Bank, in Carshalton, in Surrey," the S.S. officer announced, " and I am wondering now whether you can given me any recommendations for working again in England after the war. I am thinking that life in Germany will not be interesting. . . ."

The story of the extraordinary negotiations which Himmler carried on with Count Folke Bernadotte, the head of the Swedish Red Cross, at this time is so well known that it need not be repeated here. Himmler sought, in the last resort, through Count Bernadotte, some form of reinsurance for himself, vis-à-vis the Western Allies. In return, the Count sought the lives of as many of Himmler's slaves and prisoners as he could extract from the monstrous ex-poultry-farmer who, for twelve years, had terrorized Germany and, finally, half of Europe. The negotiations had been in desultory progress for some time, sometimes conducted by Dr Felix Kersten, who had a whip-hand over Himmler because, as his masseur, he was the only person who could relieve the Reichsführer S.S. of the agonizing stomach cramps from which he suffered. Kersten, Russian-Balt by blood, Dutchman by adoption, did not hesitate to use the power which he alone possessed to blackmail Himmler into sparing human lives. He came to Stockholm several times, and negotiated with the Swedish Government at the highest level, but as the war drew into its last weeks a certain S.S. Brigadeführer, Walter Schellenberg, one of Himmler's closest associates, travelled to and fro from Stockholm on mysterious missions of which we were extremely anxious to know more than we did.

Once again the invaluable if enigmatic Potts came to the rescue. Schellenberg, he told us, kept a diary, which he posted each evening with Teutonic thoroughness. If we would guarantee not to keep the manuscript for more than three hours, at the outside, Potts could arrange for it to be stolen and replaced without Schellenberg's ever knowing that it had been missing.

Now this was not a matter for S.O.E., or for any branch of intelligence. It was, in diplomatic parlance, a " Chancery matter," and must be referred to the Minister. For once those " proper channels " of which we hear so much worked swiftly, and within a few hours some 150 pages of typescript lay on my desk. To microfilm the diary took an hour or so, and I sighed with relief when the incriminating sheets were again on their way back to their owner. I sighed with mortification, though, when it was revealed that I should be expected to translate the whole diary in a few hours, so that it could be flown to London without delay. While relays of secretaries relieved one another I sat, glaring at the screen of a projector, while I translated what was, as far as I can remember, a document in which banality and *naïveté* were drearily blended. As a revelation of the mind of a man who was an S.S. general and one of Himmler's closest associates, the diary had great interest, but I cannot think that anybody in London gained much from it. Since the war, Schellenberg has appeared in one capacity or another, at war-crimes trials either as witness or accused, and we have had ample opportunity of assessing the quality of his mind, as we have had of judging some of his more eminent colleagues. But at that time the insight into the Nazi mentality which Schellenberg's diary afforded was fascinating.

II. SIDELIGHT FROM SAN FRANCISCO

THE THEFT AND restitution of the Schellenberg
diary was our only part in the negotiations which, as we knew,
were in progress between Count Bernadotte and Heinrich
Himmler. These were not our affair, since they were a matter
of high policy, with which S.O.E. was not concerned.

The repercussions of those negotiations were, however, far
more widespread than is generally realized, and the forged
stamps, and the rumours which we had circulated from
Stockholm, perhaps did something to bring them about.

At all events, my old friend Jack Winocour, at this time a
British civil servant in America, played a vital part in the whole
affair, which he has now, very kindly, agreed to reveal. Since
it has a strong bearing on the culmination of the war in Sweden,
it is not out of place in this book, and Mr Winocour tells it in
his own words :

" I didn't know it till years later, but, in a sense, I am the
man who killed Adolf Hitler by remote control from San
Francisco, seven thousand miles away from the Berlin bunker
in which he took his life. I beat the Russians to the punch.

" I was guilty of what the diplomats call a calculated
indiscretion, or, in other unmincing words, a deliberate leak
to the Press. I was a British Government official at the time,

so I had to cover up hard and fast. Looking back after all these years, I am not altogether dissatisfied with what I did.

" Of course, I don't claim that Hitler wouldn't have died anyway in that apocalyptic spring of 1945. His death, however, followed almost automatically with the inevitable force of a chain reaction as a result of my hesitant decision to leak the story of the negotiations between Heinrich Himmler and the Swedish Count Folke Bernadotte for the surrender of Germany.

" The leak had lesser but more comic consequences. It made an honest woman of Hitler's mistress, Eva Braun, for a few hours before her death by poison at her lover's feet. It gave Grand Admiral Karl Doenitz a few fleeting hours of power as the Nazi Reich crumbled into rubble. It also prompted a premature armistice report which ran riot through many American cities nine days before the actual termination of hostilities in Europe. It caused a great deal of bother and inconvenience to Mr Churchill and to Mr Truman, for which formal if belated apology is now made. But it may have also hurried on VE day a little. That, anyway, may justify it in retrospect.

" So rapid was the pace and so confused the order of events that to my knowledge no attempt was made then or since by any competent authority to investigate how and why the first news of the Himmler-Bernadotte negotiations for the surrender of Germany to the Western Allies reached the outside world from the lobby of the Palace Hotel, San Francisco, instead of through proper channels in Stockholm, London, or Washington.

" Until the present time, only one person besides myself has known the facts of this footnote to history. The other is Paul Scott Rankine, then Reuter's chief correspondent in Washington D.C., and now counsellor at the British Embassy, who filed the story I hesitantly gave him in the early hours of Saturday April 28, 1945. Since that time Paul and I have remained mum, even to each other. It was one of those things you don't talk about again.

" I was an added starter to an imposing contingent of British public relations advisers to the United Kingdom delegation which bivouacked in San Francisco for three hectic months from April 1945. We were attending the United Nations Conference on International Organization. It was UNCIO, as we conveniently but not too affectionately named it, which wrote the much-vexed charter of the United Nations. We were led by Francis Williams, a former editor of the London *Daily Herald*, then a high official of the war-time Ministry of Information, subsequently Clement Attlee's first Press Secretary at No. 10 Downing Street, and recently appointed a life peer. Francis had flown out from London to minister to a flock of British delegates which included Foreign Secretary Anthony Eden, Deputy Prime Minister Attlee, British Ambassador Lord Halifax, Viscount Cranborne (now Lord Salisbury), and an all-party group of M.P.'s drawn from the ranks of the coalition Government which broke up during the conference.

" There had been a general mobilization of British public relations officers stationed in the United States to reinforce Francis Williams. He himself attended the higher councils of the delegation, instructed us in matters of policy, and was at the daily service of a score or more of British correspondents. From New York, René MacColl and Bill (Sir Berkeley) Ormerod were on hand to cater to a diverse troupe of editors, reporters, columnists, and radio commentators, including foreign affairs experts like Elsa Maxwell and Walter Winchell. John Leaning, our regular San Francisco man, kept an eye on the needs of his local clientele. Victor Gordon Lennox, our aristocratic representative in Los Angeles, coped with an invasion of Hollywood stars and other movie personalities who had infiltrated Northern California to get into the act. Among them were Darryl Zanuck, Charles Skouras, Rita Hayworth and her current spouse, Orson Welles, Charles Boyer, who was also officiating as a radio commentator, Hedda Hopper and her many hats, and Peter Lorre, who haunted nightly the Palm Court of the Palace Hotel.

" The late Charles Campbell, who had already become a legendary figure at international conferences, and myself comprised the Washington contingent. Charlie was first secretary at the embassy, and I was director of the British Information Services office in downtown Washington.

" The man responsible for this colossal production remained in the background. He was Aubrey Morgan, a brother-in-law of Charles Lindbergh. Aubrey was then Deputy-Director-General of British Information Services in the United States, under Ewan Butler's father, who was Director-General. To-day, he has escaped from it all, and is happily farming some-where south of Walla Walla, Washington.

" Charlie Campbell and I set up shop in Room 8002 at the Palace Hotel, which was to be British Press headquarters for the duration of the conference. We were a comfortable distance away from British delegation headquarters at the Mark Hopkins, which gave us a welcome freedom of action. It was a pleasant two-room suite out of earshot of the din of Market Street below, but after two months it began to feel like a prison cell. Neither of us had bargained for so long a siege. Anthony Eden had spoken optimistically of a four-week conference. By the time it was all over we felt like the oldest inhabitants.

" UNCIO itself got off to a slow start on the afternoon of Wednesday, April 25. Jo Mielziner, the Broadway scene-designer, had composed a simple setting for the occasion. A sky-blue backcloth, broken by four golden columns representing the Four Freedoms of the Atlantic Charter, stretched across the stage of the Opera House. In front of it were ranged the floodlit flags of the 46 United Nations. That of the 47th, Poland, was absent. At the right of the stage sat Alger Hiss, secretary-general of the conference, who was so little known to us that the London *Times* correspondent pallidly described him as ' a young official of the State Department, who has shown administrative ability under Secretaries of State Hull and Stettinius.' None of us really ever got to know Alger Hiss at San Francisco, concerned as he was with the purely formal work of conference arrangement. My sole contact with him was a disapproving look he gave me when I arrived late for the closing session of UNCIO two months later.

" There was some hitch in the timing of President Truman's radio address from Washington. A concealed U.S. Navy band whiled away the time melodiously with an incongruous selection of popular tunes. After *Anchors Aweigh*, we heard *Lover come back to Me*, and *Wanting You*, which provoked some suppressed giggling in the balcony. It took some time for the band to reach *The World is waiting for the Sunrise*, which was the conference's theme-song. I remember only one phrase in President Truman's address, which was delivered flatly, dryly, and hurriedly, and with little apparent thought to the drama of the occasion. ' If we do not want to die together in war,' the President said, ' we must learn to live together in peace.' Mr Stettinius, Mr Eden, Mr Molotov, Mr T. V. Soong, Mr Bidault, Mr Spaak, Field-Marshal Smuts, and all the rest of us looked solemnly into space. None of us, I'm sure, saw a mushroom cloud with a heart of fire billowing up above the Pacific.

" Two days later, I attended a private delegation meeting held in a conference-room on the eighth floor of the Mark Hopkins. It was Mr Eden's first meeting with his colleagues. He was affable, but slightly preoccupied with the Polish crisis, in which he told us of the latest developments. The British Foreign Secretary, as he was then, rarely appeared disturbed, and he was not on this occasion. Almost as an afterthought at the close of the proceedings, he remarked with an air of joviality, ' By the way, there's one item of news from Europe that may interest you. We've heard from Stockholm that Himmler has made an offer through Bernadotte to surrender Germany unconditionally to the Americans and ourselves. Of course, we are letting the Russians know about it.' There were about thirty of us present, and we all received the information as casually as it was made known to us. After all, we were in San Francisco, and Stockholm was seven thousand miles away from UNCIO. We went about our business.

" Back at the Palace Hotel, and later at the Veterans Building and the Opera House, I went about mine, too, in an increasingly excited frame of mind. My first concealed reaction to

Eden's calm, unsensational recital of the facts was to exclaim to myself, ' My God, what a story ! ' In the demi-monde of government public relations, in which I had reluctantly plied my trade for the past five years, one of my chief consolations for an almost daily frustration in not being able to report the war myself was the ability to make it possible for others to do so.

" I had been on the verge of completing negotiations with a London newspaper at the beginning of 1942 to cover the war in the Pacific, when a cable was intercepted by the Ministry of Information and I was ordered to remain in the Government service in Washington. The following year I had been called up under U.S. Selective Service regulations as a resident in the United States. I had elected to serve with the British Forces, so I said good-bye to all my friends and colleagues and went off to New York to await sailing-orders. Two weeks later I was ordered back to Washington. The British Government had asked for my deferment. Somewhat sheepishly I said hello to my friends again. It had not been a particularly pleasant experience. As far as I was concerned, I had the uncomfortable feeling that I was engaged in the war effort at second-hand. I had a brief sense of relief after I had undergone my own share of bombardment by flying-bombs in London, in the summer of 1944, but even then it had been a passive experience. My own contribution to the war effort was to assist in telling Britain's story to her American ally. I was never really convinced in my heart that this was what I should have been doing. For the greater part of the war I had been stationed in Washington. I was barely in my thirties, and I had not struck a blow against an enemy who had behaved with the utmost savagery to Britain, my native land, and to my kinsfolk, the Jews of Europe.

" I mention all this because it has some bearing on this story. For me, Hitler, Himmler, and the rest of their monstrous crew were intensely personal devils. I was not to discover until much later how thorough was the act of revenge to which I had contributed.

" At this point it might be well to draw the threads of events

together. Many of the great participants in these hectic last
days of the war in Europe have already told their story.
Churchill, Eisenhower, Leahy, Forrestal, and Bernadotte
himself have written about the final climatic days, each as a
principal actor or intimate observer of events. Let me place
for the first time what each has recalled individually in the
perspective of historical narrative.

" In February 1945 Count Folke Bernadotte, head of the
Swedish Red Cross, flew to Berlin to negotiate with the Nazis
for the release and transfer to Sweden of Danish and Norwegian
P.O.W.'s. He met S.S. Brigadeführer Walter Schellenberg,
head of the political section of the Nazi intelligence service,
who arranged a first meeting with Himmler on February 12.
After protracted discussion, Himmler agreed to release the
prisoners from the concentration camps, of which he was in
control. Bernadotte returned to Berlin on April 2 for a
second meeting. Schellenberg was again the go-between, and
he took Bernadotte aside after the meeting with Himmler to
suggest that the Swedish envoy might sound out Eisenhower
on the possibility of a German capitulation on the Western
Front, leaving the Germans to continue the war against
Russia. Bernadotte guessed that this was an attempt to split
the Allies, and insisted that the initiative had to come from
Himmler himself. If he was prepared to depose Hitler, dissolve
the Nazi party, and guarantee German surrender in Denmark
and Norway as well, Bernadotte might be prepared to approach Eisenhower. Himmler sent for Bernadotte again on
April 21, but the discussion was devoted solely to Bernadotte's
original mission. Next day Schellenberg renewed his approach.
He declared that Hitler was finished and could not live longer
than a day or two more. Himmler wanted to get in touch with
Eisenhower, and Bernadotte was to arrange this for him. The
Swede said that only his Government could act with propriety
in the matter. Later that night Himmler and Bernadotte met
again during an air raid at Lübeck. Himmler declared that
Hitler had arrived in Berlin earlier in the day and could not
last much longer. He conceded that Germany was defeated,

and requested Bernadotte to transmit an offer of capitulation to the Western Allies through the Swedish Government. Bernadotte agreed, securing the promise that the surrender would include German troops in Scandinavia. The meeting ended at 3.30 A.M., Tuesday, April 24. Bernadotte made his way back to Stockholm later in the day, and immediately met with the Swedish Prime Minister and Foreign Secretary, who agreed that Himmler's message should be relayed. At 11 P.M. the American and British Ministers were summoned to a meeting, and Himmler's offer placed before them. They telegraphed Washington and London for instructions.

" Sir Victor Mallet's report of this conference reached London in the early hours of Wednesday, April 25, and was immediately brought from the Foreign Office cypher-room to No. 10 Downing Street for the attention of the Prime Minister. Churchill at once called an emergency meeting of the War Cabinet, and it was decided to notify President Truman without delay that the British would not consent to any German surrender which excluded Russia, and would so inform Stalin. At 8 P.M. Churchill, unwilling to trust the matter entirely to cabled advices, put through a telephone call to Washington.

" It was 2 P.M. in Washington, where White House reporters were suddenly mystified by an emergency conference of President Truman and the high brass at the Pentagon. The President, General Marshall, and Admiral King gathered in the second-floor communications centre, where there was a direct line to No. 10 Downing Street. They were soon joined by Admiral Leahy, who had been summoned from his lunch-table at the Army-Navy Club. Churchill repeated the contents of his telegram, and urged Truman to cable in similar terms to Stalin. Leahy did this forthwith on Truman's instructions. At the same time the commander-in-chief in Europe was advised of developments. General Eisenhower's reply was as follows : ' I regarded the suggestion as a last desperate attempt to split the allies and so informed Mr Churchill. I strongly urged that no proposition be accepted or entertained unless it involved a surrender of all German forces on all fronts.'

" The Allies thus maintained their solid front in spite of their bitter differences over the Polish question, which they were debating with Molotov on the far side of the United States. Himmler's attempt to divide them and to strengthen his own position had failed. Secret reports of this rapid-fire exchange between Stockholm, London, Moscow, Washington, and Allied G.H.Q. in Europe were made immediately available to the Allied Foreign Ministers in San Francisco. And Stalin's reply to Churchill came back late that evening. He paid rare tribute to his British ally : ' Knowing you, I had no doubt that you would act this way.'

" This, then, was the sequence of events during the long day of Wednesday, April 25, as it extended from Moscow to San Francisco. The 26th was a day of inaction, as Himmler's reply was awaited. Early on the 27th Bernadotte conveyed the stern Allied reply to Schellenberg. A further meeting between Bernadotte and Himmler was scheduled at Lübeck for the evening of the 28th, but by then it was too late. The secret was out.

" I knew nothing of this, of course, until I had finally pieced the story together years later, but as the day wore on the impact of the news hit me with increasing force. I discussed it briefly with Charlie Campbell as we returned to the Palace Hotel. We both agreed it was a terrific story but we should have to keep quiet about it, as it didn't belong in San Francisco. But then I lost track of Charlie at the Veterans Building, and I began to try to think the thing through on my own.

" Surely this was the end. Military victory in Europe had long been certain, but this meant much more. How could the Werewolves in the Redoubt hold out or continue guerilla warfare if the Nazi myth were now destroyed ? An essential part of that myth was the complete loyalty of the Party to Hitler. As far as we knew, there had been no serious crisis in the Party itself since the Blood Purge of 1934, when Hitler had eliminated Röhm and the Brown Bolshevik wing. The quarrel with Goering was not yet known to us, but the Luft-waffe chief had been in eclipse for months since Allied planes had destroyed Germany's air potential. It was Himmler who still controlled the ghastly administrative apparatus of the Nazi State. It was he who would surely be Hitler's heir, and who would attempt to perpetuate the legend. Surely Hitler now knew of Himmler's treachery? Or if he did not know why had we not begun to tell the world with every means at our command that Hitler's comrade-in-arms had betrayed him?

" There had been a long silence throughout the day. I had earlier been convinced that Eden was merely announcing to us what must soon be a matter of common knowledge in the nerve centres of war in Washington and London. The Foreign Secretary would not have taken thirty people into his confidence on a matter of this kind, if it was intended that secrecy should be maintained.

" At 3 P.M. San Francisco time it was already midnight in London, but the silence continued. I spent the late afternoon and early evening at the Veterans Building, paying my respects to the busy bureau chiefs of the wire services, and sneaking an occasional glance at the batteries of newsprinters, which were pounding out every kind of news except the story I was looking for. The big story of the day was the drawing of lines for the battle over the seating of Argentina.

" I returned to the Palace for dinner. There was still no news. What had happened? Some one must surely be asleep at the switch in London. The customary shop-talk in the Pied Piper and Happy Valley bars seemed even more banal than usual. Up in Room 8002 we had our usual late complement of welcome and unwelcome guests. I kept repeating to myself : ' This is *the* story. It must get out. We are losing valuable time. This could end the war overnight. This could finish the Nazis for ever.' But to whom could I tell it? It was impossible for me to take the chance of telling it to an American correspondent. He would inevitably try to check it with his own delegation, and then the British would be accused of leaking it. ' If I break it and I'm found out, I might as well say good-bye to Government service.' And then there was the Official Secrets Act. I recalled, too, the sad fate of two high-ranking officers for whom I had arranged Press conferences in Washington. One of them had quite fortuitously described the possible strategy of an Allied invasion of Sicily two months before it took place. He didn't even know it was being contemplated. Another had attributed our failure to break out the Anzio beach-head to our reluctance to be as lavish as the Russians in expenditure of manpower. The first of them spent a stationary war in North Africa, and the second was exiled to Peking. Both of them received tremendous rockets from Churchill himself. I was getting into deep water.

" Should I break the news to one of the British correspondents ? Most of them were personal friends and would do their best to protect me. But would it really serve any purpose to confide in the correspondent of one newspaper ? What I needed was not an exclusive story to one newspaper, which its rivals would either try to squelch or seek revenge for, which wouldn't be picked up by the B.B.C. and beamed to the heart of Germany, where it belonged, straight to Hitler's headquarters.

" Earlier in the evening Arthur Webb of the London *Daily Herald* looked in, just in case I had anything that might make a flash for the Stop Press. It was too late for the last edition of the Saturday morning paper. I was sorely tempted to tell Arthur, an old and dear friend of mine, but I held back. He was the correspondent for the official Labour Party newspaper. If I gave him the story the Conservative Press would raise a howl of jealous anger, and would surely point their finger at Francis Williams, a former colleague of Arthur and close adviser to Attlee. ' Sorry, there's nothing new,' I told him. He must have noticed a hesitancy in my voice, and he looked curious, and wanted to stop and chat. I was rather hasty with him, and regretted it afterwards. Well, I thought to myself, the opportunity has gone. By midnight I had almost reconciled myself to keeping quiet about the whole business. I wanted very badly to unburden myself to Charlie Campbell, but he was attending one of our dinner-parties at the St Francis, which I had decided to skip. I resolved to turn in.

" A little before 1 A.M. the bedroom phone rang, when I was just about to get into bed. ' Paul here,' a familiar voice introduced itself. ' Anything going on. I need something for the afternoon papers.' It was Paul Scott Rankine of Reuter's. We had worked together years ago on the night-cable desk of the British Press Service in New York, preparing daily summaries of the trend of American opinion for dispatch to London, where Cabinet Ministers read them over their early-morning tea. Later, he had been transferred to the Washington Embassy, and I to the Information Services there. Walton Cole, Chief Editor of Reuter's in London, had picked him out as his Washington correspondent, and as such he was covering UNCIO.

" I hesitated again as I had done with Arthur Webb, and then, realizing that this might be the last chance that day, I pulled myself together and made my decision. Every newspaper in Britain would carry a Reuter's story. It would be picked up by the B.B.C. The trail might lead back to San Francisco, but it would stop at Paul, and I knew it would go no further. I hurriedly gave him the facts, suggested that he might try to get confirmation from an American source, which might provide an out for both of us. I pointed out that I didn't want the story to get back to me. ' Of course,' said Paul, laconically for once, and hung up. I began to relax and went to bed.

" From that day until a few months ago, when I decided to tell this story for the first time, Paul Scott Rankine and I have never exchanged a word about this conversation. As far as we were concerned, it never took place. ' How did you finally file it ? ' I eventually asked him. ' Were you able to check it ? ' ' I couldn't get hold of Mac [1] or Linc White,' he told me, ' so I just went down to the Press Wireless desk in the lobby of the Palace and sent it off just after one in the morning.' This was the message he sent :

PRESS REUTERS LONDON
SAN FRANCISCO APRIL 28—IT WAS AUTHORITATIVELY

[1] Michael Macdermott, the State Department Press Officer.

STATED IN OFFICIAL CIRCLES HERE YESTERDAY THAT ACCORDING TO INFORMATION SENT TO STET-TINIUS EDEN MOLOTOV A MESSAGE FROM HIMMLER GUARANTEEING GERMAN UNCONDITIONAL SUR-RENDER BUT NOT TO RUSSIA HAS BEEN CONVEYED TO BRITISH AND U.S. GOVERNMENTS STOP HIMMLER AUTHORITATIVELY STATED HAVE INFORMED WEST-ERN ALLIES HE IS IN POSITION ARRANGE UNCONDI-TIONAL SURRENDER AND HE HIMSELF IN FAVOUR OF IT RANKINE

" Paul had carefully brought the other two Foreign Ministers into his dispatch to widen the possible sources of leakage and to obscure the trail. My part was done, and I receded into the background. I hardly wanted any more to know what the consequences would be. The story was in London within half an hour without any intervention by censorship. While we were still asleep in San Francisco the British evening papers were blazoning Paul's dispatch across their front pages. By 11 A.M., London time, Churchill felt compelled to issue the following statement from No. 10 Downing Street :

" ' It has been recorded by Reuter that unconditional surrender was offered by Himmler to Britain and the U.S. only. Further that Britain and the U.S. had replied saying they will not accept unconditional surrender except on behalf of all the Allies including Russia.

" ' . . . It must be emphasized that only unconditional surrender to the three major Powers will be entertained and that the closest accord prevails between the three Powers.'

" But by now a more potent force than British newspapers was carrying a report of Himmler's treachery and its rebuff deep into Europe. The B.B.C. and the clandestine radio stations were at work. In the late afternoon Bernadotte heard the news over the ' Atlantic ' radio station (one of Sefton Delmer's network of clandestine stations, of which Ewan Butler was the Stockholm correspondent) at the small Danish village of Aabenra, where he was awaiting Schellenberg's return from Himmler.

" ' My first thought,' he wrote afterwards, ' was that this

leak had spoiled everything and there was no further possibility of negotiations.

" ' I have since somewhat altered my views,' he added. ' As a matter of fact the publicity that my negotiations received at this early stage, was to be of crucial importance . . . Instead of Himmler, Grand Admiral Doenitz was appointed leader. It is very doubtful if the Allies could ever have entered into negotiations with Himmler because of his terrible reputation. It was far easier with Doenitz.'

" The news reached Berlin at 9 P.M. A radio monitor at the Ministry of Propaganda picked up the B.B.C. report, and it was brought to the Bunker by Foreign Press Chief Heinz Lorenz. One copy was handed to Martin Bormann and Josef Goebbels. Hitler's personal servant took the other in to his master. Hitler was white with indignation. The one Nazi leader whose loyalty had always been above suspicion had now stabbed him in the back. From that moment the events in the Bunker acquired a new momentum. There can be no doubt that to Hitler the treachery of Himmler was the signal for the end. During the night of April 28–29 he disposed finally of Himmler's claim to the succession, wrote his last will and testament, and married Eva Braun. Himmler's defection, he declared, was the worst act of treachery he had ever known. He wanted blood, and after a brief formality Fegelein, Himmler's emissary to the Bunker, was taken out into the Chancellery garden and shot. As he mentioned Himmler's name, Hitler's voice became more unsteady, and his hands and lips trembled. ' A traitor must never succeed me as Führer,' he shouted. He contrasted Eva Braun's fidelity with the gross treachery of Goering and Himmler, in whom he had trusted. He spoke of his plans for suicide. National Socialism was finished and would never revive ; death would be a relief to him now that he had been deceived and betrayed by his best friends.

" In San Francisco we knew nothing of this staggering reaction. At 10 A.M. Francis Williams held his usual background conference in Room 8002. I avoided his eye and kept well in the background. The British correspondents, who had been bombarded by frantic cables from their editors, were demanding more details. Francis told them of Himmler's report to Bernadotte that Hitler had suffered a brain haemorrhage and could not last much longer. I picked this up and gave it a fresh start with the embroidery that Himmler had offered to deliver Hitler's body to the Allies as an earnest of good faith. I wanted that to get back to Hitler, too. The United Press obliged. The affair had become a comedy on the grand scale.

" Reuter had scooped the field, and the American wire services were in desperate mood. Late that afternoon the Associated Press's Jack Bell cornered Senator Tom Connally, Chairman of the Senate Foreign Relations Committee and a member of the U.S. delegation, outside the Veterans Building. A few minutes later, after a preparatory ' flash,' the following story, heralded by urgent bells, emerged from A.P. newsprinters across the length and breadth of the United States :

BULLETIN
SURRENDER
SAN FRANCISCO, APRIL 28 (AP) GERMANY HAS SURRENDERED TO THE ALLIED GOVERNMENTS UNCONDITIONALLY, AND AN ANNOUNCEMENT IS EXPECTED MOMENTARILY, IT WAS STATED BY A HIGH AMERICAN OFFICIAL TODAY SF 430 P

" Senator Connally had been caught off guard, and had allowed himself to be carried too far in advance of events. He had stipulated that his name was not to be used, but A.P., which soon found itself in dire straits over this false report, subsequently persuaded him to allow his name to be quoted with the explanation that ' his information was that the surrender offer originated with Himmler, because Hitler was ill.' This was now a long way away from our original story, and I must confess I was privately delighted that I was now in the clear. There was much bigger game at large.

" The false armistice report made rapid headway across the country. Tens of thousands of New Yorkers gathered in

Times Square to watch the electric bulletins there, and did not disperse until late that night. In San Francisco, Hearst's *Call-Bulletin* rushed out an extra with the bannerline NAZIS QUIT, which was carried into the Opera House and presented to Molotov, who was then presiding. The Soviet Foreign Minister adjusted his pince-nez, rapped his gavel, and the session continued, although the majority of delegates flocked out into the lobbies to discuss the glad tidings. Miss Virginia Gildersleeve was the only American delegate to remain soberly in her seat. In Chicago, the *Tribune* also announced the premature German surrender, and the local police were mobilized at their station houses throughout the city. But it was in Washington where the reaction was most dramatic. Crowds gathered outside the White House to sing *God Bless America*, and hundreds of newspapermen, photographers, and newsreel cameramen converged on the Executive Offices to await an official announcement by the President. Mr Truman himself crossed over from Blair House shortly after 7.30 P.M., accompanied by Stephen Early, Jonathan Daniels, William D. Hassett, and Elmer Davis, his Press and Information advisers, and allowed himself to be quoted as follows :

" ' Well, I was over here, as you can see, doing a little work, and this rumour got started. I had a call from San Francisco and the State Department called me. I just got in touch with Admiral Leahy and had him call our headquarters' commander-in-chief in Europe [General Eisenhower], and there is no foundation for the rumour. That is all I have to say.'

" It was past midnight in London by then, and the city was asleep. On Sunday afternoon *The Times* diplomatic correspondent wrote in disapproving terms, ' It is probable that the Allied Governments would have preferred to say nothing at this still undeterminate stage and to await Himmler's reply before making a public announcement. Their hands were forced, however, by a leakage of news in the United States.'

" Theirs were not the only hands that had been forced. At 3.30 A.M. on Monday, April 30, 1945, Adolf Hitler put a pistol to his mouth and pulled the trigger."

12. REAPING THE WHIRLWIND

WHILE JACK WINOCOUR, in the unreal atmosphere of San Francisco, played his single card, with vast consequences upon great events, we, in the no less unreal world of Stockholm, watched, breathless, the death agony of the Third Reich.

On April 29 the German Forces in Italy surrendered unconditionally. Four days earlier spearheads of the U.S. First Army met the Russians near Torgau, on the Elbe. In the meantime British Forces were driving towards Lübeck, which they reached on May 2. In all these great events the fate of eight Danish officers, who had for months been awaiting that day, hidden in Germany, and the part which they might hope to play, was very small beer.

Yet our arrangements worked perfectly. One by one our men reported to the nearest British unit and gave the recognition signal. Just for once there was no slip. The British commanding officers were even on the look-out for these valuable allies. Quartermasters produced battledress, boots, equipment, and the badges of rank appropriate to that which each officer held in the Danish Army. Then the round-up began.

I have since heard, many times, that our eight lone wolves were invaluable, and I am sure that they were. Knowing every inch of the district in which they lived, and having kept careful dossiers on its principal denizens, they were able to point to those Germans who must be arrested without delay and also to those who had genuinely opposed Hitler and his Party, even though only mentally, and who could therefore be trusted to help the invaders. Stores of arms, looted treasure, caches of food were uncovered. The demolitions which the Danish officers had carried out may have been relatively trivial, but their work in Germany immediately after the collapse of enemy resistance was not.

In the meantime I felt that I must go to Copenhagen without delay. Packing a uniform in a suitcase, I took off, on May 2, the day before the German surrender, in an aircraft which had been chartered by the Swedish Red Cross. Count Bernadotte had finally managed to negotiate with Himmler, through Schellenberg's mediation, an agreement by which the Red Cross took charge of all Norwegian prisoners in Nazi concentration camps, and a party was going to Copenhagen to superintend their repatriation. My own principal purpose was to find Johan Bøge. He had not returned from his last visit to Germany, and we feared greatly for his safety. My arrival was notified to the Danish Resistance Movement by the excellent and speedy system of communications which had long since been perfected.

I need not have worried about Bøge. At Kastrup airport, in Copenhagen, there he was, flanked by some very tough-looking Danes in civilian clothes, but wearing steel helmets and brassards and carrying Sten guns. I had changed in the aircraft and stepped from it in all the glory of tartan trews, glengarry bonnet, and the other distinctive accoutrements of my regiment. Bøge's face, usually impassive, lit up as he saw me. He and his companions rushed forward. It was the first time a British uniform had been seen in Denmark for more than five years.

The Germans, knowing that the end was imminent, had already virtually surrendered, but spasmodic firing was still in progress as we drove into the city. The last shots were

exchanged between members of the Danish resistance, and
their traitor fellow-countrymen, the so-called Hilfspolizei, or
auxiliary police, a small and much despised body recruited by
the Germans from among the followers of the Danish Nazi
Clausen.   These desperate men, ensconced on rooftops or in
the embrasures of windows, kept up a desultory fire against
the steel-helmeted resistance men in the streets.   But the
outcome was never in doubt, and we ignored the snip-
ing.

Over a glass of beer, Bøge told me of his last adventure.   As
usual, he had had the most devilish good luck.   When crossing
the German-Danish frontier, on his way back to Sweden, a
few days before, he had been arrested by the Gestapo.   They
had nothing positive against him, but they were suspicious,
and they decided to hold him in custody and to send to Copenhagen for his record, if he had one.   Bøge had a record indeed,
and he knew enough about the Gestapo filing-system to realize
that it would very soon be unearthed.

As he waited glumly for the damaging documents to arrive
—and they would certainly condemn him to a painful and
probably slow death—a single Mosquito aircraft attacked the
Shellhuus, headquarters of the Secret State Police in the Danish
capital.   These selective raids by Mosquitos had proved highly
successful in the last stages of the war.   A single aircraft of this
type, for instance, blew away the wall of a French prison,
allowing dozens of members of the resistance to escape.   Now
a " Mossie " was to perform a rather similar service for the
Danish resistance.

The raid was a complete success.   The Shellhuus was
virtually destroyed, and with it Bøge's dossier.   As his captors
waited in vain for news from Copenhagen, their captive decided
to take matters into his own hands.   A large party of Norwegian
prisoners was waiting to be handed over to the Swedish Red
Cross, and, while confusion became chaos, as German resistance
collapsed, Bøge contrived to join the Norwegian party.   He had
consistently protested that he was a Norwegian, and the Germans, dismayed and confused, were willing to believe, in the

absence of any proof to the contrary, that this was so. Bøge lost no time in making his way to friends in Copenhagen.

We walked through the streets of the city, which was just beginning to awake from a bad dream which had lasted for five years. The sight of my uniform was the signal for a frantic outburst of joy. While the traitors still sniped sullenly from their rooftops, girls and women clustered round to embrace me. Men rushed forward vowing—which was probably quite true—that they had saved a bottle of whisky to share with the first British officer whom they saw after the war, and that I was he. People tried to snatch my bonnet, with its heavy silver badge, to cut the buttons from my tunic. We dived into the Hotel d'Angleterre, and there encountered the two Danes with whom I had celebrated the outbreak of war. They sat, still plump and apparently prosperous, in the precise position in which I had found them on September 3, 1939. My military fancy dress notwithstanding, they recognized me at once. "Well!" they said, "the war's over now. Have a drink!" We celebrated again.

But Bøge and I had another appointment. Among the most intrepid members of the Danish Resistance Movement was a middle-aged lady, by profession a masseuse. She still lives, as far as I know, in a town in Western Denmark, and I shall not mention her name. To us she was "Two Gun Fanny," and she was the executioner of the resistance. She had killed several Germans in cold blood, including the head of the local Gestapo, whom she had shot dead in his office in a carefully planned raid, and made her escape unscathed. This lady was to be our guest at luncheon at the Wivex Restaurant, in the Tivoli Gardens.

I had never met a murderess before—and "Two Gun Fanny" was just that, however laudable her motives. The whole thing was something of an anticlimax. Could this pleasant, undistinguished-looking woman really have the blood of several men on her hands. She could, she did, and she was proud of the fact. We had a delightful lunch.

I did not linger in Copenhagen. Bøge was safe, and would

return to Germany, this time in uniform, to help the British Forces. There was much to be done in Stockholm.

On that day of the German capitulation I was back in the Swedish capital. In my absence, the British, American, French, and Russian embassies had been pulling every possible string to induce the Swedish Government to assent to our taking possession of the German Legation. They were extremely reluctant to do this, and they were within their rights in refusing. News of the German surrender reached Stockholm about noon, but no authorization arrived from Utrikesdepartementet—the Swedish Foreign Office—which would allow the Military attachés of the victors to take over the rather drab brick building which must still hold so many secrets from us. But the clouds of smoke which billowed from the tall chimneys of the Legation showed clearly enough that by the time permission did reach us we should find little of any value.

In the meantime the streets of Stockholm were in turmoil. For the Swedes, VE day, which they had played no part in securing, may have come as a relief, but was not a matter for open rejoicing. The Danish and Norwegian refugees felt differently. They formed up in two great processions, led by the flags of each nation, and, as they marched through the streets of the city towards the British Legation, they made no secret of their feeling towards the people lining the route who had not actually taken part in the war. It was not a pleasant moment, but the scene outside our legation as, in the dusk, Sir Victor Mallet, the British Minister, addressed our Allies from a balcony was moving indeed.

Next day we were at last allowed to enter the German Legation. Dressed in our best uniforms, American, Russian, French, and British attachés took formal possession, in the name of the victorious Allies, of an ugly building of staring yellow brick, which, needless to say, contained nothing of the slightest interest or value. Every fireplace held charred and incinerated paper. Cupboards and filing-cabinets were as empty of bones as Old Mother Hubbard's celebrated piece of furniture. In one cupboard we did find a pile of flimsy cardboard boxes. These contained dozens of insignia of the Order of the German Eagle, Hitler's lollipop for deserving foreign dupes. There they lay, grosses made of some light metal, and cheaply gilded, some of them intended to hang round the neck from their tawdry rayon ribbons of scarlet, white, and black, others mere medals to be worn on the breast, all equally cheap and shoddy. We held an investiture, and decorated one another liberally.

" Nous voilà chamarrés de merde ! " said my French colleague. " Here we are fairly plastered with muck ! "

That was all we found to interest us in the enemy stronghold. The ebb-tide of defeat was washing up some strange and interesting creatures in Stockholm. An officer of the S.S., in his full black-and-silver uniform, black riding-boots twinkling under a shabby mackintosh, which he wore as a concession to Swedish feelings, swaggered into the British Legation and demanded sanctuary both from the Swedish police and more particularly from the Russians. He was deeply offended when I turned him out into the street to take his chance.

" But here," the S.S. man said, " I am on British soil."

" Certainly, that's just the point. If you were actually in Britain I should arrest you. You can count yourself damned lucky simply to be kicked out."

" I claim British protection ! "

I picked up the telephone and spoke to the hall porter. The Swedish police were waiting for the man as he came out of the legation.

Another and more interesting refugee claimed more of our attention. This was an official of the German Foreign Office who had been political adviser to Army Group " C," which, under Field-Marshal Ritter von Leeb, an old acquaintance of mine, had failed, but only just failed, to capture Leningrad. This man was in Stockholm to negotiate with the Swedish Government for the reception of several hundred anti-Communist but pro-Nazi citizens of the Baltic States—Latvia, Lithuania, and Estonia. Their fate, once the Russians reached their countries, was not in doubt, and the effort to secure for them asylum in Sweden was a perfectly natural and proper one. Nevertheless, I had the man—whose name I now forget and cannot trace—arrested and held by the Swedish police, who by now were more than anxious to oblige us in every possible way. I asked that he should be brought to my flat.

Two tall, solemn Swedish policemen, their heavy sabres almost trailing on the marble of the landing, accordingly delivered to me, one afternoon, a small and extremely frightened gentleman aged about sixty. I knew that my guest was an East Prussian country squire who had made a special study of Russia, as a hobby, and who possessed one of the finest libraries in existence on Russian affairs in his little manor-house, which lay somewhere among the Masurian Lakes. He had suddenly been summoned to Berlin by Ribbentrop, just before Germany's attack on Russia in June 1941, and virtually flung into the front line.

I had expected my visitor to be frightened. Sometimes a frightened prisoner is easier to interrogate than one who shows and feels no fear, but I did not think that this would apply to the little " Man from Leningrad." So I prepared a large shaker of dry Martinis, made with the excellent Argentine gin which was one of our standbys in war-time Stockholm— and when my guest had seated himself gingerly on my sofa I thrust a brimming glass into his hand.

" I expect you could do with a drink," I said.

He looked at the glass incredulously, and then drained it at a single gulp. I took the glass from him and refilled it.

This time the " Man from Leningrad " sipped, and then he sighed.

" If this is how you're going to treat me," he said, speaking for the first time, " I don't mind talking."

" What did you think I was going to do ? " I inquired. " Beat you up ? "

" I have known it done elsewhere," he said, dryly. " I do not know much about British customs."

He took another sip of Martini.

" I suppose," my guest said, after a pause, " that if any of our administrators in German-occupied Russia fall into British hands they will be handed over to the Russians."

" Certainly," I said. " They'd be liable for trial as war criminals."

" Yet a man like Gauleiter Koch deserves the highest decoration that your King can bestow."

I looked as startled as I felt. Koch's brutalities in the Ukraine were notorious.

" That's an unusual suggestion," I said. "Why do you make it ? "

The little man spoke with a sudden almost savage vehemence.

" Because it was bloody fools like Koch who kept the Red armies in the field. When we entered Russia we were welcomed as liberators. If we had known how to behave ourselves, if we had given the poor devils of Ukrainians even a little more than they had—and that wouldn't have been asking much—we'd have had sixty Russian divisions fighting at our side, we'd have swept into Leningrad and Moscow, and I shouldn't be sitting here now."

" And what happened instead ? " I asked—as if I did not know.

" Instead we get a horde of brutes like Koch, who descend on Russia, hanging and murdering and burning, and every atrocity which they commit is worth another regiment to the Bolsheviks. We gave the Russians no alternative but to fight us. I myself have driven into a village with Koch. The head-man came out offering us bread and salt, as is the custom with distinguished visitors. Instead of accepting the gift graciously, Koch hit the man across the face with his whip. ' We didn't come here to gorge,' he said to the headman, ' but to make you swine work.' Well, of course, that single incident was worth a company of troops to Stalin."

I gave the man another Martini. We talked for an hour. At last :

" Are you going to hand me over to the Russians ? " my guest asked.

" Are you a war criminal ? " I retorted.

" Do I sound as though I was one, after what I have just said ? "

" No, not if those are really your views."

He drank.

" If the Russians take me it's a one-way ticket," he said, earnestly.

" Whatever happens to you," I told my visitor, " you'll be in custody here for another fortnight or so. I think it would help you quite a lot if, during that time, you would write down, as fully as possible, everything that has happened to you since 1941 and all that you know about the Russian campaign and the behaviour of the Germans in Russia. I'd forward whatever you wrote to our people in Lübeck, and then they'll be able to make up their minds about you. It's not my job to do that."

I rang the bell, and the two policemen appeared. The " Man from Leningrad " rose, and we shook hands.

" I'll work hard, Herr Oberstleutnant," he promised.

Ten days later a massive folio was delivered—page after page—covered with neat, scholarly handwriting. I sent the document to Lübeck, and a few days later the British authorities agreed to accept its author and undertook that he would not be handed to the Russians. But one thing is certain. My East Prussian squire never saw his little manor-house or his library again. He became one of the millions of refugees from the lost provinces of which Hitler's folly robbed Germany. The manor-house, if it still stands, is in the Soviet Union now.

Now that the war was ended it was possible and permissible for those of us, including myself, who had no faith whatever in the purity of Russian intentions or the value of Soviet promises, to be rather more frank with our Swedish friends than we had been able to be when we and the Soviet Union were fighting a common enemy. The Swedes were divided in their feelings towards Germany, but in their sentiments about Russia, the ancient, traditional enemy, they were completely united. They loathed and feared our Allies, and they still do.

It was a relief, therefore, to be free to confess, in private, to one or two Swedish friends, that one saw the future in very bleak terms indeed. My friends were relieved to find that I was not quite such a fool as continued professions of confidence in Russian loyalty and good intentions, made during the war, had led them to suppose. " We didn't see how you *could* have believed some of the things you used to say about Russia," they would exclaim. To which it was now possible to reply, " I didn't."

Although the work which had occupied Janet and myself for almost two years was now formally ended, the collapse of Germany left an almost unbelievable number of loose ends to be tied up, of odd jobs to be done—and some of the jobs were very odd indeed. Our " friends," of course, were all preparing to return to the countries from which they had been exiled for so long. Ernst Paul itched to get back to the Sudetenland, " Freund B " could hardly wait to return to Bavaria. We tried to warn these good people, whose joy and enthusiasm was as natural as it was pathetic, that their dreams of a peaceful social-democratic Germany were likely to be long in being fulfilled, and indeed we did not believe—and events have since proved that we were right—that they would ever be realized. Most of these ageing politicians belonged to a breed which was, even in 1945, as extinct as the dodo.

Kreisky, now Foreign Minister of Austria, was an exception to a pretty valid general rule. The rest of them might indeed return home, but it was almost certain that all the hopes nurtured by long years of exile would prove to be illusions. It was difficult for Janet and me, younger and in some ways less experienced than our friends, but at the same time better aware than they that the world had irrevocably changed since 1939, to explain this, as our helpers packed their bags and prepared to go home, but we did our best. Nor was it easy to make them understand that the British military authorities in Germany were not willing to let exiles, however impeccable their record of hostility to Hitler, return forthwith to Germany and resume political activities. Had we not, our friends demanded, been fighting for democracy? Very well, then, democracy had won the day, and now it was for democratic Germans to show their misguided compatriots how to govern themselves. We replied that this would, in time, obviously be necessary, but not yet. For the present the power lay with Military Government in the four zones of Germany, and to this fact our friends must learn to accommodate themselves for some time to come. They did so with ill grace. One by one they drifted away from Stockholm. Only Willi Jesse, the survivor of the July 20 Plot, returned to Germany with his future relatively assured. As a man who had actually taken an active hand against the Nazis *in Germany* during the war, and whose knowledge of the country was therefore up to date, he was of very definite interest to the British authorities. He returned to Lübeck, and to an important post in the German civil administration. Before he left Stockholm he gave Janet a beautiful and costly piece of Orrefors glass. It was no more than a return for much kindness which she had shown Jesse, but she took it with misgiving. How much painful penny-pinching might that ornament not represent?

In the meantime, to the south of us, the concentration camps had given up their dead and their near-dead. Of the latter, the Swedish Red Cross received a large number, for treatment and rehabilitation, in particular women from the ill-famed Ravensbrück camp. They were brought to Sweden by the hundred, many of them stricken with typhus, all so emaciated as to be unrecognizable to their closest relatives, and were cared for in hospitals and clinics until they died of their sufferings—as very many did—or were restored to some semblance of normality.

I received, one day, orders from London to go to Gothenburg, with a secretary, and to interrogate as many of the British subjects among these unhappy women as were capable of undergoing such an ordeal. The purpose of the expedition was twofold—to obtain as many accurate descriptions of concentration-camp personnel as possible, in order that they might be tracked down, arrested, and brought to trial, and to discover anything which it might be possible to learn of the British girls sent to France by S.O.E. who had been betrayed, arrested, and sent to Ravensbrück. Violette Szabo, the Brixton girl, to whom a plaque was unveiled, was one of them, and there were several others.

I took a small suite in a Gothenburg hotel, and, with the help of the Swedish Red Cross, I went to work. The number of British subjects who were available for interrogation was small—in fact, the number of women of any nationality who were able or willing to talk of their experiences was very limited. I widened my scope to include French nationals, and here I found some admirable witnesses. There was, for instance, Mademoiselle Germaine Tillon, of the Musée de l'Homme, in Paris, at that time already a well-known anthropologist and now far more celebrated. The day that this quiet, studious, unobtrusive little woman entered Ravensbrück was an unfortunate one for many of her German tormentors. Trained in scientific observation, accustomed to hardship, Mademoiselle Tillon looked upon her stay in the concentration camp much as she might have regarded a sojourn with a remote and barbarous tribe in the High Atlas. She observed with clinical precision, and her tenacious memory filed away every fact which she had noted.

Could Mademoiselle Tillon, I asked, give me a full description of S.S. Oberaufseherin Binz—a particularly bestial woman whom we were determined to hang? Ah, yes, indeed, said Mademoiselle Tillon, and gave a full and highly detailed description which would have delighted the most meticulous C.I.D. officer. And S.S. Obergruppenführer Pohl (the head of Hitler's whole concentration-camp system)? Had Mademoiselle Tillon ever seen him? Indeed she had. A most interesting type, anthropologically speaking. There followed a full description, including estimated cranial measurements, which proved, after Pohl's arrest, to have been accurate to within a millimetre or two. Pohl, Binz, and several others were duly hanged, and I like to think that their arrest was largely due to Mademoiselle Tillon, and to our talks in the Gothenburg hotel.

There were nuns, too, who made excellent witnesses. They also were trained and dedicated women who took Ravensbrück in their stride, so to speak, and whose spirit had remained completely serene in that horrible place. But the person whom I must *really* see, every one agreed, was the Comtesse de Chaverny. She was, perhaps, the most remarkable woman in Ravensbrück. How, I asked, could I get in touch with her ? Well, said her fellow-prisoners, she had just recovered from typhus, and they believed that she was staying with friends, of whom she had many in Sweden. Eventually I tracked the comtesse down, and invited her to dinner. She accepted with pleasure.

On the appointed evening the comtesse appeared, punctual to the minute. She was a woman of about fifty, who must once have been extremely beautiful. Her good looks shone even through the frightful emaciation of her face and body. She was literally skin and bone. Nevertheless, she appeared for dinner, on that June evening, in a flowered chiffon dress of great elegance and a large hat, her ravaged face carefully made up. She might have been strolling into the Ritz, in Paris, *à l'heure du cocktail.*

We went out to a restaurant, and the comtesse, scanning the menu critically, ordered her meal with discrimination. " When one has been eating only once a week," she observed, casually, " one takes a great interest in food."

I offered the comtesse the wine-list. She looked at it with some disdain.

" Nothing in the way of champagne but non-vintage " she complained. " It's the same everywhere in Sweden."

I explained that the Swedish Wine and Spirit Monopoly had had little opportunity, in recent years, of importing champagne.

" Yes, of course," said the comtesse. " Still, when one has been in solitary confinement in a dark cell for fourteen months one does appreciate decent champagne."

I told her that I had a bottle of really excellent cognac in my sitting-room, and she brightened considerably.

" We'll go back and have a party," the comtesse said, " and I'll tell you all about it."

After dinner we settled down with coffee and a splendid brandy in small balloon glasses, and the comtesse told her story, which is worth telling again.

During the First World War the comtesse had married a British officer, who had been killed in action soon afterwards. Reverting to her maiden name, but never renouncing her British nationality, of which she was very proud, she spent the years between the wars in search of adventure. She was a rich woman. She owned her private aircraft and was a first-class pilot and navigator. She had flown all over the world, and some of the adventures which she recounted during the long evening's conversation were alarming, and some very funny. A strongly ironic sense of humour was one of Madame de Chaverny's strongest points. In fact, it probably saved her life and her reason.

The comtesse was also a trained nurse, and when war broke out in 1939 she organized a military hospital at her own expense, and became its matron. France collapsed—Madame de Chaverny spoke bitterly of the behaviour of certain French officers and of some of her own staff in the crisis—but the matron stayed at her post with the best of her nurses and doctors, and watched the Germans take over the hospital.

The conquerors allowed the comtesse to retain her position, and the hospital, which was, as far as I can recall, somewhere near St Omer, continued to treat patients, French, German, British, without discrimination and, I should think, with great efficiency.

But the British patients recovered, and, having recovered, some of them wanted to escape. The Germans had not discovered that the matron was a British subject—her title overawed them, and so, I should imagine, did her manner of dealing with them. It never occurred to them that she might be, technically, anything but the French aristocrat which she very obviously was. But the Comtesse de Chaverny was made of the same stuff as Edith Cavell, and she did, in the second

German War, what Miss Cavell did in the first. British airmen, shot down, wounded, and healed at that little hospital, found that the matron was willing to help them to escape. She provided maps, clothes, money. One day, in 1943, the Germans at last realized what was happening, and they arrested the comtesse, as they were quite entitled to do.

She was tried by court-martial, found guilty of giving aid and comfort to the enemy, and sentenced to death, as was Miss Cavell.

" They asked me what I would like for breakfast on the last morning," the comtesse told me, " and I said that I'd like a nice, juicy tournedos and a bottle of decent Burgundy. They gave it me, and very good it was, too. Then I was marched out and tied to a stake, and the firing-squad loaded and presented their rifles . . . I refused to have my eyes bound. Then, just as I was expecting the officer to give the order to fire, he marched towards me, halted, saluted smartly, and made a little speech. He said that the German Army did not shoot women and that I should not be shot. Instead, I should be handed over to the Gestapo. I didn't know whether to feel relieved or not. I'd heard quite a lot about the Gestapo."

The Comtesse de Chaverny travelled to Ravensbrück by very slow stages in a crammed cattle-truck. On arrival at the camp her head was shaved, as were those of all the other women, and she was given the sack-like uniform of the camp. But while the other new arrivals were marched away to their huts, the Comtesse de Chaverny was driven, with blows of a heavy whip, in the opposite direction. She was thrown into a tiny, windowless cell, quite unfurnished, and there she was left for several days, with a jug of water as her only nourishment.

" They fed me every Tuesday," my guest went on. " Why Tuesday I don't know—it might just as well have been Thursday or Saturday. But once a week they brought a bucketful of soup—quite good soup—potatoes and other vegetables and a bit of meat here and there. I was allowed to eat as much as I could cram in at a sitting. But I was never allowed to keep any of the soup back. Once I had eaten until I could eat no more the bucket was taken away, and that was all for another week."

" But you couldn't possibly survive on that regime," I said.

" I wasn't meant to survive. But I did, thanks to people who used to slip me morsels of food through the grating in my cell door—a carrot or two, a raw potato, a turnip—things like that. I don't know who those people were—whether they were S.S. with some sparks of human feeling, or fellow-prisoners, but whoever they were, if I could discover their identity there's nothing I wouldn't do for them now. Let's have another brandy ! "

I poured another golden measure into the balloon glasses, and the Comtesse de Chaverny continued her story.

" I think," she said, " that when the Germans came round on Tuesdays with my soup and found that I was still alive——"

" And still damned insolent to them, I should judge," I interpolated.

The comtesse smiled.

" Well, yes, perhaps just a little—enfin quels sales individus, hein ? I think the fact that I insisted on living made them furious. At any rate, they used to take me out on to the parade-ground and whip and kick me a good deal. They stove in most of my ribs. The Swedes had to put in two metal plates—look ! "

She raised her elegant skirt and pushed up the bodice of her dress. I protested, in acute embarrassment.

" Really, Madame—there's no need, I assure you . . ."

The comtesse laughed heartily.

" Non, mais voyons, mon Colonel—in Ravensbrück one loses much of one's sense of modesty. I'd like you to see what they did."

I saw and felt a little sick. The comtesse sat down again.

" They used to whip me every now and then. After that I was put back into the cell, and I saw no one for another week."

My guest fell silent.

" Then there was Christmas," she said at last.

" Christmas ? "

" Last Christmas—1944. They came to my cell and beat
me out of it. I was taken over to the S.S. barracks. They were
having a party there—roast goose, cream cakes, pork, schnapps,
gallons of that filthy German imitation of champagne—
everything. I hadn't eaten for six days. They lashed me to a
chair and made me watch while they ate and drank. The
children of the garrison were at the party too—their mothers
were our torturers. The little darlings were encouraged by
their parents to come over to me and spit at me. They seemed
to enjoy doing so."

I was speechless.

" When they had quite finished their meal they untied me
and locked me up again, in my dark cell. Then, I expect,
they sang carols."

I nodded.

" Yes, I expect they did. *O Tannenbaum !* and all those
touching ones about the Christ-child in the manger. Even the
S.S. remember God at Christmas."

" Well," said the comtesse, " perhaps . . . in a way."

At last the Comtesse de Chaverny was released and brought
to Sweden. She had won her solitary battle. The King of
Sweden, a personal friend, sent her a porcelain bowl filled
with chocolates, and other Swedish friends, learning of her
arrival, had sent presents of all kinds. For the present, the
object of all this solicitude was hardly able to appreciate it,
since she was at the gates of death with a raging attack of
typhus. But this battle too she won, and, having won it, she
tried to return these kindnesses.

This brought us to a question which I had been wanting to
ask for some time. The expensive clothes, the champagne,
parties given to Swedish friends—how had Madame obtained
the money to do all this ?

The comtesse smiled.

" Have you ever tried swallowing diamonds every day for
eighteen months or so ? " she asked.

" Well—no, I haven't got any diamonds, anyhow."

"I did have some, and when I knew that I was to be arrested I swallowed some of them. I used to retrieve them—you can imagine how—and swallow them again and again. Not having anything to eat made that part a little easier. At any rate, the diamonds came to Sweden with me—how furious the S.S. would have been to know what they missed—and when I left hospital I was able to sell them for quite a good price, and that's how I manage for money at the moment."

We parted vowing to see one another again. We never did. I do not know even whether the Comtesse de Chaverny is still alive. But if she is I hope that she reads this. I do not think that her story has ever been told, and I have tried to set it down here just as it came from her lips, for of that evening, the intervening years notwithstanding, I remember every detail.

We have erected a statue to Edith Cavell near the Church of St Martin-in-the-Fields, in London. I think that Madame de Chaverny equally deserves to be remembered by the country of which she was a subject by marriage, and which, with her own France, she glorified by her courage. But the comtesse would not thank me for making this suggestion.

13. "THE CURTAIN IS DOWN"

THE DAYS WHEN Stockholm was linked to the Western World only by a tenuous air service were over. We were accessible once again, and visitors came pouring in.

One of our more welcome visitors was Colonel Shamus Macgill, head of the British Military Mission in Helsinki. Finland had been, at best, an unenthusiastic ally of Germany. For obvious reasons, the Finns loathed the Russians, who had treacherously attacked them in 1940, and since Germany was at war with Russia, they supported her. But they had little use for the Nazis or for the system which they represented.

The British Government fully understood this, and at the Teheran Conference, at the end of 1943, Mr Churchill had, by hard bargaining, managed to modify the harsh terms which Stalin had intended to impose upon his small and gallant neighbour. But the Allied Military Mission, which went to Helsinki at the end of the war, was under the overall command of a Soviet general, and the British contingent were thus under Russian orders.

Shamus, whom I had known since we used to play together as small boys, and who had been at school with me, was a natural choice as commanding officer of the British mission, since he was one of the very few officers in the British Army—indeed, perhaps the only officer—who spoke fluent Finnish.

In civilian life, Shamus was in the timber trade, and as a very young man had served a rigorous apprenticeship in the logging camps of Northern Finland. This early experience was now rewarded by a pair of scarlet gorget-patches.

The purpose of Shamus's visit to Stockholm was to buy food for his mess, and, incidentally, on his own account, for a number of Finnish friends who, like the rest of their compatriots, were on the verge of starvation. In order to make the trip he had been forced to ask his Russian superior for leave, and he had realized that if he revealed the real object of the journey it would almost certainly not be granted. So he explained to the Soviet general that he felt completely sex-starved. Might he be allowed to go to Sweden, and there find consolation and assuagement in the arms of one of the beautiful blondes which that country was known to produce in gratifyingly large numbers ?

The Russian general demurred.

" There are plenty of girls in Finland," he said, reasonably enough.

" Oh, yes, of course sir," Shamus said. " But I don't think it would be much to the credit of the Allied mission if I—er —let myself go here. We have a proverb in England which says that one does not foul one's own doorstep."

The Russian nodded.

" Da ! da ! A very proper attitude, Colonel. Very well, you may go to Stockholm for ten days—and good hunting."

Shamus, who was happily married, spent an impeccably chaste leave with me in Stockholm, and returned to Helsinki with many crates of provisions. We passed our last evening together in devising an elaborate series of erotic adventures with which Shamus would satisfy the curiosity of his Soviet colleagues, who would certainly insist on knowing how his amorous expedition had fared. If he told them all the stories which we invented I should think that his reputation as a twentieth-century Casanova spread from Leningrad to Vladivostok.

Air Chief Marshal Sir Arthur Tedder, Deputy Supreme

Commander, another distinguished visitor, flew into Bromma
Airport and shocked the rank-conscious Swedes by the in-
formality with which he treated the crew of his aircraft.
General Nordenskjöld, Commander-in-Chief of the Swedish
Air Force, whose dark good looks had earned him the nickname
" Bildsköne Bengt," or " Pretty-as-a-picture Bengt," greeted
our distinguished visitor, while we stood at attention behind
him. Tedder shook hands with us all, and then turned back
towards his aircraft.

" You all right, George ? " he called up to the squadron-
leader in the cockpit.

" O.K., sir," said the captain of the aircraft.

" Well, see that you and the boys don't have too good a time
to-night. We've got an early take-off to-morrow."

" Roger, sir."

Nordenskjöld looked deeply shocked. Later he said to me :
" Do officers of Sir Arthur Tedder's rank in the Royal Air
Force call junior officers by their Christian names ? "

" Yes, sir, if they're working closely with them, as the Air
Chief Marshal is with his own personal crew."

The Swedish general shook his head.

" *I* don't know how you managed to beat the Germans," he
said.

This little incident, insignificant in itself, was only one of
many such which I encountered during my tour of duty in
Sweden. On one occasion I was asked by the Swedish General
Staff to explain to them the workings of the Army Bureau of
Current Affairs, or A.B.C.A. This excellent organization, it
will be recalled, issued specially written pamphlets and other
documentation upon topics and problems of the day to units
throughout the Army. Commanding officers and adjutants
were then expected to organize debates, in which these topics
were freely discussed by all ranks, with very few holds barred.
I explained this to the Swedish officers.

" But that would mean that a private soldier would be entitled to argue with an officer," they said, in tones of horror.

" Of course. That is one of the objects of the exercise."

" It would never do for us," they replied, and no more was heard of the matter.

As air communications opened up, the British Council lost no time in sending lecturers to the Swedes, who, they felt, must have been starved for too long of British culture. They were probably quite right in this supposition, although Ronald Bottrall, the distinguished poet who was their representative in Sweden throughout the war, had struggled manfully to keep the flame alight with such unpromising material as lay to hand. Anybody in the British Legation who happened to have an evening, or better still, a day, off, was recruited by Bottrall to travel, often to a remote part of Sweden, and to deliver a lecture to the local branch of the Swedish-British Society, a flourishing organization which thrust up strong shoots in the most out-of-the-way places. I myself lectured on countless evenings in trim little towns, to eager groups of people, ate many simple suppers with them, and slept in countless provincial hotels, which in Sweden are always excellent, however small the town in which they stand.

My subject was " Winston Churchill as a Soldier," and the lecture became very popular, not on any particular merits of its own, but because I took a slightly irreverent attitude towards the military career of the great man, who had indeed been a somewhat unorthodox young officer in many ways. Often, at the end of the lecture, some one in the audience would get up and ask how I could speak thus lightly of my great leader. I always hoped that this question would be asked because it enabled me to give the reply which, as far as I was concerned, was one of the main points of the lecture.

" Certainly I can speak as I have of Mr Churchill," I would reply. " But ask the German Military attaché to give a lecture on Hitler's military career, and see what answer you get, and what sort of a lecture he would give if he would ever agree to deliver it. That is the difference between the two sides in this war. We have no Gestapo, and we are not afraid to tell the truth, even about our greatest men—not that Mr Churchill would object to anything which I have said this evening."

This always impressed the audience.

But, as things turned out, I had spoken a little too soon. One day, after the war was ended, I found on my desk a letter from No. 10 Downing Street. The Prime Minister, it said, had learned that I was in the habit of giving a lecture on his military career which was, he understood, very popular. The Prime Minister would be obliged if I would forward a script of this lecture.

We might not have a Gestapo, but we obviously had a leader who kept his ear very close to the ground indeed. As it happened, I had no script, and had never had one. When I first gave the lecture I had done so from a little sheaf of notes written in minute characters, and small enough to be carried in the palm of the hand—I hate lecturers who read what they have to say from a great wedge of manuscript. Before long I knew the lecture by heart, and even the notes were discarded.

I wrote to the Prime Minister explaining this, and adding that I was very willing to dictate the whole lecture and to send him a transcript, except that he might think that, having done this after hearing from him, I had watered down my remarks. I assured him that the lecture contained nothing disrespectful, and added that I was certain that Mr Churchill himself would agree that he had not entirely conformed to the accepted pattern of a young subaltern in his early days. I then awaited the counterblast with some anxiety.

When it came it was no blast at all. " I am rather fond of the Swedes," Mr Churchill wrote, " because they buy my books in large numbers, which gratifies me." He added that he was sure that my lecture contained nothing offensive (as it certainly did not), and that he wished he could have heard it. When I got this letter I went home and had a stiff drink. To incur the anger of Winston Churchill would have been no light matter.

Now I could forget the whole affair. The British Council had no further need of my services, and in any case my evenings were all fully occupied in the pleasantest manner. Victory brought with it a round of festivity and the time to enjoy it. I decided that I must give a dinner-party for the assistant Military attachés of the Allied Powers. Little flag-staffs bearing silk flags of the Allies adorned the table. We began with Martinis and continued the liquid part of the evening with a dry Chilean white wine—no Rhine wine for us—claret and champagne. When the time for speeches came I said very little, my American colleague was straightforward and to the point, my French colleague eloquent. Ironically enough, a good deal of German had been spoken at table, since our Soviet colleague, Major Pinyugin, spoke no English or French, and German was our *lingua franca*. But when he rose, champagne glass in hand, he announced that he intended to speak in Russian. Fortunately we had an interpreter in the person of the French Military attaché, and when he translated Pinyugin's remarks they came as something of a shock. We had beaten Germany, the Soviet major said. Now the Soviet Union would play her part in the defeat of Japan. We drank to this with an enthusiasm which was more apparent than real, and I took the first opportunity of getting to a telephone and telling my Minister of what had been said.

Winston Churchill had, if we had but known it, just sent to President Truman the celebrated telegram in which he said, of the Russians, " An iron curtain is drawn down upon their front. We do not know what is going on behind." The sinister phrase which the Prime Minister thus coined had not yet become a part of our language as, to our sorrow, it now has. But we in Stockholm were, perhaps, more aware than many people at home of the threat which the Soviet Union already presented, and we had no wish to see it extended to Japan.

After dinner Major Pinyugin, who had obviously enjoyed himself very much, drew me aside.

" Tell me," he said, looking round my drawing-room, with its high ceiling and tall windows, " is this the way you usually live ? "

" Well, no," I admitted. " I get a rent allowance, and this flat is rather grander than anything I should be likely to have in London."

" But in any case you would have several rooms in London, as you have here ? "

" Oh, yes—a drawing-room and a dining-room, I suppose, and two or three bedrooms, as I have here. But the rooms probably wouldn't be as large as these."

" At home," said Pinyugin, " I and my family would be very lucky to have two small rooms—and that was before the war, when the Germans had not destroyed everything. What it will be like now I can't imagine." His eyes, to my great surprise, filled with tears. Then he said, " We have a reception at the Embassy to-morrow, I shall see you there. I shall be wearing my new uniform for the first time."

This was important. A year or so before the end of the war Stalin devised a new dress uniform for his officers—olive-green tunic, with heavy rectangular epaulettes, covered with gold lace, dark trousers, a smart forage-cap. Our Russian colleagues had been sent set patterns and samples of the cloth. They had promptly formed up in a body to Reggie Sutton-Pratt and to me.

The British, said the Soviet delegation, were known to have strong views about uniforms and tailoring. What did we think of the design for the new uniform ? We examined the drawings which had come from Moscow, and said, quite truthfully, that it looked very smart indeed. We inspected the samples of material and approved them. Would it be better, our visitors asked, to have the material sent from Moscow and the uniforms made by Swedish tailors in Stockholm, or to rely upon Muscovite talent ? We strongly advised the former course of action. Swedish cutters, we said, were celebrated throughout the world, and if the uniforms were made in Stockholm our friends could have as many fittings as were needed. Nothing looked worse than a dress uniform which was not perfect in every respect. The Russians agreed and departed.

Months later they reappeared at the legation, in the new uniforms, and Reggie's office was transformed into a salon. They paraded before us, and we inspected them critically. The uniforms were extremely smart, and we congratulated their wearers. They departed, delighted with themselves and with us.

And now Seraphim Pinyugin was to wear his uniform in public for the first time. I regretted I had not brought with me the full undress uniform of my own regiment—dark-green patrol-jacket, patent-leather crossbelt, heavy with silver ornament, strapped trews, dress wellingtons. The strapped trews and the wellingtons, however, I had. A service tunic would have to serve. After all, we go on church parade in this dress, and so it should be good enough for the Soviet Embassy.

I had been many times to the Soviet Embassy, a somewhat daunting place. The porter's lodge was equipped with an elaborate system of mirrors, which allowed unseen eyes to scrutinize visitors from who knows how many hidden points of vantage. But on the night of this victory party the front door stood wide open, and although no doubt we were all carefully watched on arrival, the fact was not made as obvious as usual.

The enormous reception room was ablaze with light. The last time I had seen it was at a memorial gathering for the wife and children of Captain Taradin, the Soviet Naval attaché, who had been shot down into the sea in a Swedish civil aircraft by German fighters as they flew from Scotland to Stockholm to join him. That had been a mournful occasion, the great room almost in darkness, the strictly secular ritual, offering as it did no hope of eternal life or of a meeting with the dear dead beyond the grave, was infinitely depressing.

Now the room was ablaze with light. The Soviet diplomatic corps, too, had been granted new uniforms by Stalin, and they stood about stiffly in dark suits which sparkled with gold embroidery on collars and lapels and the shining gilt of many buttons. The military contingent looked very smart indeed in their finery, and well they knew it. In the centre of the gathering, seated in a high-backed chair, sat the formidable Ambassador of the Union of Socialist Soviet Republics, Madame Alexandra Kollontay.

Madame Kollontay was a legendary figure. At that time she and Stalin himself were almost the only authentic creators of the Revolution of 1917 who had not been eaten by the monster which they had brought to life. The daughter of an aristocratic family, Alexandra Kollontay had fallen in love with a rating of the mutinous Imperial Navy and married him. Cast off by her parents, she had thrown herself heart and soul into the revolution, and she had been rewarded by being admitted into its inner councils. Now, twenty-eight years later, she was almost the last of the Old Bolsheviks. Witty, immensely intelligent, and possessed of great charm, the Ambassador sat very upright in her chair, like a queen who was gracing by her presence a rather barbaric festival. The British party greeted her formally, and moved on towards a phalanx of Russians, who plied us with vodka and caviar. Very few of our hosts spoke any language but Russian, but this fact did not inhibit their good humour or their hospitality. Presently I saw that Madame Kollontay was beckoning to me. I went over to her.

" Are you enjoying yourself? " she asked, in perfect English.

" Very much indeed, your Excellency."

She made a gesture towards her staff, most of them now a little flushed and garrulous with vodka.

" Look at all my silly little boys," the Ambassador said.

" Silly little boys, Madame . . . ? "

" Yes. They none of them know anything. Moscow sends them to me, and I have to teach them everything. They have no *savoir-vivre*."

" They are very good hosts, Madame," I said.

" Oh, yes, they know how to hand round vodka and zakouska, but not much else. I have lived in so many worlds . . . seen so much . . . probably I expect too much of them. I am too *exigeante*. But now that Germany is beaten, Russia will be great. You will see. In twenty years there will be no more silly little boys."

There are certainly none now.

July passed in a flurry of visits. Baker Street sent out a small contingent, which we were very glad to see, to help us all in compiling a report of the activities of the mission as a whole. People began to drift away from the legation. Almost every night saw a farewell-party, almost every day one stood on the tarmac of Bromma Airport waving good-bye to a colleague. The prefabricated offices, only two months before filled with life and activity, lay empty and forlorn. It was almost time for Janet and me to make good the promise given to our Danish officers before they went to Germany.

We left for Copenhagen on the first Saturday in August, by the early morning flight, and arrived in the Danish capital at eleven o'clock. An hour later we were seated at a long table, laid for twelve people, in the terrace of the Hotel d'Angleterre. We had not been in touch with any of our protégés (if that is the right word) since they were overrun by British troops. Would they remember our rendezvous, would all eight turn up?

We need not have worried. Sharp at noon a small cavalcade of splendid cars—Mercedes, Horch, Borgwardt—drew up outside the hotel. A couple of officers in battledress descended from each car, and we rushed towards them. Our boys had returned, every one of them.

From the boots of the cars came loot of all sorts—wine and liqueurs, presents for Janet, a splendid 12-bore shotgun for me. All chattering at the tops of our voices, we moved to our table, and waiters brought champagne.

The terrace of the Hotel d'Angleterre is at street level, separated from the pavement only by an ornamental iron railing. We drank our champagne beneath an awning, while on the other side of the low railing strolling Danes enjoyed the hot sunshine and gazed with amusement at the cheerful party of British officers and the solitary girl who seemed to be enjoying themselves a great deal.

Then a passer-by looked very hard at our table, walked on a few paces, turned back, stared again, and finally leaned over the railing and addressed one of our party.

" Look, aren't you Paul Jensen ? " he said, in Danish.

" Yes, that's me . . . well, if it isn't Alan Larsen ! "

" What the hell are you doing in British uniform ? Last I heard of you, you were in Sweden."

" Oh," Jensen said vaguely, " I've been getting around, here and there." I called upon the newcomer to join us, and he did so. I might not have done this had I been able to foresee that this little scene was to repeat itself four times within the next half hour, so that we had to ask that an extra table should be added to ours. By the time we were ready to go to lunch our original party of twelve had become one of twenty.

The rest of that week-end was spent in reminiscence. We heard, at long last, the full story of these Odysseys into Germany, and I wish that I could remember them in detail. They were enshrined in a report which Janet wrote, but is now destroyed, and Janet herself can remember little of what it contained.

There was nothing particularly sensational in the stories which the returned wanderers told, but, then, intelligence work is, as a rule, lacking in sensation. Theirs were modest achievements, and so, in the context of the war as a whole, they were, according to the narrators, but they called for great courage, intelligence, and tenacity, and the warmth with which the British Army spoke of the Danes' work since the collapse of Germany was testimony enough that they had wrought well and that their missions had been valuable. And we had not lost a man. That may seem a negative achievement, but it pleased Janet and me very much.

In Stockholm the machine was slowly running down. Soon the career diplomats would be able to resume the normal, leisurely routine of peace-time, unembarrassed by the presence and the activities of a gang of amateur thugs like ourselves. More than once, in the previous six years, I had watched clouds of smoke billow up as documents were burned. They had always been harbingers of disaster, or at least of possible disaster. Now the same acrid smoke rose again, into the pale blue sky of Swedish late summer, but this time we were making burned offerings to victory. *Valkyrian* made many cruises in August 1945. Laden with food and drink, and feeling rather guilty, since at home things were still so very tight, we sailed out of Smedslätten every week-end, and sometimes even during the week—a thing unthinkable in war-time. But we took with us also on each voyage a number of bulky sacks, which contained a strange assortment of goods—explosives and detonators, leaflets, malingering kits, itching-powder, stink bombs, and many other things even less avowable. We would sail to an isolated cove, far from prying eyes, lunch, and weight the bags with heavy stones. Then they were sunk in deep water. Soon our own cupboards began to look almost as bare as those which we had found in the German Legation.

It was nearly time to go home. I was due for demobilization in October, on the principle of " first in, first out." I had been a soldier of a sort for more than six years. During a brief duty visit to London some months earlier I had called upon Lord Rothermere, at the suggestion of his Stockholm correspondent, and he had offered me a job when I left the Army. I did not wish to return to *The Times* for two reasons. In the first place, they wanted me to go back to Germany as their correspondent, and I felt that I had had quite enough to do with the Germans to last me for a long time to come. In the second place, some people in Printing House Square had, in the months which preceded the war, called me a " war-monger," because, contrary to the policy of the paper, I had continually warned, in my reports from Berlin, of Hitler's evil intentions and of the danger of war. *The Times* had duly printed all I wrote (sometimes taking the edge off it in a leading article), but they had not liked me for writing what I did, or, at least, some of my colleagues had not liked me. I felt that I needed a spell in England and a fresh start.

At last it was ended. The entire S.O.E. Mission in Stockholm, under the chairmanship of our chief, Ronald Turnbull, dined together, for the first and last time, in great amity and with some sadness. We put those who had greatly helped us, notably Johan Bøge, in for decorations, and our recommendations were accepted. The first few snowflakes of winter, which comes early in Sweden, were drifting in still air as my Dakota took off for home.

In Baker Street I found the same air of dissolution which

we had left behind us in Stockholm. This was well expressed in some verses written by one of our most senior staff-officers, which ran, in part :

> Farewell to the tumult and shouting :
>   Group-Captains and Colonels, depart !
> It has been a remarkable outing,
>   And leaving it goes to the heart.
> But let us give thanks to our maker
>   That now it is over and done,
> And empty is 64 Baker
>   Street, W.1. . . .
>
> Return to the ease of the City :
>   Hey now for the Bank and the Brokerage
> (Assuming the Kennet Committee
>   Don't send us out East in the Stokerage).
> What fun and what freedom, what frolic ! . . .
>   And yet, I will frankly allow,
> That sentiments quite melancholic
>   Come over me now . . .
>
> Demobilized soldiers aforetime
>   Were faced with despair and decay.
> Let us, I suggest, make our war-time
>   Subversive experience pay.
> For life will be real, lad, and earnest,
>   And branches will grow as you bend ;
> And crook thou has been, and returnest
>   To crook in the end . . .
>
> And X could teach F, as he wanders,
>   To vex his trade opposite numbers
> By mud in the sumps of Lagondas
>   And sand in the axles of Humbers !
> " Strike ! " stickers would start off a panic
>   In Morris or Austin or Singer ;
> And each Studebaker mechanic
>   Would learn to malinger.
>
> Well, close the door gently behind you,
>   And say your farewell to the show,

(I now for the last time remind you
    To turn off the light as you go).
The stage is deserted, and fled
    Tragedian, mummer and clown.
The voice of the prompter is dead.
    The curtain is down.

I had two days to waste before travelling to Ayr, for the first stage of my demobilization, and I asked whether I might see Lord Rothermere. He received me very kindly and inquired whether I would be willing to become Foreign Editor of the *Daily Mail* at a more than adequate salary. I was very willing, and said so.

" Well, then," said Lord Rothermere, " I think you'd better meet the editor."

We passed through two intervening rooms from Lord Rothermere's office to that of the Editor of the *Daily Mail*, Stanley Horniblow. Lord Rothermere made the introductions and left us together.

Horniblow looked at the Scottish officer who stood before him with undisguised loathing. He tried to be civil, but failed dismally.

" I gather," he said, " that you're to be my Foreign Editor."

" That was the general idea," I replied.

" Have you ever done any journalism before ? " Horniblow inquired.

" Well, I used to earn my living that way before the war," I said.

His forbidding manner became slightly less forbidding.

" Oh, really. What did you do ? "

I told him.

" By God," said Horniblow, smiling suddenly, " you're a newspaper man."

" I used to think so. Do you suppose Lord Rothermere would have offered me the job if I wasn't one ? "

" Well, no—except that we have the most extraordinary lot of chaps after jobs nowadays. People who have written a

couple of poems in the *Cherwell* and done a spell in the com-
mandos and think they ought to be News Editor of this
newspaper. You wouldn't believe what I have to put up with.
Come on, I'll take you to lunch at the Dorchester."

That was the beginning of a friendship with a good man and
a fine editor.

Two days later I travelled to Ayr and back to London.

My last journey in uniform was not destined to be without
incident. About five hundred troops were travelling south on
my train for demobilization, and as senior officer present I was
appointed O.C. Train. This meant, among other things, that
I had charge of the " demob books " of every soldier under my
care, and these were neatly stacked on the rack above my
head. Without those documents there could be no demobilization in London.

Just before the train reached York a corporal came to my
compartment to report that he had been robbed of a sizeable
sum of money. When we reached York I posted guards on
the coach in which the corporal was travelling and told the
other officers in my compartment that I was going to telephone
ahead to Grantham, to arrange for military police to board the
train there and begin inquiries. If by any chance I was left
behind at York I would catch the next train to London. But on
no account was the next senior officer—a captain—to forget to
take the " demob books " with him to the London barracks
which was our final destination. That officer vowed that he
would not forget.

The train left without me, but another was due to leave for
London in half an hour, so little time was lost. From Euston
station I drove to Albany Barracks to find the place in pande-
monium. Five hundred men were waiting to say good-bye to
the Army without a single " demob book " among the lot of
them. My captain had failed in his duty.

After telling that officer what I thought of him, I rushed back
to Euston. The station master could not have been more helpful. The train in which we had travelled had already been
shunted out to Chalk Farm marshalling-yards. A telephone

call to Chalk Farm got the search under way, and the authorities there were instructed to hand the books, when found, to the first train, light engine or whatever, which was bound for Euston.

For half an hour or more I waited in a horrible state of anxiety. Then an engine-driver and his stoker appeared, clutching the books to them. Honour was saved, the adventure had ended, and I could return to Albany Barracks, near Regent's Park, without fear of being lynched.

A soldier no longer, I took a taxi to Olympia and drew a strange demobilization suit (for which my tailor credited me with £10), shirt, shoes, a pair of socks, and a very odd hat, constructed, as far as could be judged, of cardboard. Then I drove to Harrods and went up to the pet department. I knew exactly what I wanted.

I found it, too. A bulldog puppy, aged about eight weeks, was looking morosely through the bars of a cage. I asked how much it would cost to become his master. The assistant produced a formidable pedigree. The little creature had a most distinguished family tree, fairly studded with champions, and the price which was asked for him reflected this fact.

" I do hope you'll decide to have him, sir," the assistant said. " It's Saturday, you see, and we were wondering what to do with him over the week-end."

I could not resist the little creature. He lay, snug in my greatcoat, while a taxi drove us to King's Cross. There, on the bar of the buffet, Brewer—that was to be the puppy's name—tottered about, and was made much of by the barmaids, while I drank a pint of water faintly flavoured with beer and ate a glutinous and anonymous pie.

Then we went home together.

EPILOGUE

ABOUT A YEAR after I had left the Army, Johan Bøge came to stay a week-end with me in my house in Essex. During his adventures in Germany a considerable amount of pay had accumulated to his credit in a London bank, and he had come to England to spend some of it.

Bøge was deeply distrustful of the Russians, and he wished to have nothing to do with them. He planned to spend the next few years manning an isolated weather-station in Greenland. At all costs, he said, he had to get away from it all.

The only memento which Bøge had kept of his service with us was the tiny " Minox " camera which travelled with him through Germany, and which had given us many valuable pictures. He had asked whether he might keep this as his personal property, and London had agreed that he might.

One morning at breakfast, while the sun streamed through leaded windows, I inquired about this camera.

" Have you still got it ? " I asked.

Bøge held out his hand. The " Minox " lay in the palm.

" I've just taken a photo of you," he said.

Old habits die hard.

At about this time, too, I received a letter from the United States Embassy, in London. It informed me that the President had awarded me the Medal of Freedom, with Bronze Palm. I duly went and received the decoration from the Ambassador. The citation was highly flattering and much exaggerated. Why I was so honoured I have never been able to make out.

INDEX

940.54

Butler
Amateur agent